Commercialism and Frontier
Perspectives on
the Early Shenandoah Valley

Commercialism and Frontier

Perspectives on
the Early Shenandoah Valley

Robert D. Mitchell

University Press of Virginia

Charlottesville

THE UNIVERSITY PRESS OF VIRGINIA
Copyright © 1977 by the Rector and Visitors
of the University of Virginia

First published 1977

Library of Congress Cataloging in Publication Data

Mitchell, Robert D   1940-
  Commercialism and frontier.

  Includes index.
  1. Land settlement—Shenandoah Valley—History.
2. Shenandoah Valley—Economic conditions. I. Title.
HD211.V8M58   333.7′09755′9   76-26610
ISBN 0-8139-0661-X

Printed in the United States of America

For Karen

Contents

Figures

Tables

Preface

The colonization process is a fascinating topic for geographic inquiry because it provides an opportunity to study human behavior in new environments through the formation of new societies. Such societies are a blend of the old and the new, the product of tradition and cultural change. Tradition itself is modified because of selective trait retention by the culture bearers as they negotiate and settle the new environments. The core culture undergoes trait reduction and simplification, while those traits which are retained are intensified and become the framework to which innovative or borrowed traits are added to form the configuration of a new society.

Commercialism was a key contributor to the European configuration of early American society and a dominant force in the creation of Europeanized landscapes. Commercialism was a set of attitudes, a particular way of viewing the external world. Exchanges between man and land and between man and man were interpreted from a utilitarian, exploitive perspective, and surplus items from productive enterprise were regarded as potential sources of trade and profit within a money-based economic system. The belief in private property, freedom of trade, and competition, within an economy understood to be inclined toward some kind of internal, self-adjusting, market equilibrium, was a characteristic trait of most of the European colonists who undertook the transformation of the colonial environment.

Because so many of the European immigrants to the North American colonies in the seventeenth and eighteenth centuries were commercially minded settlers, or becoming so, rather than communally oriented peasants, the kinds and rates of social and environmental change that occurred were more substantial and more rapid than in any other part of the Americas. However, the new societies were not composed solely of self-interested, pragmatic individualists, for many social needs and wants had to be met and new social and political orders had to be established. Commercialism in the colonies was in part the creator of a widely accepted individualism, a consequence of the depersonalized effects of a money and credit economy and a sparsely occupied territory where the acquisition and alienation of land became the principal source of personal and public wealth. The commercialization of the soil was the most revolutionary institutional aspect of European occupance.

The interpretation of this occupance can be pursued at a number of levels. An evaluation of the meaning of individualism per se requires analysis of individual and family behavior in relation to community functions, insofar as this is possible. This study is focused more at regional and county levels because the objectives were to examine how the processes of commercialization influenced land utilization and social evolution in newly settled areas over time and to evaluate the degree to which the emerging stuctures and patterns may have been modified by considerations of environmental variation, external political control, and different cultural heritages. How did commercial factors operate in the initial choice of settlement sites, and how were these factors modified by cultural and environmental constraints? What were the motivations for frontier migration, and how were they reflected in the market for land? How widespread was land speculation, and what were its effects on the distribution of landholding and the rates of settlement? How rapidly did the commercialization of pioneer economies occur, and what factors were most important in their formation? What direct and indirect effects did governmental policies have on settlement processes, population composition, and the direction of economic development? What were the relationships between commercialization of the economy, the emergence of urbanism, and the changing stratification and differentiation of society over time? And how and where were economic linkages and exchanges made with the outside world, and what consequences did they have for the distinctiveness of frontier areas?

The area chosen in which to examine these questions was the Shenandoah Valley of Virginia. The choice was the result of both interest and design. My interest in the westward movement of the early eighteenth century directed attention to those areas actively being settled during this time. I perused the settlement history of the area west of the fall line from Pennsylvania to the Carolinas, with particular reference to the population movements originating in southeastern Pennsylvania and spreading southward and westward through the Appalachians. The Shenandoah Valley lay in the path of these movements, and its function as a kind of migration corridor seemed likely to provide a potential dynamism to the interaction between population, land, and society there. The earliest European reconnaissance of the valley was made during the first decade of the eighteenth century; the peak of the area's economic importance in relation to the westward movement came at the turn of the nineteenth century before the opening up of the Middle West. I therefore focused the study on the eighteenth century, and in order to obtain a perspective on the meanings of the terms *frontier* and *pioneer*, I examined the valley through the period immediately after these phases of its occupance.

The settlement history of the northern half of the valley (the lower valley) is reasonably well documented, but the settlement of its southern half (the upper valley) is not. Although county records are quite comprehensive for the entire valley, those for the lower valley lack some materials necessary for exploring the processes of economic development. It is more difficult to reconstruct the evolution of trade in the lower valley and to fill in the specifics of Winchester's growth and service functions. In terms of detailed settlement reconstruction, I have placed more emphasis on the upper valley.

Virginia has been given more attention by scholars than any other southern colony. Most of this attention, understandably; has concentrated on the economic, social, and political history of eastern Virginia. These writers have presented a general impression of the early Shenandoah Valley as a backcountry area far removed from the Tidewater. This image was also held by many colonial officials, who regarded interior areas remote from the coast as being politically inconsequential, though strategically significant, and who equated their backwardness with the settlement of people of different origins and background from their own. It seems necessary not only to correct such impressions but also to dispel the notion of undifferentiated western frontiers displaying few regional variations in their occupance patterns.

Commercial behavior in new environments is a very significant, but only one, aspect of the entire theme of European colonization. The operations of the commercial aspects of the economic system were important only insofar as they provided consistent support for socially acceptable standards of living and ways of life. Measurable changes usually occurred more frequently in the economic system than in the social or political system, so that interpretations of change in colonial endeavors will tend to differ depending upon the part or parts of these endeavors specifically isolated for study. Within the commercial components themselves, changes in marketing and transactional activities often occurred more frequently and less discernibly than changes in land use, and in some instances may not have been reflected in the landscape at all or only imperfectly after a time lag. Thus, although change is inherent in the settlement of new areas, different aspects of settlement change at different rates and seldom are completely synchronized. Modifications and adjustments within and between the aspects are rarely in equilibrium at any given time but, at best, are in a constant state of steady motion. *Culture* and *society* remain among the most complex and most difficult wholes to comprehend.

For the encouragement and constructive criticism I received in beginning this work, I am most indebted to David Ward, Morton Rothstein, Clarence Olmstead, and the late Andrew Clark. William Pattison and Norman Thrower did much to stimulate my initial interest in American historical problems; the work of James Lemon and Roy Merrens helped to maintain that interest. Special thanks goes to Gary Dunbar, who gave me liberally of his time and his extensive knowledge of Virginia. Wally St. Clair, Karen Pearson, Joe Poracsky, and especially Charles Murphy labored long in translating my scribbles into polished maps which, in part, reflect their own varied cartographic styles. Mary Terry typed two earlier drafts of the manuscript, and Bonnie Dunn, with the assistance of Dana Delaney, typed the final draft. I also express my thanks to Howard Wilson of Staunton, whose intimate knowledge of the history of early Augusta County I tapped on several occasions; to Raymond Hildebrand of Roanoke, who kindly provided me with copies of his cadastral maps of Beverley Manor and Borden's Tract; and to Henry and Bobby Lederer, formerly of Richmond, whose hospitality will long be remembered.

The archival research and the field work for this study were largely financed by the University of Wisconsin, through a University Fellowship, a Wisconsin Alumni Research Foundation Fellowship, and two travel grants. The Association of American Geographers provided additional research aid from its Gibson fund, and a General Research Board grant from the University of Maryland allowed me a summer in which to tie many loose ends together.

The research could not have been accomplished without the assistance of the staffs of the various libraries and other institutions whose resources I used: the Henry E. Huntington Library, San Marino, California; the William L. Clements Library, Ann Arbor, Michigan; the Manuscript Division, New York Public Library, New York; the Library of Congress, Washington, D.C.; the Wisconsin State Historical Society, Madison; and, in Virginia, the University of Virginia Library, Charlottesville; Augusta County Courthouse, Staunton; Frederick County Courthouse, Winchester; College of William and Mary Library, Williamsburg; the Research Department, Colonial

Williamsburg, Williamsburg; Rockingham County Courthouse, Harrisonburg; Union Theological Seminary Library, Richmond; and the Virginia Historical Society, Richmond. I am especially indebted to the late William J. Van Schreeven, formerly State Archivist, and John W. Dudley, Assistant State Archivist, and their most helpful staff at the Virginia State Library, Richmond, on whose advice and assistance I relied heavily.

Figures 2, 10, 12, 21, and 24 are reproduced with permission from material I had published in the *Annals of the Association of American Geographers*, Volume 62, 1972.

Greatest thanks must go to my children, Mark and Kim, and most especially to my wife, Karen, for putting up with me throughout the entire enterprise.

Commercialism and Frontier
Perspectives on
the Early Shenandoah Valley

1 Temporal and Spatial Frameworks

WHEN the dawn of the eighteenth century broke upon the American colonies, active settlement had been in progress for almost a century. Except for southern New England, the Hudson River valley, and the Chesapeake Bay colonies, scarcely a dent had been made in the interior. South of Virginia a sparse population was confined to a few isolated settlements along the coast. By the end of the century, American farmers, although stymied temporarily in the Southeast, had expanded their living space north to the present Canadian boundary and as far west as the Ohio Valley and western Kentucky (fig. 1). The first sustained settlement of this western interior began during the 1720s as the increasing European immigration to already occupied coastal areas of the Middle and Chesapeake Bay colonies pushed settlers into the adjacent interior.

The tenor of this seventeenth-century coastal phase of the American frontier was distinctly commercial, whether in Puritan Massachusetts or Cavalier Virginia. "Starving times" gave way quickly to steady settlement expansion and economic output. Parts of larger European cultural wholes had broken off, survived, and grown. The commercial achievements are documented convincingly. It seems rather odd, therefore, that in conceptualizing the first phase of interior expansion during the eighteenth century, scholars until recently have tended to emphasize the further reduction and simplification of colonial culture as settlers attempted to transform the primitive wilderness into an American garden. Renewal and rebirth were considered the essence of frontier experience. In the vivid language of the most famous exponent of this view, Frederick Jackson Turner:

American development has exhibited not merely advance along a single line, but a return to primitive conditions on a continually advancing frontier line, and a new development for that area. American social development has been continually beginning over again on the frontier. This perennial rebirth, this fluidity of American life, this expansion westward with its new opportunities, its continuous touch with the simplicity of primitive society, furnish the forces dominating American character. . . . In this advance, the frontier is the outer edge of the wave—the meeting point between savagery and

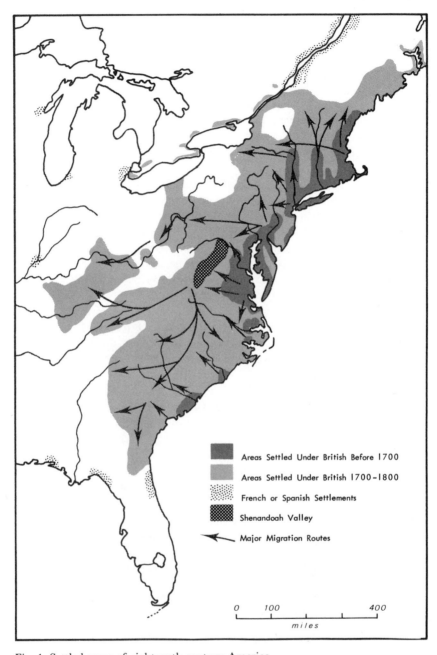

Fig. 1. Settled areas of eighteenth-century America

civilization. . . . at the frontier the environment is at first too strong for the man. He must accept the conditions which it furnishes, or perish, so he fits himself into the Indian clearings and follows the Indian trails. Little by little he transforms the wilderness, but the outcome is not the old Europe. . . . here is a new product that is American.[1]

There is no doubt that the early American frontiers lacked the sophisticated trappings of longer occupied areas, but seldom were they reduced to a raw state of economic evolution distinguished by geographical isolation, complete self-sufficiency, and marginal living standards. Such conditions were, at most, a temporary feature of the first year or two of initial permanent settlement. In this sense, the self-sufficiency issue has long been laid to rest.[2] What remained was the belief in a developmental framework which postulated dual, even dichotomous, modes of economic existence, the "subsistent" and the "commercial," and a typology of discrete stages of self-sufficient, subsistent, and commercial enterprises.[3] The pioneer economy was equated with subsistence, the production of goods primarily for local, on-site consumption rather than for sale; a commercial orientation was said to have come later, if at all.

Such a conceptualization has had important consequences for the interpretation of the economic foundations of frontier areas. It has led to an overestimation of the duration of a primarily subsistent agricultural economy and an underevaluation of both the rate of economic specialization and the creation of external trading and transportation linkages. When applied to specific localities, it has frequently overemphasized the constraints of local environmental conditions;[4] when related to political conditions, it has contributed to the notion that recently settled areas emerged largely independent of, and in opposition to, existing policies;[5] with respect to cultural issues, it has been equated with the primacy and persistence of ethnic

1. Turner, *The Frontier in American History* (New York: Holt, Rinehart, and Winston, 1920), pp. 2–4.

2. Rodney C. Loehr, "Self-Sufficiency on the Farm, 1759–1810," *Agricultural History* 26 (1952): 37–42; Richard Hofstadter, "The Myth of the Happy Yeoman," *American Heritage*, 2d ser. 7 (1956): 43–53. On regional food supply, see Sam B. Hilliard, *Hog Meat and Hoecake: Food Supply in the Old South, 1840–1860* (Carbondale and Edwardsville: Southern Illinois University Press, 1972).

3. This typology is articulated most fully in Lewis C. Gray, *History of Agriculture in the Southern United States to 1860*, Carnegie Institution of Washington publication no. 430, 2 vols. (Washington, D.C., 1933), 1:437–61.

4. Walter P. Webb, *The Great Plains* (Boston and New York: Ginn and Co., 1931), is an extreme example.

5. The antagonism often may have been justified, but see William A. Schaper, *Sectionalism*

contributions to early American development;[6] and when applied to social characteristics, it has frequently produced static and repetitive categorizations of socioeconomic change.[7]

Instead, it seems more realistic to see eighteenth-century frontier areas as progressing from a brief phase of primary subsistence and nascent commercialism through various degrees of commercialism and to interpret westward settlement expansion as a process of diffusion of a steadily increasing commerical bias. Commercial tendencies were present from the beginnings of permanent settlement and were the most dynamic element in the emerging pioneer economy (fig. 2). The great majority of settlers were eager to exploit any profit-making opportunities available. In their acquisition of land for settlement, they viewed land less in terms of a carefully nurtured garden to be transmitted intact to the next generation than as a commodity to be bought, sold, and leased in the open market. In their daily affairs they were primarily concerned with providing the basic requirements for life and, of necessity, being as self-sufficient as possible. Yet the migration of other settlers to and through frontier areas and the need for materials that were not available locally promoted early trading. The earliest phase of development included local commercialism within the context of unspecialized general farming and a brisk land market. The proportion of total production comprising farm and hunting items available for sale was typically less than one

---

and Representation in South Carolina, Report of the American Historical Association, 1900 (Washington, D.C., 1901), pp. 237–463; Thomas P. Abernethy, *From Frontier to Plantation in Tennessee: A Study in Frontier Democracy* (Chapel Hill: University of North Carolina Press, 1932).

6. Conrad Arensberg, "American Communities," *American Anthropologist* 57 (1955): 1143–62, is a thought-provoking example. Compare E. Estyn Evans, "Culture and Land Use in the Old West of North America," *Heidelberger Studien zur Kulturgeographie* 15 (1966): 72–80.

7. Turner, *Frontier in American History*, p. 12, exemplifies the repetitive stages approach. In an attempt to attach a developmental component to a static classification, Jackson T. Main, *The Social Structure of Revolutionary America* (Princeton, N.J.: Princeton University Press, 1965), p. 8, labeled his socioeconomic categories as pioneer, subsistence farm ("or more accurately subsistence plus," p. 277), commercial, and urban. Despite the inconsistencies in his scheme, Main was one of the first scholars to attempt a comprehensive view of economic patterns and social structure using a wide array of primary sources. For criticism of the premises of such a study, see James T. Lemon and Gary B. Nash, "The Distribution of Wealth in Eighteenth-Century America: A Century of Change in Chester County, Pennsylvania, 1693–1802," *Journal of Social History* 2 (1968): 1–24; Andrew H. Clark, "Suggestions for the Geographical Study of Agricultural Change in the United States, 1790–1840," *Ag. Hist.* 46 (1972): 155–72; Robert D. Mitchell, "The Shenandoah Valley Frontier," *Annals of the Association of American Geographers* 62 (1972): 461–86.

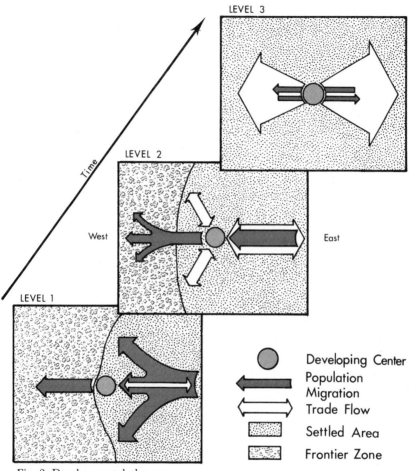

Fig. 2. Developmental change

tenth. As population increased and spread out and as links with external market centers were consolidated, the proportion of farm products used for subsistence declined, for family demand for basic foodstuffs remained relatively inelastic. Output of commercial commodities expanded, and an increasing number of goods and services were acquired in the open market. These changes necessitated the creation of small central places as points of consolidation within an increasingly competitive trading environment. As agriculture became more specialized, in response to demands from external areas for products they lacked, and as the local economy became more diversified, because of a larger, more occupationally varied and credit-dependent population, individual settlement communities became more identifiable and social patterns more complex and stratified. During this phase of development, as the area entered the world of a more regionally distinct postpioneer interior, the proportion of goods for sale increased typically from one-third to one-half or more of total output.

A number of critical factors affected the timing of these phases in various frontier areas—the extent and availability of agriculturally productive land, the characteristics of population growth and distribution, the type of agricultural system, the availability of other natural resources, the timing of long-distance trading and transportation connections, the structure and orientation of local and regional marketing systems, and the availability and application of capital.

Geographical changes are inherent in such a developmental scheme. American frontier areas were located in a continually changing space-time matrix within which their relative locations can be measured over time. Frontier areas have fixed locations but the importance of the location varies with the direction and continuity of settlement expansion and the economic evolution of recently occupied areas. Figures 2 and 3 illustrate this point for areas undergoing development within a frontier zone. The levels diagrammed in these figures should not be interpreted too literally, for the processes involved are not always synchronized in space and time. An area no longer on the frontiers of settlement may remain a sort of pioneer inlier maintaining a low level of commercial activity in comparison with adjacent areas. Conversely, specifically located resource exploitation may occur in advance of a permanent agricultural frontier in a sort of commercial outlier, such as a mining camp, committed to a high level of commercial activity from its inception. The degree of coincidence of locational and developmental changes ultimately will be reflected in the area's internal economic structure and the characteristics of its external trade flow.

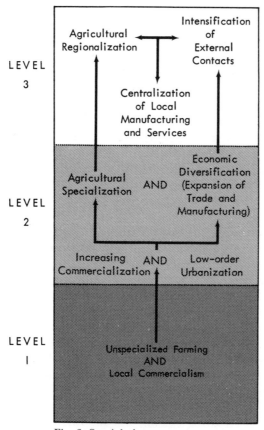

Fig. 3. Spatial change

The critical ingredients in the initial phases of settlement are the formation of an agriculturally active population and a regular supply of new settlers through immigration. As areas became more fully occupied and as the frontier zone moved farther inland (west), the contributions of immigration to population change were replaced by those of natural increase and emigration. As informational and economic exchanges with the longer settled East were multiplied and intensified, the links between the frontier and the East became associated less with the migration of people and more with the transaction of activities. From a Turnerian perspective the modification of the initial occupance patterns by frontier settlers independent of the East created distinctive American characteristics, so that the linkages between East and West were of lesser importance. This viewpoint greatly underestimates the dependence of frontier areas and the fact that the development process there was mainly induced from the outside. As interaction between the West and the East increased, frontier areas became part of the expanding hinterlands of the Atlantic seaport cities and, with adjacent frontier areas, merged into regionally identifiable economies. As the western edge of the settled area extended farther inland, former frontier areas acquired a different role within the westward movement; they became links in a long-distance trade system between the seaport cities and the new frontier zones. How well they integrated into this emerging national system depended upon their accessibility and the level of their commercial enterprise. Areas along major transportation routes operated as entrepôts channeling interior products to the coast and redistributing eastern goods and services to the interior. Areas that remained less accessible tended to decline or to stabilize at low commercial levels unless additional natural resources were discovered and exploited. Thus what became distinctly American was the product of the mutual relationships between eastern urbanization, industrialization, and overseas trading, on the one hand, and western resource exploitation and landscape modification, on the other.[8]

It is within this conceptual framework that the Shenandoah Valley of Virginia is here examined. An area of some 6,500 square miles stretching southwestward 180 miles from the Potomac River to just south of the Natural Bridge, the valley was strategically located with respect to the major directions of interior population movements during the late colonial period. It was a meeting place for settlement expansion westward across the Virginia Piedmont and southward from southeastern Pennsylvania through the Great Valley of the Appalachians to the backcountry of the southern colonies and, after the Revolutionary War, to Kentucky and Tennessee. The valley itself was a major settlement point for these migrations between the 1730s and 1770s. The region's population derived primarily from small-proprietor southeastern Pennsylvania and planter Tidewater Virginia. Thus, this valley offers an opportunity not only to examine commercial evolution in an area

8. For the possible integration of this framework with a wholesale trading model, a regional development model, and a spatial integration model, see respectively, James E. Vance, Jr., *The Merchant's World: The Geography of Wholesaling* (Englewood Cliffs, N.J.: Prentice-Hall, 1970), pp. 1–14, 80–101; David Ward, *Cities and Immigrants: A Geography of Change in Nineteenth-Century America* (New York: Oxford University Press, 1971), pp. 11–49; D. W. Meinig, "American Wests: Preface to a Geographical Interpretation," *Annals Assoc. Amer. Geog.* 62 (1972): 159–84.

being effectively occupied but also to observe both the spread and interaction of two different agrarian systems and modes of commercial life and their integration into the emerging economy and society of the frontier. In theory, the survival of both plantation and nonplantation forms of economy would depend most heavily upon the structural flexibility of the two production systems in new environmental circumstances and the relative numerical and distributional strengths of the representatives of the two systems within the valley. In terms of labor, capital, and commodity options, the more flexible characteristics of the general farming, nonplantation economy introduced from the north would suggest that, the other factors being equal, a small-proprietor, mixed agricultural structure would eventually become dominant.[9] Moreover, the southern half of the valley (the upper valley) presented a somewhat more difficult physical environment to settlers than the northern half (the lower valley), and it was more physically and socially isolated from the longer settled areas along the Atlantic coast. Consequently, one could hypothesize that the less accessible the area, the slower would be its rates of economic development and integration and, consequently, its predisposition for social change.

Few clear trends in the regional variation of economy and society were established immediately in the valley, but elements of potential regionalism were inherent in the area's initial territorial organization. The absence of clearly defined western boundaries posed few problems for the Virginia government until the first decade of the eighteenth century, when interest was first shown in settling west of the Blue Ridge. Three sets of territorial claims were extended westward: those of Lord Baltimore, proprietor of Maryland; of the colony of Virginia; and of Lord Fairfax, proprietor of the Northern Neck in Virginia. A dispute between the Virginia government and Fairfax during the 1730s over the western extent and southern boundary of the Northern Neck proprietary influenced the territorial configuration of the Shenandoah Valley (fig. 4B).[10] The main problem was the vagueness in the Northern Neck charter of the term "First heads or springs"

9. See Robert E. Baldwin, "Patterns of Development in Newly Settled Regions," *Manchester School of Economic and Social Studies* 24 (1956): 161–79.

10. For interpretations of the background to this dispute and its eventual resolution, see Josiah H. Dickinson, *The Fairfax Proprietary* (Front Royal, Va.: Warren Press, 1959); Stuart E. Brown, Jr., *Virginia Baron: The Story of Thomas 6th Lord Fairfax* (Berryville, Va.: Chesapeake Book Co., 1965); Fairfax Harrison, *Virginia Land Grants: A Study in Conveyancing in Relation to Colonial Politics* (Richmond: Old Dominion Press, 1925), pp. 60–134, and Harrison, "The Northern Neck Maps, 1737–1747," *William and Mary Quarterly*, 2d ser. 4 (1924): 1–15.

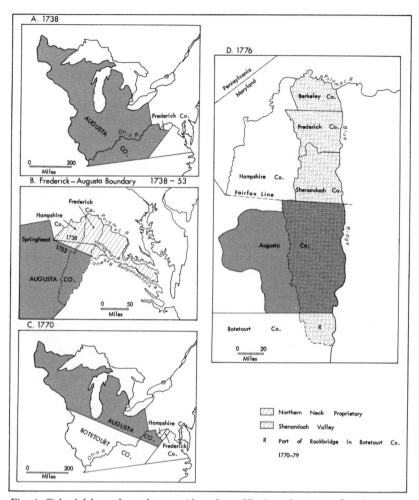

Fig. 4. Colonial boundary changes (data from Hening, *Statutes at Large*)

of the Potomac and Rappahannock rivers. While the problem was being resolved in London, Lieutenant Governor William Gooch took the initiative and subdivided Virginia's claims west of the Blue Ridge into the new counties of Frederick and Augusta in 1738 (fig. 4A).[11] Frederick's southern boundary was a straight line drawn from the crest of the Blue Ridge at the headwaters of the Hedgeman River, the Virginia government's interpretation of "First heads or springs," to Springhead at the head of the Potomac. Augusta, by far the larger of the two counties, stretched "to the utmost reaches of Virginia." The Shenandoah Valley was divided in such a manner that the northern two-fifths was located in Frederick County and the southern three-fifths in Augusta. However, the English Privy Council settled the boundary dispute in 1745 in favor of Lord Fairfax. The decision extended Fairfax's domain west of the Blue Ridge to Springhead, thus including Frederick County within the proprietary, and southward to a new survey line drawn from the Conway River to Springhead part of which, the Fairfax Line, became the revised Augusta-Frederick boundary within the Shenandoah Valley in 1753 (fig. 4B).[12] This boundary line was of little geographical significance at first, for society and economy on either side were basically similar, but Fairfax's ownership of the lower valley later virtually guaranteed the westward penetration of eastern Virginia social and economic influences.

The subsequent formation of new counties from the counties of Frederick (particularly Berkeley and Shenandoah) and Augusta (particularly Rockingham and Rockbridge) diminished their size and eventually, in 1791, produced a close coincidence between the valley as a political and as a physical entity (figs. 4 and 5).[13] It is the 1791 set of boundaries that constitutes the territorial framework of the present study. During the early nineteenth century the final county outline took shape, and by 1836 the present county boundaries had been formed (fig. 5). Only the secession of West Virginia in 1863, and with it Berkeley and Jefferson counties, broke the political unity of the Shenandoah Valley.

The colony of Virginia in the eighteenth century never developed the variety of local administrative units that characterized New England or some of the Middle Colonies. Except for incorporated towns and

11. *The Statutes at Large: Being a Collection of All the Laws of Virginia* . . ., ed. William W. Hening, 13 vols. (Richmond, 1809–23), 5:78–80.

12. Ibid., 6:376–79.

13. Ibid., 8:395–98, 597–99, 9:262–66, 420–24, 10:114, 351, 12:637–38, and 13:165–67.

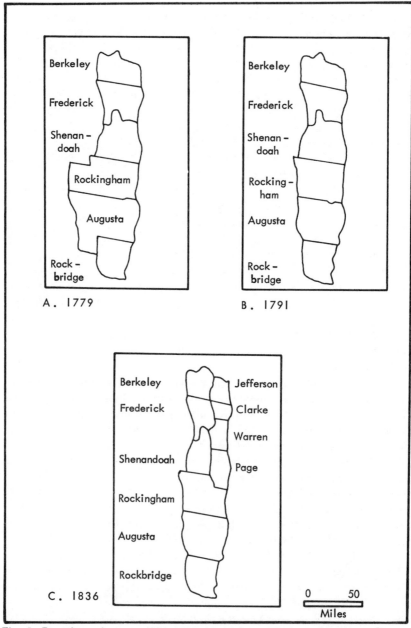

Fig. 5. Boundary changes, 1776–1836 (data from Hening, *Statutes at Large*; Shepherd, *Statutes at Large*)

boroughs, no administrative subdivisions existed by which the individual county unit was reduced into parts for the purposes of local government. The only local functional unit that was as widely distributed as the county was the parish organized by the Anglican church. In many cases, including Frederick and Augusta counties, parish and county boundaries coincided.[14] Thus each individual county in interior Virginia during the eighteenth century was the sole source of local public records until the appearance of incorporated towns after 1778. Although the Revolutionary War produced few immediate geographical changes in the shape of the Virginia frontier, the political change from colony to commonwealth had important repercussions on the reorganization of local government and its records and, consequently, on the availability and structure of the materials needed to interpret the past. County records before 1775, while less well organized, are more varied than those after 1783 when new rules reduced the comprehensiveness but increased the standardization of local records.[15]

Historically, the establishment of a county seat in Virginia did not guarantee the formation of an urban settlement. County seats in several eastern Virginia counties consisted of no more than a courthouse and a jail, often contained in the same building. However, in the Shenandoah Valley the crossroads location of county seats with respect to the main roads in and out of the valley provided these points with a function that went beyond their initial administrative

14. Ibid., 5:78–79; map opposite p. 96 in Charles F. Cocke, *Parish Lines, Diocese of Southwestern Virginia*, Virginia State Library Publications, no. 14 (Richmond, 1960). The significance and functions of the parish and the county are traced in William H. Seiler, "The Anglican Parish in Virginia," in *Seventeenth-Century America*, ed. James M. Smith (Chapel Hill: University of North Carolina Press, 1959), pp. 119–42; Isobel Ferguson, "County Court in Virginia, 1700–1830," *North Carolina Historical Review* 8 (1931): 14–40; Albert O. Porter, *County Government in Virginia, a Legislative History, 1607–1804,* Columbia University Studies in History, Economics, and Public Law, no. 526 (New York, 1947).

15. County records provide a variety of geographical information. For land data the most useful are the land patent books, survey records, deed books, and land tax books (introduced in 1782); for information on population, the court order books and tithable records; for social and economic data, the order books, personal property tax books (introduced in 1782), will books and inventories, court judgments, and petitions and claims (entered after 1775). All of these records are contained in the Virginia State Library, Richmond, in the original, facsimile, or on microfilm, except the court judgments, which are located in the county courthouses.

Because of the concern with trade and the processes of commercialization in this study, the most useful supplementary materials have proved to be local merchant records. A number of Tidewater and Piedmont merchant records also were examined, but other than those mentioned in the text, references to Shenandoah Valley customers were rare.

responsibilities. The seats of the original Frederick and Augusta counties, Winchester and Staunton respectively, had an initial advantage in establishing their commercial functions over later seats established when new counties were formed.[16] In 1800 the valley had a total population of almost 84,000 people. Although most of the towns founded by that date were county administrative centers, all of them had solid commercial foundations. It is a most intriguing question as to how far this condition reflects a departure from the commercial traditions of eastern Virginia in favor of those derived initially from farther north where plantation influences were absent. Part of the answer lies in the motivations for settling the valley and the time of arrival of migrants from the different source areas.

16. The relationships between county seats and the development of urban settlement have been explored for two different areas in H. Roy Merrens, *Colonial North Carolina in the Eighteenth Century* (Chapel Hill: University of North Carolina Press, 1964), pp. 142–72, and James T. Lemon, *The Best Poor Man's Country: A Geographical Study of Early Southeastern Pennsylvania* (Baltimore: Johns Hopkins Press, 1972), pp. 118–49.

2 Initial Occupance and Subsequent Migration

THE westward movement basically consisted of the migration of people and their persistent spread into and occupance of new environments. Newly settled areas in eighteenth-century America were not occupied in a vacuum but as part of a broad internal expansion of populations whose members displayed a variety of attitudes toward place attachment. The attitude that most typified these populations was a predisposition for geographical mobility, as reflected in rapid population turnovers and low rates of settlement persistence.[1] These rates varied from place to place and over time, but all frontier areas were affected by four sets of migration processes: immigration, through-migration, internal movement, and emigration. The interaction of these processes and their relative timing and rates of change influenced and were influenced by a variety of economic, social, political, cultural, and environmental factors. At both national and regional levels the locational consequences of eighteenth-century population movements have been examined in a general way, but very little has been done at subregional and local levels where the more specific clues to explanation lie.

The whole structure of record taking runs counter in many respects to the objectives of migration research. The basic recording unit in Virginia, the county, can provide information as the result of its role as the destination for some population movements and as the point of departure for others, but it can provide few clues to the processes of through-migration or internal movement at the local level. Other records are scarce and provide a meager supplement to county sources. The large size of frontier counties and their periodic boundary changes make consistent measurement of the timing, direction, and distance of movements, as well as the numbers of people involved, very difficult. The probability of measuring both internal migration and emigration accurately, for example, increases as the size of the counties decreases.

1. For interpretations of mobility, persistence, and turnover, see James C. Malin, "The Turnover of Farm Population in Kansas," *Kansas Historical Quarterly* 4 (1935): 339–72; and, for the late eighteenth century, Lemon, *Best Poor Man's Country*, pp. 73–77, and Main, *Social Structure of Revolutionary America*, pp. 164–96.

Internal Movements of Population

The immigration of European settlers to the American colonies during
the eighteenth century was unevenly distributed among colonial ports.
It was focused on the ports of the Northeast, particularly Philadelphia
and adjacent Delaware centers, between 1710 and about 1755. The
most prominent demographic consequence of this migration was the
growth of the Middle Colonies, especially Pennsylvania. Between 1700 and
1780 Pennsylvania increased its share of population from 7% to
over 13% and ranked second only to Virginia by the outbreak of
the Revolution.[2] Through Philadelphia and southeastern Pennsylvania
came a major segment of the population that later settled the southern
interior. The pattern of coastal immigration in the South was much more
diffuse and, except for Negro slaves, less substantial. Consequently, the
eighteenth-century settlement of the southern interior came from two
directions. Settlers moved south and west from Pennsylvania and adjacent
areas and occupied the Southern Colonies from the landward
side, while other immigrants and settlers were moving inland from
Tidewater areas (figs. 2 and 6). The Shenandoah Valley was a
meeting place for settlers from both directions.

The Valley of Virginia, of which the Shenandoah Valley is
the northern part, was known to fur trappers and Indian traders
by the middle of the seventeenth century. It was viewed or explored in
part by John Lederer in 1669 and 1670 (the Shenandoah Valley),
by John Batts and Robert Fallam in 1671 (the Roanoke area), and
probably by Cadwallader Jones in the late 1690s.[3] The Shenandoah
Valley had not been inhabited by any resident Indian tribes for
a considerable period of time before the earliest of these travels. The
absence of sedentary Indians allowed for a more peaceful and orderly
settlement of the area than in many other eighteenth-century frontiers.
However, with the expansion of European settlement inland from the
Virginia Tidewater after 1700, the main routes for war and trading
paths through Virginia between rival northern and southern tribes
moved west to the Shenandoah Valley by the early 1720s.

2. U.S., Bureau of the Census, *Historical Statistics of the United States, Colonial Times to 1957*
(Washington, D.C., 1960), p. 756.

3. John Lederer, *The Discoveries of John Lederer*, trans. Sir William Talbot (London,
1672); *The Discoveries of John Lederer*, ed. William P. Cumming (Charlottesville: University
of Virginia Press, 1958), especially pp. 75, 89–95; Clarence W. Alvord and L. Bidgood, *The
First Explorations of the Trans-Allegheny Region by the Virginians* (Cleveland: Arthur H. Clarke
Co., 1912), pp. 64–73, 131–71, 181–205; Fairfax Harrison, "Western Explorations in Virginia
between Lederer and Spotswood," *Virginia Magazine of History and Biography* 30 (1922): 323–40.

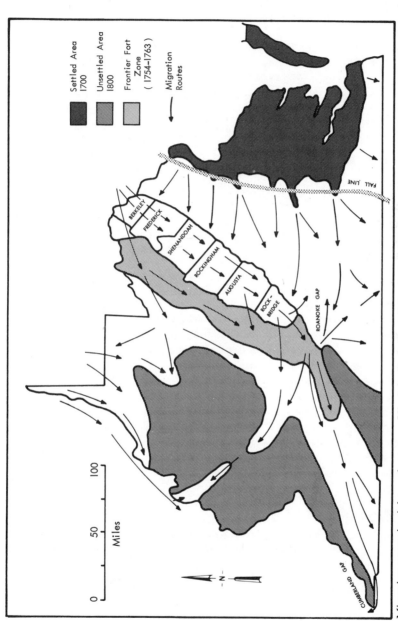

Fig. 6. Migration routes in eighteenth-century Virginia (data from Friis, *Series of Population Maps;* and Mitchell, "The Presbyterian Church as an Indicator of Westward Expansion in 18th Century America," *Professional Geographer* 28[1966]: 293–99)

Consequently, much of the Indian life seen by early settlers was the periodic passage of rival Indian tribes up and down the valley.[4]

By the early 1720s also, recent European immigrants to Pennsylvania were finding it increasingly difficult to acquire suitable land for settlement. As land prices rose, longer-established settlers sold their farms and moved on, and many more recent arrivals began also to move farther inland. Some moved northward to the Lebanon and Lehigh Valleys, while others migrated westward via the lower Susquehanna Valley to the Cumberland Valley, part of the Great Valley of the Appalachians.[5]

Many writers on frontier settlement have explained the reasons why the Great Valley rather than western Pennsylvania provided the major orientation for interior migration before the Revolution. Some have emphasized the topographic and drainage obstacles to easy movement in western Pennsylvania and the natural accessibility of the Great Valley and the attractions of its potentially good agricultural lands.[6] Frederick Jackson Turner attributed the importance of the Great Valley migration routes to ease of access, cheap lands, and fertile limestone soils, while others have emphasized the unpredictable Indian situation in western Pennsylvania, which was so well exploited by the French; the desire by colonial governments to encourage Great Valley settlements as a buffer against possible Indian and French attacks; the problems arising from the drawing of the Pennsylvania-Maryland boundary; and, most of all, the cheapness of

---

4. For Indian treaties, see Hening, *Statutes*, 4:103–6; *Executive Journals of the Council of Colonial Virginia, 1680–1739*, ed. H. R. McIlwaine, 4 vols. (Richmond, 1925–30), 3:552–53; *Calendar of Virginia State Papers and Other Manuscripts, 1652–1781, Preserved at the Capitol in Richmond*, ed. W. F. Palmer, 11 vols. (Richmond, 1875–93), 1:238. See also Walter Stitt Robinson, "Indian Policy of Colonial Virginia" (Ph.D. diss., University of Virginia, 1950), pp. 227–38.

5. Lemon, *Best Poor Man's Country*, pp. 71–97; Wayland F. Dunaway, "Pennsylvania as an Early Distributing Center of Population," *Pennsylvania Magazine of History and Biography* 55 (1931): 134–69.

6. Ellen C. Semple, *American History and Its Geographic Conditions* (Boston: Houghton Mifflin Co., 1903), p. 59; Harlan H. Barrows, *Lectures on the Historical Geography of the United States as Given in 1933*, ed. William A. Koelsch, Department of Geography Research Paper no. 77 (Chicago, 1962), pp. 62–63; Herman R. Friis, *A Series of Population Maps of the Colonies and the United States, 1625–1790*, American Geographical Society Mimeographed Publication no. 3 (New York, 1940), pp. 11–14; Ralph H. Brown, *Historical Geography of the United States* (New York: Harcourt, Brace, and World, 1948), pp. 183–86.

land in the Valley of Virginia in comparison to prices in southeastern Pennsylvania after 1725.[7]

An Environmentally Varied Setting

Although it would be inaccurate to attribute the significance of the Shenandoah Valley to any one major factor, the presence of a large area of broadly undulating, well-watered, fertile land, early perceived to be most suitable for agriculture and lacking permanent Indian settlements, could scarcely have failed to impress the earliest Europeans searching for favorable sites for settlement. The location of the valley between two formidable-looking mountain ranges merely magnified this impact.

Lying between the Blue Ridge to the east and the first ridge of the valley and ridge country to the west, the Shenandoah Valley represents the largest area of fine continuous agricultural land in the Virginia Applachians.[8] The western ridges and the Blue Ridge come closest together at the southern end of Rockbridge County, and are breached only by the James River (fig. 7). The broad continuous valley lying between these two ranges effectively ends at Buchanan. The more rugged, broken terrain of the areas to the south and west, with their isolated pockets of agricultural land, precluded the possibility that these territories would experience a physically uninterrupted pattern of settlement expansion.

The Shenandoah Valley lies open to the north, the direction from which the earliest settlers came. The likelihood that the northern part of the region (the lower valley) would be settled first was further enhanced by internal variations in the physical factors most critical for settlement and accessibility, which tended to deteriorate from northeast to southwest. Topographically, the floor of the valley is gently undulating in the north (with most slopes of less than 3% inclination) and broadly rolling in the south (with slopes increasing to 12% to 15%

7. Turner, *Frontier,* pp. 100–101; Carl Bridenbaugh, *Myths and Realities: Societies of the Colonial South* (Baton Rouge: Louisiana State University Press, 1952), pp. 120–30; Robert W. Ramsey, *Carolina Cradle: Settlement of the Northwest Carolina Frontier, 1747–1762* (Chapel Hill: University of North Carolina Press, 1964), pp. 15–21.

8. For general treatments of the valley, see William Couper, *History of the Shenandoah Valley*, 3 vols. (New York: Lewis Historical Publishing Co., 1952); John W. Wayland, *Twenty-Five Chapters on the Shenandoah Valley* (Strasburg, Va.: Shenandoah Publishing House, 1957); Jean Gottmann, *Virginia in Our Century* (Charlottesville: University Press of Virginia, 1969).

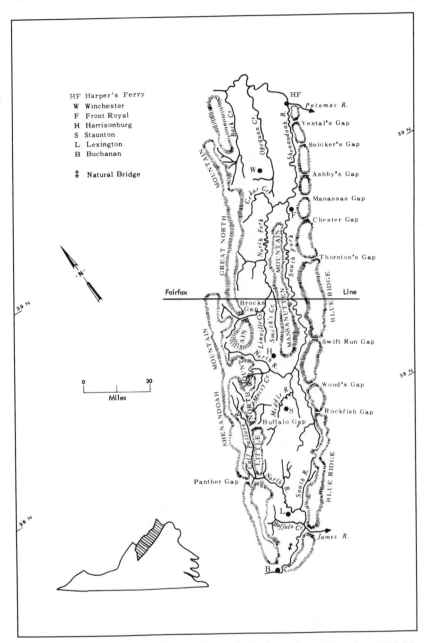

Fig. 7. Shenandoah Valley of Virginia: physical setting (data from USGS Topographic Sheets; Wayland, *Twenty-Five Chapters on the Shenandoah Valley*)

inclination).[9] In width the floor narrows from twenty-six miles at Winchester to less than twenty miles at Staunton and only eight miles at Lexington; it slopes gradually away from the base of the Blue Ridge and increases in elevation to the southwest (570 feet at Front Royal, 1,380 feet at Staunton, and almost 2,000 feet in western Rockbridge County). Although Massanutten Mountain, rising steeply 1,000 to 1,500 feet above the valley floor, divides the central part of the region into two sections and isolates the main fork of the Shenandoah River from the major path of migration immediately to the west, it did not provide a significant barrier to the early southward movement of settlers through the valley.

Climatically, these topographic variations cause temperatures and precipitation, modified by altitude and the mountainous environs, to become less favorable for agricultural activities toward the southwest and the valley sides, with marked deteriorations as altitude increases. Mean temperatures for the warmest months in summer range from 70° to 75° F with a gradual increase from west to east; winter means range from 30° to 34° F, usually being lowest in the western part of the valley.[10] Average annual precipitation varies from thirty-two inches along the western foothills to forty inches in the southwest; snow is common during the winter but rarely lies for long periods on the valley floor.[11] The growing season varies from 165 to 180 days, increasing

9. See Charles Butts, *Geologic Map of the Appalachian Valley of Virginia with Explanatory Text*, Virginia Geological Survey, bulletin no. 42 (Richmond, 1933), and Butts, *Geology of the Appalachian Valley in Virginia, Pt. 1, Geologic Text and Illustrations*, Virginia Geological Survey, bulletin no. 52 (Richmond, 1940). For comments on physiography and drainage, see P. B. King, "The Floor of the Shenandoah Valley," *American Journal of Science* 247 (1949): 73–93; Dorothy Carroll, "Sedimentary Studies in the Middle River Drainage Basin of the Shenandoah Valley of Virginia," *Geological Survey* 314 (1959): 125–54. Some contemporary observations are contained in Thomas Jefferson, *Notes on the State of Virginia*, ed. William Peden (Chapel Hill: University of North Carolina Press, 1955), pp. 21–25.

10. U.S., Department of Agriculture, *Climate and Man, Yearbook of Agriculture* (Washington, D.C., 1941), pp. 1159–69; Gottmann, *Virginia in Our Century*, pp. 19–27.

11. Although snow does not often lie for long periods, it could accumulate to considerable depths. During the winter of 1750, James Patton noted that the weather was so bad that he did not venture out except for church meetings on Sundays (Preston Papers, 10061, Draper Manuscripts, Wisconsin State Historical Society, Madison). Contemporary comments like this on the weather are rare, and they generally refer to unusually harsh winters. One of the most vivid is Fithian's description of the valley for Dec. 23, 1775: "Perhaps I never felt a more cold Day than the 23d. of Decem. The Wind Northeast, and cloudy too—All the Morning we see the Snow falling on the Tops of the high Mountain; none is on the low Lands—Ice in large Cakes passes floating down the rapid River . . . But the River almost never freezes over." At the end of January 1776, he reflected: "People may talk of Virginia's mild Winters, but my Observation is

generally in a northeasterly direction so that the area experiencing 180 days is much more extensive in the lower valley. Settlers who arrived directly from northwestern Europe would have found summers warmer and more humid than they were accustomed to. Otherwise, despite local physical gradients, conditions were not unlike those across the Atlantic, and the crop and livestock patterns which the settlers brought, and to which they added New World domesticates, were well adapted to the seasonal rhythm of the valley.

The region's vegetation patterns have been altered more radically than any other element of the physical environment. Prior to European settlement the valley was most likely covered by oaks and chestnuts with hickories, poplars, maples, and pines in lesser abundance. Early land records indicate that there was still abundant tree growth throughout the Shenandoah Valley at the time of pioneer settlement, when the area was dominated by white oaks with hickories, black oaks, red oaks, chestnuts, pines, and walnuts as the major component species. Pines (scrub, pitch, and white varieties) appear to have been most abundant on the slopes of the Blue Ridge and Massanutten Mountain and along both forks of the Shenandoah River (fig. 8).[12] Adjacent Indian groups had long used the area as a hunting reserve. Their periodic, systematic use of fire to drive and trap game undoubtedly led to changes in the composition and density of the forest and grass cover, favoring the selective growth of grasses and tree species that were relatively fire resistant or exhibited a more open growth pattern. But the frequency and extent of grassland areas has been greatly exaggerated by later writers, and there was certainly no single

---

a convincing Evidence with me that this has been long, and most of it, extreme cold" (Philip Vickers Fithian, *Journal, 1775–1776*, ed. R. G. Albion and L. Dodson [Princeton N.J.: Princeton University Press, 1934], pp. 147, 178). For general observations on eighteenth-century winters, see David M. Ludlum, *Early American Winters, 1604–1820* (Boston: American Meteorological Society, 1966).

12. Of the boundary trees denoted by surveyors in the 455 land surveys recorded for the upper valley between 1735 and 1755, white oaks were mentioned 1,144 times (40%), hickories 594 (20%), black oaks 440 (15%), red oaks 201, Spanish oaks 123, chestnuts 116, walnuts 68, pines 66, locusts 53, poplars 41, and chestnut oaks 28. Many of these surveys were carried out by Thomas Lewis, the first surveyor of Augusta County, who was also employed in the official survey of the Fairfax Line in 1746. For a fuller description of early vegetation patterns, see Robert D. Mitchell, "The Upper Shenandoah Valley of Virginia during the Eighteenth Century" (Ph.D. diss., University of Wisconsin, 1969), pp. 33–42. The precise distribution of pine species cannot be reconstructed because Lewis uses the term *pine* to refer to a group of species. The distribution pattern of individual species appears to have changed little in the last two hundred years. See Alan H. Strahler, "Forests of the Fairfax Line," *Annals Assoc. Amer. Geog.* 62 (1972): 664–84.

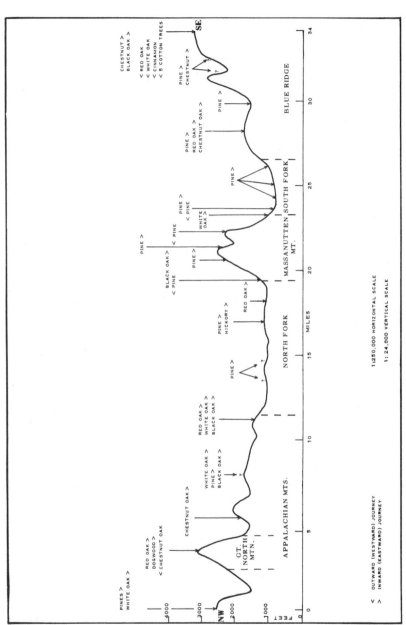

Fig. 8. Boundary tree transect along Fairfax Line, 1746 (data from Thomas Lewis, Journal of 1746–Field Notes, Brock Collection, Huntington Library, San Marino, Calif.)

uninterrupted grassland covering the valley floor.[13] Rather, the early settlers would have encountered a region covered with predominantly open to relatively dense woodlands of hardwoods and pines in various phases of succession interspersed with relatively open grassland areas of varying extents.[14] Prior Indian hunting activities together with evidence from early European accounts testify that the valley abounded in a large variety of game, especially deer, elk, buffalo, and bear.

Access to the settled outside world was easiest to the north, where crossing the Potomac River was the only major obstacle. The main northeast-to-southwest topographic alignment of the valley and its mountain borders is followed by the northward-flowing Shenandoah River. North of the Massanutten Mountain the valley has a gradient of less than two feet per mile, and the river meanders broadly in a shallow channel bordered by a series of floodplain terraces which the early settlers perceived to be excellent for grazing land. In the section divided by Massanutten Mountain, the Shenandoah exhibits a remarkable series of meanders entrenched 100 to 150 feet into the valley floor. This section interrupted any use of the river for navigation above Front Royal. The valley of the James River produces a less meandering and entrenched pattern, but it breaks through the Blue Ridge in a narrow, steep-sided gorge which can be negotiated only with great difficulty. Stream flow and river depth

13. The origin of the view that the valley was covered with prairies by the early eighteenth century seems to derive from Samuel Kercheval, *A History of the Valley of Virginia* (Winchester, Va., 1833), p. 69, or p. 52 in the more accessible 4th edition (Strasburg, Va.: Shenandoah Publishing House, 1925). It was further expanded in William H. Foote, *Sketches of Virginia, Historical and Biographical* (Philadelphia: Lippincott, 1850), p. 13, and William Meade, *Old Churches, Ministers, and Families of Virginia*, 2 vols. (Philadelphia: Lippincott, 1857), 2:279n. The "prairie idea" has been reiterated by writers ever since. See, for example, Hu Maxwell, "The Use and Abuse of Forests by the Virginia Indians," *William and Mary Quarterly*, 1st ser. 19 (1910): 73–103; John W. Wayland, *The German Element of the Shenandoah Valley of Virginia* (Charlottesville, 1907), p. 5, and Wayland, *Twenty-Five Chapters on the Shenandoah Valley*, pp. 18–19; Couper, *History of the Shenandoah Valley*, 1:1; Howard McK. Wilson, *The Tinkling Spring: Headwater of Freedom* (Fisherville, Va.: Tinkling Spring and Hermitage Presbyterian Churches, 1954), pp. 2–3; Gottmann, *Virginia in Our Century*, pp. 233–34; Merle C. Prunty, "Some Geographical Views of the Role of Fire in Settlement Processes in the South," *Tall Timbers Fire Ecology Conference Proceedings* (Tallahassee, Fla., 1964), pp. 164–65.

14. William C. Robison, "Cultural Plant Geography of the Middle Applachians" (Ph.D. diss., Boston University, 1960), p. 162, concluded that "the Shenandoah Valley probably was burned to a greater degree than any other part of the Middle Applachians but that this burning was spotty and did not produce continuous prairies of great extent." See also Edmund Ruffin, "Inquiry into the Causes of the Formation of Prairies, and of the Peculiar Constitution of Soil Which Favors or Prevents the Destruction of Forests," *Farmer's Register* (1825): 334–35.

in the Shenandoah and James rivers show marked seasonal variations, with both rivers attaining their highest levels in late winter and early spring.[15] Both are at their lowest during late summer and early fall, just when local farmers were marketing their crops. Thus, even where they were navigable, the region's rivers proved of little worth for transportation.

To the east the Blue Ridge creates a barrier to movement which becomes progressively more difficult toward the south. Bordering the lower valley the Blue Ridge seldom rises above 3,000 feet and is pitted with numerous low wind gaps, ranging from 1,000 to 1,800 feet above sea level, which rarely posed serious problems for early road builders. Along the upper valley the mountains become steeper and increase rapidly in height to between 3,500 and 4,000 feet. Wind gaps are higher and more widely spaced. In this section only Rockfish Gap at 1,850 feet and Swift Run Gap at 2,400 feet were penetrated by roads before 1785 (fig. 7). The western mountain boundaries of the valley, known collectively as the North Mountain during the eighteenth century, average 2,000 feet in height in the north and almost 3,500 feet in the south. Interest in penetrating these mountains to the west developed only after the Revolution.

Strategic and Commercial Rationales for Initial Settlement

The first recorded attempts at settlement occurred soon after the early explorations of the region. Louis Michel, with some other Swiss companions who had traveled in Pennsylvania, probably explored the lower Shenandoah Valley around Harper's Ferry in 1704 or 1705. Regarding the valley as a desirable area in which to establish a Swiss Protestant colony, they sent petitions to Queen Anne requesting land grants in the lower valley to accommodate 400 to 500 initial settlers. The early financing of the project would be undertaken by Her Majesty's government, but once the area was settled by the Swiss, "We hope and expect Minerals Hemp flax Wine Salt and other

15. J. J. Dirzulaitis and G. C. Stevens, *Water Resources of Virginia*, Virginia Geological Survey, bulletin no. 31 (Richmond, 1927), pp. 37–47, 55–58, 73–74, 80–81, 176–79, 225–27. The average discharges for the Shenandoah River at Harper's Ferry for January through April were between 4,000 and 6,000 second-feet. In the James River basin, for the same period, average discharges ranged from 2,500 to 5,000 second-feet. In the fall, the Shenandoah averaged 750 to 2,000 second-feet and the James only 300 to 500 second-feet.

16. Charles E. Kemper, "Documents Relating to Early Projected Swiss Colonies in the Valley of Virginia, 1706–1709," *Va. Mag. Hist. Biog.* 29 (1921): 12.

Necessarie improvements will soon appear."[16] The British government
approved the project in 1709, but they refused to allow the settlement
to become a separate colony and the whole scheme failed to
materialize. In that same year, Christopher de Graffenreid, another Swiss
who had been associated with Michel, obtained an order authorizing
the establishment of a settlement on the Shenandoah River, "as
benefit and advantage by strengthening the frontier of Virginia
against the French of Canada and Mississippi."[17] On arriving in
Virginia, Graffenreid discovered that the area he proposed to settle was
in dispute between Lord Baltimore and Lord Fairfax. He abandoned this
project and instead established a settlement at New Bern in North
Carolina. The two earliest proposals for occupying the Shenandoah Valley
were, therefore, based on planned group settlement, justified on grounds
of defense, religion, and potential commercial contributions, but unable to
overcome doubts concerning independent colonies and landownership.

Twenty years elapsed before any other large-scale colonization schemes
were attempted in the Shenandoah Valley. In 1730 Jacob Stover (Stauber),
a Swiss farmer in southeastern Pennsylvania, and several associates
requested permission from the Virginia House of Burgesses to establish
a German-speaking, Swiss Protestant colony "behind the mountains,"
thus forming a settlement wedge between the French in Canada
and in Louisiana. They sought a 10,000-acre grant on the south
fork of the Shenandoah River. Stover previously had taken a three-month
exploratory trip to the Shenandoah Valley to view the soil and
topography. In his estimation it possessed good pastureland and soils
suitable for the production of hemp, flax, and grain. Prospects for
making saltpeter and potash seemed good, the mountain slopes could
be used for vineyards, and the climate seemed suitable for silk
production.[18]

Stover and his associates planned an ambitious colony of considerable
size which, if it had been established, would have radically altered
patterns of settlement and economy in western Virginia during the

17. Brown, Jr., *Virginia Baron*, p. 41. See also Harrison, *Virginia Land Grants*, p. 148.
18. See Kemper, "Documents Relating to Early Projected Swiss Colonies in the Valley of
Virginia, 1706–1709," *Va. Mag. Hist. Biog.* 29 (1921): 1–17, 180–82, and Kemper, "Documents
Relating to a Proposed Swiss and German Colony in the Western Part of Virginia,"
ibid., 29 (1921): 183–90, 287–91. See also Ann V. Strickler Milbourne, "Colony West
of the Blue Ridge Proposed by Jacob Stauber and Others, 1731," ibid., 35 (1927): 175–90, and
36 (1928): 58–70; *Calendar of State Papers, Colonial Series, America and West Indies*, ed. A. P.
Newton et al. (London: H.M. Stationery Office, 1860), 38 (1731): 77, 212, 247–49;
Great Britain, Board of Trade, *Journal of the Commissioners for Trade and Plantations*, 14 vols.
(London: H.M. Stationery Office, 1920–38), 6: 188–89, 232.

eighteenth century. Sir William Keith, a future governor of Pennsylvania, who was officially requested to give his opinion of the proposed colony, believed it to be strategically and commercially propitious. Because the project would be largely financed by the settlers themselves once they were established, settlement of the area should be "on much easier Terms than would in all likelyhood be obtained from Persons of overgrown Estates and opulent Fortunes." However, it was one of those "Persons of overgrown Estates" who objected most strongly to the establishment of the Stover colony. Thomas Fairfax, sixth Baron Fairfax of Cameron, who had become sole proprietor of the Northern Neck in 1719, objected to the Board of Trade about Stover's proposals because they intruded on his claims west of the Blue Ridge. The colony was never established.[19]

Stover himself, nevertheless, acquired from the Virginia governor and Council lands on the south fork of the Shenandoah River. It was in this vicinity that the earliest permanent settlements in the Shenandoah Valley were established. In December 1733 Stover patented two 5,000-acre tracts of land on the south fork of the river. His northern (lower) tract was located on both sides of the river from the mouth of Hawksbill Creek (opposite Thornton's Gap) to just north of the Fairfax Line as drawn in 1745. His southern tract was located on both sides of the river in Rockingham County between Cub Run (opposite Swift Run Gap) and the northeastern corner of Augusta County.[20]

Two questions related to Stover's patents require some reexamination. The reason why Stover's lands were located so far up in the valley has never been satisfactorily explained. The usual suggestion has been that they were in open, grassy areas which would have been easy to settle. It is more likely, however, that the location of the patented tracts was influenced by Stover's desire to avoid further disputes with Lord Fairfax. Both patents were located just south of the Northern Neck boundary recognized by the Virginia government. The northern boundary of Stover's lower tract corresponded to the southern boundary of his

19. *Journal of Commissioners for Trade and Plantations*, 7: 189, 234ff. Compare Thomas P. Abernethy, "The First Transmountain Advance," in *Humanistic Studies in Honor of John Calvin Metcalf*, University of Virginia Studies, vol. 1 (Charlottesville, 1941), pp. 120–38.

20. See *Executive Journals*, ed. McIlwaine, 4:223–24; Spotsylvania Co. Patent Book 15:127; Harry M. Strickler, *Massanutten, Settled by the Pennsylvania Pilgrim, 1726: The First White Settlement in the Shenandoah Valley* (Strasburg, Va.: Shenandoah Publishing House, 1924), map opposite p. 120. F. B. Kegley, *Kegley's Virginia Frontier: The Beginning of the Southwest, the Roanoke of Colonial Days, 1740–1783* (Roanoke: Southwest Virginia Historical Society, 1938) is a useful source of information on the westward movement in Virginia.

earlier colony project. In addition, his proximity to Thornton's Gap provided access to eastern Virginia.

A second question concerns the timing of the earliest settlements in the valley. There may have been German and Swiss settlers in the valley by 1726 in the vicinity of Hawksbill Creek, although Stover does not mention them in the report of his travels.[21] Adam Müller and his fellow settlers, who seem to have been living on Hawksbill Creek as early as 1727, had been buying land from Stover even before the latter secured a patent for his two tracts. It seems probable, therefore, that the presence of the Müller settlement was also an important factor in the location of Stover's tracts, although Müller might have been encouraged to settle in the valley by prospective northern land speculators.[22] Immediately after he acquired his lands, Stover sold his upper tract to a group of German settlers from Lancaster County, Pennsylvania, for over £400. By the end of that year there were fifty-one settlers on this 5,000-acre tract.[23] The Stover patents thus provided impetus to the settling of the south fork of the Shenandoah River in the upper part of the valley.

Land Grants in the Lower Shenandoah Valley

Further evidence of commercial motivations for settlement and the impact of large land grants on the distribution of pioneer settlement is provided by the contributions of Jost Hite (Hans Jost Heydt), Robert McKay, and their associates. In June 1730 John and Isaac Van Meter applied to the Virginia governor and Council for a tract of land west of the Blue Ridge on which to settle themselves, their families, and friends from the colony of New York. Between them the two brothers received three grants: a 10,000-acre tract in the forks of the Shenandoah River and extending up Cedar Creek; a second tract, of 20,000 acres, between the Potomac, the Shenandoah, and Opequon Creek; and a

21. See Charles E. Kemper, "The Early Westward Movement," *Va. Mag. Hist. Biog.* 13 (1905): 116–17.

22. See the reproduction of Müller's naturalization paper in "First Settler in the Valley," *Wm. and Mary Qtly.*, 1st ser. 9 (1900–1901): 132–33. Müller is reputed to have come from Lancaster County in 1726 or 1727 and eventually to have acquired 820 acres in Rockingham County in 1742 which had expanded to 1,300 acres by his death in 1783. These events cannot be verified from extant county records, but see Charles E. Kemper, "The Settlement of the Valley," *Va. Mag. Hist. Biog.* 30 (1922): 172–73; Richard L. Morton, *Colonial Virginia*, 2 vols. (Chapel Hill: University of North Carolina Press, 1960), 2:543.

23. *Calendar of Virginia State Papers*, ed. Palmer, 1:219–20.

third tract of 10,000 acres between the Shenandoah and the Opequon.[24] Two general stipulations had to be met. One family had to be settled for every 1,000 acres of land granted, and this settlement had to be accomplished within a two-year period.

Because of lawsuits filed against them by Fairfax's agent and their difficulties in complying with the settlement requirements, the Van Meters sold their grants to Jost Hite, a relative and former Hudson River valley neighbor, in August 1731. Hite moved from Pennsylvania to Opequon Creek, and in October he, McKay, and associates received another grant for 100,000 acres located immediately south and west of the lower Van Meter grants.[25] Since the family settlement stipulations had to be met for this huge area, Hite in particular became active in recruiting settlers in Pennsylvania for all of his group's tracts in the lower valley. By Christmas 1735 the settlement requirements on the Van Meter grants were judged to have been fulfilled, and twenty-seven valid surveys had been made totaling 37,834 acres. At least sixty-seven families were settled on these lands in Frederick and Berkeley counties by this time, although fifty-four families was the total number that Hite and McKay had actually settled on their tract.[26] Clearly, the efforts by recipients of large grants of what the Virginia government considered to be crown land to comply with the settlement stipulations attached to them was a major factor in the early prominence of the Shenandoah Valley as a settlement magnet.

On the other hand, two local factors may have operated against a regular, systematic settlement of the lower valley. Lord Fairfax and Jost Hite and his heirs carried on a long dispute over land ownership. The dispute derived from Fairfax's insistence that Hite had failed to comply with the government's family settlement requirements and that the surveys which had been made were not "regular." In 1712 the Virginia Assembly had passed an act which provided that the breadth of a patented tract should be at least one-third of its length except where interrupted by rivers, creeks, or swamps.[27] The act had been subject to broad interpretation, and Fairfax's accusation that

24. *Executive Journals*, ed. McIlwaine, 4:223.

25. Fairfax vs. Hite, 1735–39, Report to the Lords of the Committee of His Majesty's Privy Council, Virginia Miscellany, Manuscript Division, Library of Congress, Washington, D.C. For Hite's background and movements, see Klaus Wust, *The Virginia Germans* (Charlottesville: University Press of Virginia, 1969), pp. 32–35; [Francis] Richardson Hillier, "The Hite Family and the Settlement of the West" (M.A. thesis, University of Virginia, 1936), pp. 1–13.

26. Brown, Jr., *Virginia Baron*, pp. 166–67.

27. Hening, *Statutes*, 4:38.

Hite had established many illegal, odd-shaped plats could have been applied equally to many other frontier landowners. However, some of the families whom Hite had settled never had their land surveyed, while other plats were calculated to have enclosed areas of up to twice the size of the original acreages circumscribed in the patents.[28]

Several writers have suggested that the confusion over land titles retarded the settling of the lower valley and caused many settlers to avoid Hite's lands and move farther south within the valley.[29] The earliest tithable records provide only partial support for these opinions. In September 1745 it was reported that there were 1,283 tithables in Frederick County and 1,196 in Augusta County.[30] Although the figure for Augusta is relatively high despite the county's more limited accessibility to early migration streams, one might have expected an even higher total if the Hite-Fairfax dispute had really discouraged settlement farther north.

The attitude of Lord Fairfax and his agents toward frontier settlement also had important implications for the settling of the valley. Although Fairfax objected on technical grounds to the surveys made for Hite, he claimed to have no complaints with the settlers who were already located on his lands because he wanted to encourage settlement of the lower valley. He also claimed that Hite's behavior had discouraged the growth of frontier settlement.[31] Yet his own land-granting activities hardly spurred settlement. His agent in Virginia, Robert Carter, had initiated the first surveying of lands in the lower valley in 1727, and the first grants were made in 1728.[32] By 1740 eastern Virginians, many of whom were members of the Fairfax family or close friends, had acquired over 470,000 acres in the lower valley

28. See especially Brown, Jr., *Virginia Baron*, pp. 72–79, which is based on the papers of the Hite suit in the British Museum, and Dickinson, *Fairfax Proprietary*, appendix, pp. xi–lv, which is based on the manuscripts in the Library of Congress. Brown favors Fairfax and describes Hite and other substantial non-Virginian grantees in the lower valley as "hucksters" (see pp. 73, 113–14, 117, 163).

29. Wayland, *German Element in the Shenandoah Valley*, p. 52; J. Lewis Peyton, *History of Augusta County* (Staunton, Va.: S. M. Yost and Son, 1882), p. 66; Joseph A. Waddell, *Annals of Augusta County, Virginia* (Richmond: W. Ellis Jones, 1886), p. 10; Wilson, *Tinkling Spring*, pp. 29–30.

30. Preston Papers, IQQ29–30, Draper Manuscripts, Wis. State Hist. Soc.

31. Brown, Jr., *Virginia Baron*, pp. 116–17. A witness ventured the opinion that Hite and McKay also asked high prices for their land.

32. See "James [Thomas], Account of Expenses at Chenandoah [1727 and 1729]," Fairfax Papers, vol. 1, Brock Collection, Huntington Library, San Marino, Calif. Carter had 52,212 acres surveyed for himself in the lower valley on both sides of the Shenandoah River (Dickinson, *Fairfax Proprietary*, p. 6).

from Lord Fairfax; but since they had no settlement requirements to fulfill, these owners used their lands more as speculative ventures than as inducements to others to settle. They did have to pay quitrents, at 2s. per 100 acres, to the proprietor. Although these rents were more efficiently collected than on crown lands, this efficiency is most evident after the mid-1750s, when Lord Fairfax had taken up permanent residence in the valley, and was extended more to the smaller and middle-sized grantees than it was to the larger ones, who were often more than ten years in arrears.[33] By means of these grants eastern Virginia landowners were later able to imprint their own patterns on the economic and cultural life of the lower valley. Many of the settlers who moved onto these lands migrated from Northern Neck areas in eastern Virginia either as landowners or as persons employed by absentee owners to develop the lands into economic units. The location of the earliest of such large grants along the Shenandoah River in eastern Frederick County (present-day Clarke County) paved the way for significant concentrations of Tidewater influence in this area after the French and Indian War.[34]

Land Grants in the Upper Shenandoah Valley

The granting of 118,491 acres in the future Augusta County to William Beverley and others in September 1736 and 92,100 acres in the future Rockbridge County to Benjamin Borden, Sr., in November 1739 set the tone for the settlement of the upper valley (fig. 9).[35] By 1740, 539,000 acres within the Shenandoah Valley had been granted by

33. This conclusion is based on an examination of the Northern Neck Land Books and Quit Rent Rolls and the county abstracts of the Land Office Records in the Virginia State Library, as well as the Fairfax Papers, Brock Collection, Huntington Library.

34. Willard F. Bliss, "The Tuckahoe in the Valley" (Ph.D. diss., Princeton University, 1946); Bliss, "The Rise of Tenancy in Virginia," *Va. Mag. Hist. Biog.* 58 (1950): 427–41; Bliss, "The Tuckahoe in New Virginia," ibid., 59 (1951): 387–96. Compare Robert D. Mitchell, "Content and Context: Tidewater Characteristics in the Early Shenandoah Valley," *Maryland Historian* 5 (1974): 79–92.

35. The original patent for Beverley's grant is in the manuscript collection of the Virginia Historical Society, Richmond. See also Land Office Records, no. 29, Orange Co., Book 17:54, Va. State Lib. The best background material on Beverley is in Jane D. Carson, "William Beverley and Beverley Manor" (M.A. thesis, University of Virginia, 1937), and John McGill *The Beverley Family in Virginia* (Columbia, S.C.: R. L. Bryan Co., 1956), pp. 534–35. Information on Borden is contained in J. A. Kelly, "Benjamin Borden, Shenandoah Valley Pioneer: Notes on His Ancestry and Descendants," *Wm. and Mary Qtly.*, 2d ser. 11 (1931) : 325–29, and Kegley, *Kegley's Virginia Frontier*, pp. 148–50.

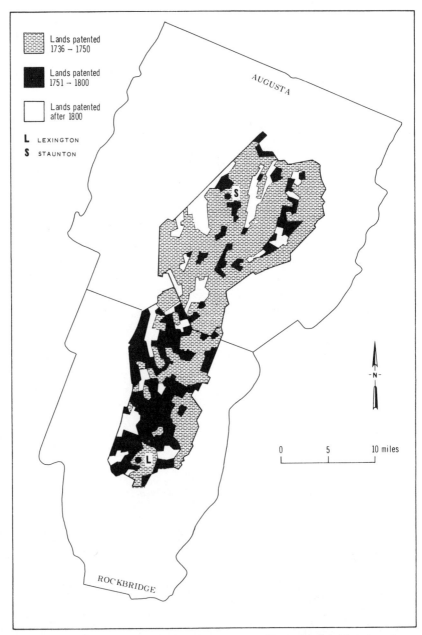

Fig. 9. Settlement of Beverley Manor and Borden's Tract, 1736–1800 (data from Orange County Deed Books 1–10; Augusta County Deed Books 1–29; Rockbridge County Deed Books 1–3; Land Office Records, Augusta and Rockbridge counties)

the Virginia government to eight individuals or partnerships.[36] Since they were obliged to follow the same general settlement stipulations as the other grantees of large areas of crown land, Beverley and Borden had to find settlers for their lands. The statement that "the settlement of the Valley was carried forward by speculators who thus became immigration agents"[37] applies more to Beverley and Borden than it does to those who received land from Lord Fairfax.

Both Beverley, a Tidewater planter from Essex County, and Borden, a former New Jersey land agent, are said to have been active in recruiting settlers for their huge grants, although there is no evidence to indicate that they ever went abroad or recruited abroad for settlers.[38] A close examination of the settlement history of Borden's tract shows that he had considerable difficulty in obtaining the required number of families within the stipulated period. Many of his early settlers came from New Jersey.[39] Beverley had much the wider range of social and commercial contacts. Yet he does not seem to have placed advertisements in the *Pennsylvania Gazette*, and only two references appear in the shipping records for the lower Chesapeake Bay to indicate that James Patton, an Ulster captain, might have imported Scotch-Irish immigrants at Beverley's request.[40] In 1737 Beverley wrote Patton that he would be happy if Patton could import families either from Pennsylvania, as mentioned in the government's order, or from Ireland.[41] By the end of 1738 Beverley had made two grants of 474 and 1,230 acres in Beverley Manor, a manor only

36. Manning C. Voorhis, "The Land Grant Policy of Colonial Virginia, 1607–1774" (Ph.D. diss., University of Virginia, 1940), p. 162.

37. Abernethy, "The First Transmountain Advance," *Humanistic Studies*, p. 137.

38. Peyton, *History of Augusta County,* pp. 64–65; Waddell, *Annals of Augusta County*, pp. 16–17; Charles E. Kemper, "Historical Notes from the Records of Augusta County, Virginia—Part 2," *Lancaster [Pa.] County Historical Society, Papers* 25 (1921): 149–50; G. Melvin Herndon, "George Mathews, Frontier Patriot," *Va. Mag. Hist. Biog.* 77 (1969): 307. The use of agents in Philadelphia and adjacent southeast Pennsylvania rather than newspaper advertisements would seem to have been a more realistic method of settlement recruitment for Beverley and Borden in view of the fact that many immigrants were either illiterate or did not read English. If this was the case, the extent to which both men actually recuited in Pennsylvania may never be known.

39. Orange Co. Deed Books 6–10, and Augusta Judgments, 1745–46 (file 385). Borden and his temporary partner petitioned successfully for a one-year reprieve on the two-year limit for settling his tract (*Executive Journals*, ed. McIlwaine, 4:408–9).

40. Virginia Shipping Returns, South Potomac and Accomac Districts, 1735–56, C.O.5/1445, British Public Record Office (on microfilm, Library, Union Theological Seminary, Richmond), specifically for Aug. 26, 1738, and Aug. 23, 1739.

41. William Beverley to James Patton, Aug. 8, 1737, and also Beverley to Patton, Aug. 22, 1737, William Beverley Papers, New York Public Library, New York. Note also Worthington C. Ford, "Some Letters of William Beverley," *Wm. and Mary Qtly.*, 1st ser. 3 (1894–95): 226–27.

in name and not in function, to Patton and promised that if Patton's relative, John Preston, emigrated, he would also receive land. When Preston did emigrate with his family, he reported that they had come "directly from Ireland," which might indicate that they landed on the Virginia coast and made their way westward to the upper valley over the Blue Ridge. About thirty-five other families between 1738 and 1740 indicated that they had emigrated in a similar manner; they may have been imported by Patton as part of his trading activities.[42]

Some of the early German settlers in Shenandoah and Rockingham counties also migrated westward from eastern Virginia well ahead of Tidewater Virginians. In 1731 a group of German Protestants petitioned for a 50,000-acre tract north of Stover's tracts on the main fork of the Shenandoah River. Of the German petitioners at least two, John Fishback and Jacob Holtzklow (Holzclaw), seem to have been from the German settlement founded in the Virginia Piedmont in 1714.[43] Thus, although the migration of Scotch-Irish and German settlers and immigrants from eastern Virginia to the Shenandoah Valley probably has been underestimated for the period before 1750, the pattern of migration was a discontinuous "leapfrog" movement which bore little connection with the more gradual but constant westward expansion of settlement in the Piedmont by eastern Virginians.

The majority of pioneer settlers in the upper Shenandoah Valley, however, migrated from southeastern Pennsylvania and adjacent areas in the Middle Colonies. This process was already in operation before the grant to Beverley in 1736. Squatters of Scotch-Irish origin with no legal title to land were probably settled in the area later contained within Beverley Manor as early as 1732, but very few seem to have settled permanently there. Although Beverley frequently took legal action against settlers on his upper valley tracts, most of the litigation was for debt for land purchase.[44] Squatting of a more prolonged

42. Augusta Co. Order Book 1:44. See also Orange Co. Order Book 2:109–10, 114, 119, 138, 155–60, 185, 205–18, 225.

43. Comparison of names of petitioners in *Executive Journals,* ed. McIlwaine, 4:250 with those of early Germanna settlers in William J. Hinke, "The 1714 Colony of Germanna, Virginia," *Va. Mag. Hist. Biog.* 40 (1932): 317–27, and 41 (1933): 41–49. For suggestions that some Germanna settlers eventually settled in the Shenandoah Valley, including Hite's lands in the lower valley, see John W. Wayland, *A History of Rockingham County* (Dayton, Va.: Ruebush-Elkins Co., 1912), p. 43; Elmer L. Smith, J. G. Stewart, and M. E. Kyer, *The Pennsylvania Germans of the Shenandoah Valley,* Pennsylvania German Folklore Society, vol. 26 (Allentown, Pa., 1962), p. 25; Wust, *Virginia Germans,* pp. 35–36.

44. See Orange Co. Order Book 2:224ff., and the two Beverley Manor Account Books contained in the Virginia Historical Society and in the Beverley Papers, New York Public Library, respectively. The account book in the Virginia Historical Society's collection

nature was most likely to occur either in the most inaccessible areas or on those lands belonging to the crown or to the proprietary which were outside the boundaries of the large land grants. On the other hand, the relationship between the settling of these large grants and the timing of pioneer settlement was such that there was relatively little opportunity for squatting. The granting of large tracts to individuals or groups occurred just before or at the same time as the first major settlement influx to the Shenandoah Valley about 1740. Moreover, the establishment of grants, with the responsibility for settling them resting with the grantees, was specifically designed to encourage a more rapid process of migration to the area. The early process of settlement, therefore, was centered on the large land grants whose grantees actively participated in encouraging settlement by one means or another.

The majority of direct immigrants to the upper valley from western Europe were Scotch-Irish who came via Philadelphia, while those moving out of Pennsylvania were from a wide variety of ethnic backgrounds.[45] The virtual absence of German names from immigrant records, even allowing for surname anglicization, suggests that German settlers in the valley by 1750 had already been farming elsewhere in the colonies, especially in Pennsylvania, New Jersey, and New York. Some had been encouraged by the recruiting attempts of Stover, Hite, and others in the lower valley, but many arrived to patent lands on their own behalf. Settlers of English and Scotch-Irish origins also set up a steady stream of migration out of Pennsylvania. Direct immigrants from Northern Ireland arrived primarily at their own expense rather than as indentured

---

contains a few details not found in the other copy. For comments on the preemptive rights of squatters, see Thomas P. Abernethy, "The Southern Frontier, an Interpretation," in *The Frontier in Perspective*, eds. Walker D. Wyman and C. B. Kroeber (Madison: University of Wisconsin Press, 1970), p. 13; Lemon, *Best Poor Man's Country*, pp. 55–57.

45. Of particular significance is *Pennsylvania Archives*, 3d ser., ed. William H. Egle, 30 vols. (Harrisburg, Pa., 1897–1901), vol. 24, which contains abstracts of land warrants for the period after 1733 in several Pennsylvania counties which provided immigrants to the Shenandoah Valley, especially Philadelphia, Chester, Bucks, Lancaster, and Cumberland. Volume 26 contains the abstracts for Berks County, but no data are available on York County warrants. For early immigration to the valley, see especially Orange Co. Order Books 1–4 and Deed Books 3–10; Frederick Co. Order Books 1–6 and Deed Books 1–3; and Augusta Co. Order Books 1–3 and Deed Books 1–3. For secondary interpretations, see Kemper's studies, "Early Westward Movement of Virginia," *Va. Mag. Hist. Biog.* 13 (1905): 1–16, 113–38; "Historical Notes from the Records of Augusta County, Virginia," *Lancaster* [Pa.] *Co. Hist. Soc. Papers* 25 (1921): 89–92, 147–155; "Settlement of the Valley," *Va. Mag. Hist. Biog.* 30 (1922): 169–82; "Early Settlers in the Valley of Virginia," *Wm. and Mary Qtly.*, 2d ser. 5 (1925): 259–65. See also Ramsey, *Carolina Cradle*, pp. 15–60; Kegley, *Kegley's Virginia Frontier*, pp. 31–47.

servants, which may indicate that they were no less economically prepared to set up house than settlers with previous experience in the colonies. They tended to concentrate on the Beverley and Borden grants in the upper valley.

Between 1738 and 1750 William Beverley was able to record 199 land patents in Beverley Manor to incoming settlers from Northern Ireland and Pennsylvania. This represented 59% of all the patents made in Beverley Manor during the eighteenth century (fig. 9). Benjamin Borden, who was probably handicapped by the competition from Beverley Manor, did not record his first patent until November 1741. By 1750, 121 patents had been made in his tract, which represented 40% of all those made during the century. The main infilling of Borden's Tract occurred during the 1750s and 1760s.[46]

The significance of Beverley Manor and, to a lesser extent, of Borden's Tract in the distribution of settlement by 1750 can be seen in fig. 10. Although by this time there were settlements in the Shenandoah Valley from the Potomac to the Forks of the James, there was no continuous line of settlement. Rather, areas of settlement were strung out along the main stream courses, with a relatively high density in the lower valley in the vicinity of the future county seat of Winchester. In the upper valley the most prominently settled areas were contained within the boundaries of Beverley Manor. Other important settlement focuses had been established in the southern end of Borden's Tract and on Linville Creek in northern Rockingham County. Fulmer Mood's statement about the plurality of frontier lines in 1740 was true also of 1750: "there yet remain numerous discrete settled areas that by no stretch of the mind can be thought of as forming integrated parts of the major population continuum . . . including backcountry settlements along the Valley of Virginia."[47]

Changing Frontiers, 1750–1776

The frontiers of settlement in 1750 were located far to the south beyond the James River. Isolated groups and individuals had settled

46. The Augusta Rent Rolls for 1761–62 (Preston Papers, Va. Hist. Soc.) indicate that there were at least 271 separate landholders in Beverley Manor and as many as 240 in Borden's Tract and adjacent areas of northern Rockbridge County. For the crown lands north and west of Beverley Manor 195 landholders were reported, and for those south of Borden's Tract as far as the Roanoke River 274 were recorded. Fifty-four landholders were located on the Calfpasture River.

47. Mood, "Studies in the History of American Settled Areas and Frontier Lines: Settled Areas and Frontier Lines, 1625–1790," *Ag. Hist.* 26 (1952):31.

at the headstreams of the Holston River and on the New River where it breaks through the Allegheny Front on its westward course to the Ohio River. Westward of these rivers, Joshua Fry, after completing the field work for his Virginia map with Peter Jefferson, reported in 1750 that "the country between our settlements and the Mississippi is uninhabited or at least has only some inconsiderable Indian villages."[48]

Although a few land grants had been made along the eastern foothills of the Blue Ridge during the late 1720s, the westward expansion of settlement in the Piedmont proceeded relatively slowly. North of the James River the first westward extension of tobacco cultivation was contemporaneous with the settlement of the Shenandoah Valley. The major routes of migration followed the main river valleys, especially the James and the Rappahannock (see fig. 6). In the Piedmont south of the James, in what was to be regionalized as Southside Virginia, settlement was also beginning in the late 1720s. The colonial government of Virginia thus encouraged the concomitant settling of both the colony's western and southern frontiers.[49] Moreover, not only did settlers arrive in Southside Virginia from both directions, there was also a through-migration function there similar to, though more diffuse than, that in the Shenandoah Valley. Both regions lay in the path of the major landward migration to the Carolinas, and through both was to run the Great Wagon Road from Philadelphia.

The period from 1750 to 1776 was one of major settlement expansion and infilling within the valley. Yet even by 1776 there was no continuous band of settlement from the Potomac to the James. The continuity of settlement seems to have broken in Rockingham County (see fig. 10). Rockingham was least affected by the pattern of large land grants in the valley. Lacking the proliferation of immigration agents that characterized much of the rest of the valley, this county was not so well publicized nor so rapidly settled as adjacent counties. Moreover, Massanutten Mountain stretched into the northern half of the county, continuing to split settlement into two prongs.

By 1776 the frontier phase of settlement had been completed in the lower valley, especially in Berkeley and Frederick counties. The overall density of population in the entire valley was just over 5 persons

48. Delf Norona, "Joshua Fry's Report on the Back Settlements of Virginia (May 8, 1751)," *Va. Mag. Hist. Biog.* 56 (1948):37.

49. See Morton, *Colonial Virginia,* 2:560–69; Kegley, *Kegley's Virginia Frontier,* pp. 48–54; Thomas P. Abernethy, *Three Virginia Frontiers* (Baton Rouge: Louisiana State University Press, 1940), pp. 48–54; Landon C. Bell, *The Old Free State: A Contribution to the History of Lunenburg County and Southside Virginia,* 2 vols. (Richmond: William Byrd Press, 1927), 1:79–101.

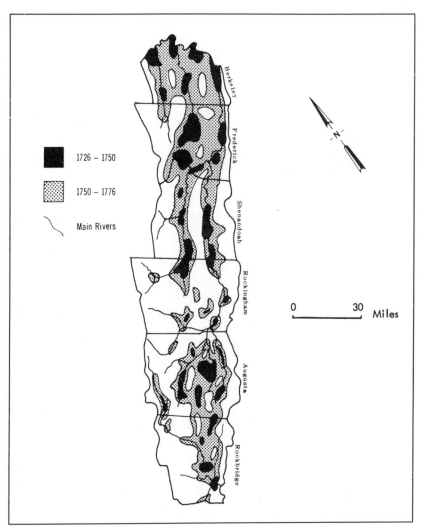

Fig. 10. Settlement of the Shenandoah Valley, 1726–76 (data from County Order Books, Deed Books, and Will Books, 1726–76)

per square mile; the lower valley had attained a density of 8 persons per square mile, compared with 3.5 in the upper valley. Uninhabited areas and sparsely settled areas within the lower valley were located in interriver zones lacking adequate water supplies and in bordering mountain zones where steep slopes and inaccessibility precluded rapid settlement. In Shenandoah County, by avoiding Massanutten Mountain the pioneers produced a bifurcation in the southward spread of settlement along both forks of the Shenandoah River. It became increasingly evident after 1750 that the north or western fork and its tributaries were being settled more actively than the south fork. Except for additional settlements along the Calfpasture River, the more mountainous western parts of all three upper valley counties remained uninhabited or only very sparsely settled by 1776. Several thousand acres of relatively good, accessible farmland remained available within the upper valley after the Revolution. Nevertheless, the frontier phase of settlement had also ended in this region, and at the beginning of the Revolutionary War the frontiers of settlement were located far to the south and west (fig. 6).

The extent of the settled areas in western Virginia by 1776 reflects the thrust of renewed migration patterns after the disruptions of the French and Indian War. Augusta County records contain few references to immigration after 1752. The sheer size of the county and the surviving reports of Indian troubles, vaguely described as being "on the frontiers of Augusta," have led many writers into the false belief that the upper Shenandoah Valley section was as prone to Indian attacks as the rest of the huge county.[50] Braddock's defeat near Fort Duquesne in July 1755 created considerable uneasiness among the settlers in the Shenandoah Valley, but the main impact of French and Indian incursions on settlement was felt west and south of the frontier fort zone which was created to protect the valley (see fig. 6).[51] Some of the settlers in more exposed areas may have retreated to the Shenandoah Valley, but the reporting of tithables was thrown into confusion during the late 1750s and such internal movement cannot be traced.[52]

50. See Ramsey, *Carolina Cradle*, p. 21; Wust, *Virginia Germans*, pp. 58–64; Freeman H. Hart, *The Valley of Virginia in the American Revolution, 1763–1789* (Chapel Hill: University of North Carolina Press, 1942), pp. 66–82.

51. The register kept by William Preston, between October 1754 and May 1758, of the number of white persons killed or captured by the Indians in Augusta County shows that of the 137 people killed, all but a handful had been settled well to the west and south of the upper valley (Preston Papers, 1QQ83, Draper Mss., Wis. State Hist. Soc.). See also Waddell, *Annals of Augusta County*, 2d ed., pp. 154–58.

52. For example, Augusta Co. Order Books 4:322, 495, 5:245, 6:85, 210. Augusta's tithables fell from 2,663 in 1754 to 1,358 in 1759 as a consequence of incomplete returns.

Through-migration to the west was clearly hindered by the war, and it was not until after 1763 that migration to areas south and west of the valley was renewed.

Processes of Land Selection to 1776

By the end of the colonial period the basic processes of land selection and population distribution had been worked out. These processes were governed by the overriding fact that the great majority of settlers were rural farm people interested in choosing land that was most advantageous for crop production and livestock maintenance. A major proposition of this study is that commercial considerations were paramount in making decisions about where to settle, especially the initial costs of land purchase. This topic will be explored in the next chapter. First, it is necessary to test the alternative propositions, so widely dispersed throughout the secondary literature, that environmental and cultural factors were equally, if not more, important in the settler's land selection.

The quality of the land a settler occupied largely depended upon topographic, soil, and drainage characteristics. Much has been claimed for the perceptiveness of colonial farmers in recognizing the inherent fertility of certain soils. German and Scotch-Irish settlers in particular have been viewed at different ends of this spectrum. Thus, "methodically the superior German husbandmen selected only limestone soils and pre-empted the best land"[53] while the Scotch-Irish "chose foothills rather than valleys; shale soils rather than limestone."[54] Because few writers bothered to examine the original land records to find out precisely where settlers located, discussion largely revolved around possible reasons for the assumed cultural differences in land appraisal. These differences have been explained in terms of both past cultural experiences and environmental conditions in western Europe. Some writers have suggested that the Germans who came from the unwooded gravels of the Palatinate appreciated sparsely wooded grassland areas, while the Scotch-

---

53. Bridenbaugh, *Myths and Realities*, p. 133. Thomas J. Wertenbaker, *The Old South: The Founding of American Civilization* (New York: Charles Scribner's Sons, 1942), tends to be more careful about cultural differences in land appraisal although he too refers to the Germans' "keen scent for good soil" (pp. 166, 170). A strong pro-German bias is evident in Richard H. Shryock, "British versus German Traditions in Colonial Agriculture," *Mississippi Valley Historical Review* 26 (1939): 39–54.

54. Stevenson W. Fletcher, "The Expansion of the Agricultural Frontier," *Pennsylvania History* 18 (1951): 124, 126.

Irish, coming from humid forestlands, were suspicious of such areas.[55] Others have suggested that the Scotch-Irish preferred foothill areas either because they were not accustomed to woodland or, conversely, because of their need for extensive woods pasture.[56]

The soils of the Shenandoah Valley are predominantly of limestone origin (fig. 11). Limestone parent materials are widely distributed throughout the valley floor except in the vicinity of the Massanutten foothills, from which a narrow band of shales extends north to the Potomac and south beyond Staunton. Figure 12 shows the distribution of national groups in the valley.[57] A comparison of figures 11 and 12 reveals little correlation between the distribution of national groups and that of soil types. All three major groups—English, Scotch-Irish, and Germans—occupied the limestone soils of the valley. The predominance of Scotch-Irish in the upper valley was a result of the land activities of Beverley and Borden; the singular importance of English settlers along the eastern part of the lower valley was mainly the result of the land policies of Lord Fairfax. The shale areas north of Massanutten were occupied primarily by Germans and English, while those to the south had been settled mainly by Scotch-Irish and German. There is no evidence that early Scotch-Irish settlers moved to more marginal hilly areas either because of cultural preferences or because of the unavailability of good land on the valley floor.

Nor was there an ethnically selective appraisal of settlement sites

55. George Tatham, "The Cumberland Valley in Pennsylvania: A Study in Regional Geography" (Ph.D. diss., Clark University, 1934), p. 90n.

56. Compare Fletcher, "The Expansion of the Agricultural Frontier," *Penn. Hist.* 18 (1951): 127 and Evans, "Culture and Land Use in the Old West of North America," *Heidelberger Studien zur Kulturgeographie* 15 (1966): 79.

57. National groups in the Shenandoah Valley are by no means clearly defined. The most intractable problem in reconstructing the ethnic origins of population is that, unless otherwise stated, estimates have to be made from the family names recorded in the tax returns and other county records. The problem is a long-standing one and has been tackled with varying degrees of success. As an attempt to narrow the range of error, first names have been used in this study as well as family names in the identification of German names which have undergone some degree of anglicization. While "John Miller" could be a British or an anglicized German name, "Ludwick Miller" is almost certainly non-British. Similarly, "Henry Carpenter" might possibly be English, but "Jacob" or "Conrad Carpenter" is most likely not. Another advantage of working on a county scale is that there is a good chance that "John Miller" types can be more precisely identified from other records. In terms of British names, the general tendency is to place names of uncertain origin in the English category, and since I have not explored the genealogical record systematically, that has probably happened to some extent in this study also, especially for the lower valley. At the same time, the number of German settlers may well be slightly exaggerated by the inability to distinguish Swiss on occasion.

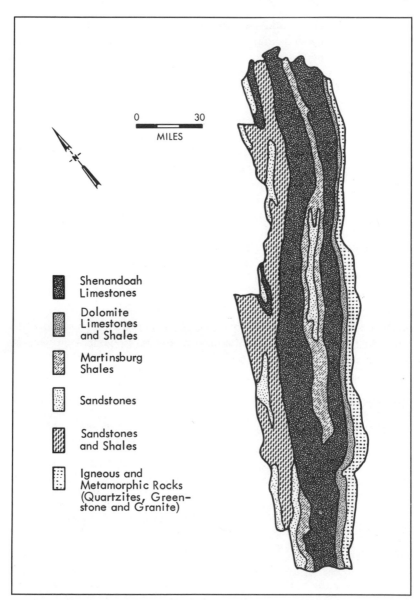

Fig. 11. Shenandoah Valley: soil parent materials (from Geologic Map of Virginia, Virginia Geological Survey, 1928)

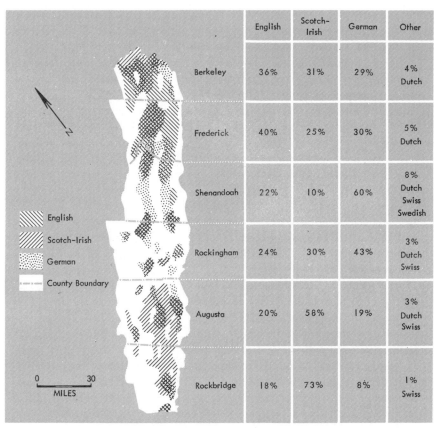

	English	Scotch-Irish	German	Other
Berkeley	36%	31%	29%	4% Dutch
Frederick	40%	25%	30%	5% Dutch
Shenandoah	22%	10%	60%	8% Dutch Swiss Swedish
Rockingham	24%	30%	43%	3% Dutch Swiss
Augusta	20%	58%	19%	3% Dutch Swiss
Rockbridge	18%	73%	8%	1% Swiss

Legend:
- English
- Scotch-Irish
- German
- County Boundary

0 ——— 30
MILES

Fig. 12. Distribution of national groups in the Shenandoah Valley, 1775 (data from County Order Books, Deed Books, and Will Books, 1775–82; Land Tax Records, 1782–83)

in terms of water supply or vegetation cover. Water supply was a prime consideration in choosing any site for settlement. Almost all colonial land grants were located along one or both sides of a stream, and references to land grant locations were always made in relation to the nearest stream. In an area so extensively underlain by soluble limestone rocks, springs were numerous both throughout the valley floor and along the mountain foothills. Fresh water was therefore easily available in most parts of the valley. As the land records show, there was only a limited amount of open grassland for any of the settlers, regardless of preference, to choose. Moreover, the need for wood for construction and fuel makes it unlikely that settlers would have occupied more easily cleared grassy tracts unless wood was available nearby.[58] Areas described as "barrens" were astutely avoided as settlement sites. The justices of Augusta County, who examined the twenty-five-acre tract which Beverley conveyed to the county for a courthouse and other county buildings in 1746, reported that it was "entire Illconvenient and useless being most part of it on a Barren hill or Mountain where the County Cannot Pretend to Sell one lot . . . afording neither firewood nor Water no spring being Included . . . tho' several are Nigh and Adjacent . . . cannot accept the s[ai]d Land unless it be so laid of[f] that the Court House be in the Center."[59] This was one of the few surveys of land quality which contained any reference to the unavailability of wood.

There is another set of cultural implications to be drawn from figure 12. In their selection of sites, settlers also had to consider the closeness and identity of their neighbors. Distance between neighbors varied in terms of topographic characteristics, the size and shape of land grants, the location of farmsteads within the grants, and the density of settlements. In the Shenandoah Valley, as in most areas of colonial America, there was no prior or orderly system of land survey. The unsystematic metes-and-bounds survey procedures allowed for an irregularly dispersed settlement pattern. Over time the spacing of settlements within the valley shifted from irregularly distributed areas of relatively close linear arrangements of settlements along streams, separated by larger areas of widely dispersed farmsteads, to more continuous areas of relatively closely spaced settlement patterns along the Shenandoah and Opequon stream courses in the lower valley and between the Harrisonburg and Lexington areas in the upper valley.[60]

The location of already established settlers of similar cultural background was a major site factor for many pioneer settlers. This

58. See Terry G. Jordan, "Between the Forest and the Prairie," *Ag. Hist.* 38 (1964): 205–16.

59. Augusta Co. Order Book 1:102–3. A similar complaint was made against the site of Lexington in 1778.

60. Contemporary comments on eighteenth-century settlement patterns can be found in Fithian, *Journal, 1775–1776*, pp. 152–53, 158–59, François Jean, marquis de Chastellux, *Travels in North America in the Years 1780, 1781, and 1782*, ed. Howard C. Rice, Jr., 2 vols. (Chapel Hill: University of North Carolina Press, 1963), 1:405; François Alexander Frédéric, duc de La Rochefoucauld-Liancourt, *Travels through the United States of North America, the Country of the Iroquois, and Upper Canada, in the Years 1795, 1796, and 1797, with an Authentic Account of Lower Canada*, trans. H. Neuman, 2 vols. (London, 1799), 2:89; Isaac Weld, *Travels through the States of North America in the Years 1795, 1796, and 1797* (London, 1799), p. 134.

was particularly true when group migration to the valley was involved, as in the case of Germans to the early Stover and Hite grants and Scotch-Irish to the Beverley and Borden tracts. But such territorial separation of national groups was rarely maintained over the long term. The residential mixing of ethnically diverse populations was the most dominant trend by the end of the colonial period. Only a few areas retained any semblance of cultural distinctiveness: the Tidewater Virginian settlement which had just begun to emerge along the main branch of the Shenandoah River in Frederick County, the Germans along both forks of the river in Shenandoah County, and the Scotch-Irish in parts of Augusta and Rockbridge counties. There is some distributional evidence to support the long-standing view that the valley's population could be regionalized in terms of national origins, but it is more apparent than real. English settlers were proportionally most numerous in Berkeley and Frederick counties, but they comprised at least two major groups, small holders from the Middle Colonies and a small number of Tidewater planters. Germans were most numerous in Shenandoah and Rockingham counties but were by no means a homogenous cultural group either. Only in Augusta and Rockbridge counties, where Scotch-Irish comprised almost two-thirds of the entire white population, did any group represent a substantial majority. Thus, the increasing locational intermingling and interaction of populations within the valley by 1776 raise the questions as to whether discrete national groups still existed in any viable form and how far different cultural heritages can be considered a significant factor at all. This question will be explored more fully in Chapter 4.

Through-Migration and Emigration during the Colonial Period

Both migration through and emigration from the Shenandoah Valley represented basic steps in the westward movement, contributing to the pioneer settlement of more recent frontier areas to the west and south. In some cases the emigrants from the valley were families who had settled in the region for only a few years; in other instances, they were younger people who had been born in the valley.

Moravian missionaries from Pennsylvania were traveling through the valley on their way to the Carolinas and Georgia as early as 1743.[61]

---

61. William J. Hinke and Charles E. Kemper, "Moravian Diaries of Travels through Virginia," *Va. Mag. Hist. Biog.* 11 (1903–4): 113–31, 225–42, 370–93, and 12 (1904–5): 134–53, 271–84.

During the next ten years other Moravians used it as a route to reach German settlers living along the New River in southwestern Virginia and in the North Carolina Piedmont. From the 1750s on, peddlers operating out of Pennsylvania were to be found throughout the valley, and cattle drives originating from as far south as North Carolina passed northward on their way to markets in Pennsylvania. Perhaps the most significant indicator of the valley's function as a migration corridor was the increasing number of ordinaries (providing food and lodgings) that were established. Licenses for at least 100 separate ordinaries were granted by the Augusta County court between 1746 and 1776, especially for the Staunton area and other areas along the Great Wagon Road. The number of ordinaries grew most noticeably in the period after 1765, when the rates of migration through the valley began to increase.

Available data on the number of through-migrants and the frequency of migrations are neither impressive nor overly helpful. In 1730 almost no settlers occupied the southern colonies south of the James River between the fall line and the Blue Ridge. By 1776 about 160,000 settlers may have been located in this area, with an additional 50,000 occupying the Virginia Applachians south of the headwaters of the James River.[62] An average of 3,900 people were added every year to these areas south of the James. If it is assumed that the contribution of migration to the area's population growth between the first settlements in 1740 and the year 1775 was twice as large as the contribution of natural increase, and that new settlers came equally from northerly and easterly directions, an annual average of 1,300 settlers passed southward through the Shenandoah Valley. However, during the 1740s and 1750s, probably twice as many settlers migrated via the Shenandoah Valley as moved inland from the coast.[63] Thus, during those twenty years, perhaps an average of 2,200 settlers passed through, or in a few cases from, the Shenandoah Valley annually.

In terms of emigration from the valley, settlers were moving out of the upper valley on a second or later phase of their migration process at least as early as the mid-1740s.[64] Such locational instability was a major characteristic of frontier migration. In January 1746 a group of settlers who had emigrated from North Ireland to

62. Bridenbaugh, *Myths and Realities*, p. 121. See also the maps in Friis, *A Series of Population Maps*, and Ramsey, *Carolina Cradle*, pp. 21–145.

63. Bridenbaugh, *Myths and Realities*, pp. 122–30; Friis, *A Series of Population Maps*, pp. 16–17 and fig. 3.

64. Orange Co. Deed Book 4:43; Augusta Co. Deed Book 1:42.

the upper valley late in 1739 petitioned the South Carolina government to settle on frontier lands to be acquired from the Cherokees. Within a year thirty more settlers were on the move to South Carolina.[65]

Figures 13 through 16 represent an attempt to depict general trends in the location of land grantors who sold or transferred land in Augusta County and left a record of their present residence. In this manner, one can map the general outlines of the migration field of settlers from the upper Shenandoah Valley.

Grantors located in areas north and northeast of the upper valley were probably mostly absentee landowners who had never actually settled in Augusta County, although some may have taken up residence on a well-established farm left them by a relative rather than take the risks of moving on to a new frontier environment and starting over again. An inability to distinguish between these two categories explains the inclusion on the maps of grantors in the lower valley, eastern Virginia, and southeastern Pennsylvania. Short-range movements within the Shenandoah Valley appear to have been relatively common and mainly involved migration from the lower Shenandoah Valley to its upper part. To the south, the most important areas to which Augusta County settlers migrated during the decade 1745 to 1755 were Southside Virginia and the Carolinas. The North Carolina Piedmont, particularly Anson and Rowan counties, was a major area of attraction for Augusta County settlers between 1756 and 1765; the physical security of the area from Indian incursions guaranteed a continuing influx of new settlers.[66] Since western and southwestern Virginia remained a part of Augusta County until after 1770, figure 13 gives no indication of migration patterns within the Valley of Virginia south of the James River. On the other hand, connections between the upper valley

65. Orange Co. Deed Book 3:450–52, and Order Book 2:109–10, 113; Robert L. Meriwether, *The Expansion of South Carolina, 1729–1765* (Kingsport, Tenn.: Southern Publishers, 1940), pp. 123–25, 138–40; Ramsey *Carolina Cradle*, pp. 28–57.

66. Some writers have pointed out that religious dissenters in the Virginia backcountry often moved to the Carolinas in order to escape paying tithes to the established Anglican church. This was probably more true of the lower valley, where the Anglican church was more firmly established after 1760, than of the upper valley. In Augusta County, although the parish framework existed and an Anglican church was built in 1762, the influence of the church was weak. Nonconformists only joined the church on a nominal basis when they were interested in holding local political office. Despite continual complaints levies were usually about the same level as general taxes and could be easily avoided. The money that was collected was used mainly for local social welfare programs rather than for the specific use of the church. See Bridenbaugh, *Myths and Realities*, pp. 127–28; Charles W. Bryan, Jr., "Morgan Bryan, Pioneer on the Opequon and Yadkin," *Va. Mag. Hist. Biog.* 70 (1962): 160–61; Augusta Parish Vestry Book (1746–80).

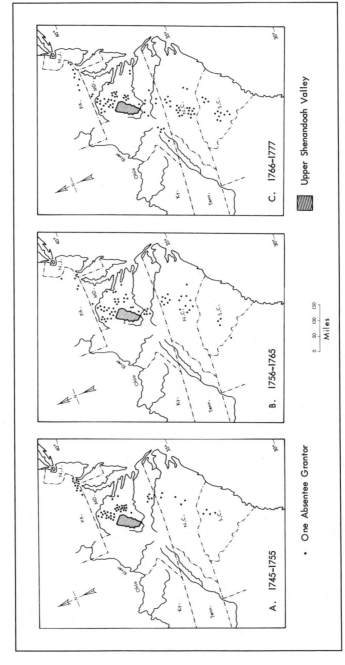

Fig. 13. Upper Shenandoah Valley: location of grantors, 1745–77 (data from Augusta County Deed Books)

• One Absentee Grantor

A. 1745–1755

B. 1756–1765

C. 1766–1777

▨ Upper Shenandoah Valley

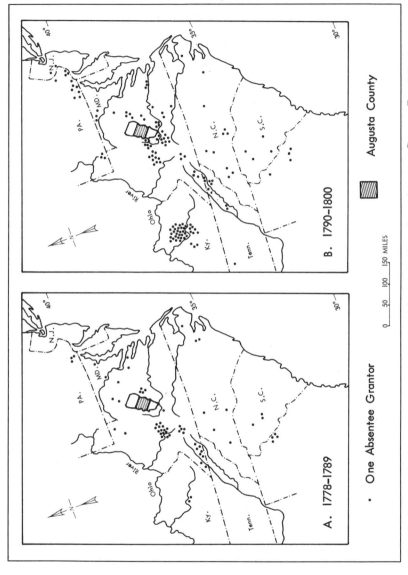

· One Absentee Grantor   Augusta County

A. 1778–1789   B. 1790–1800

0   50   100   150 MILES

Fig. 14. Augusta County: location of grantors, 1778–1800 (data from Augusta County Deed Books)

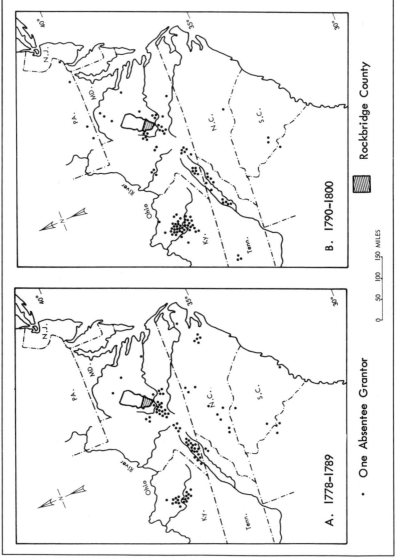

A. 1778–1789   B. 1790–1800

• One Absentee Grantor

▨ Rockbridge County

0 50 100 150 MILES

Fig. 15. Rockbridge County: location of grantors, 1778–1800 (data from Rockbridge County Deed Books)

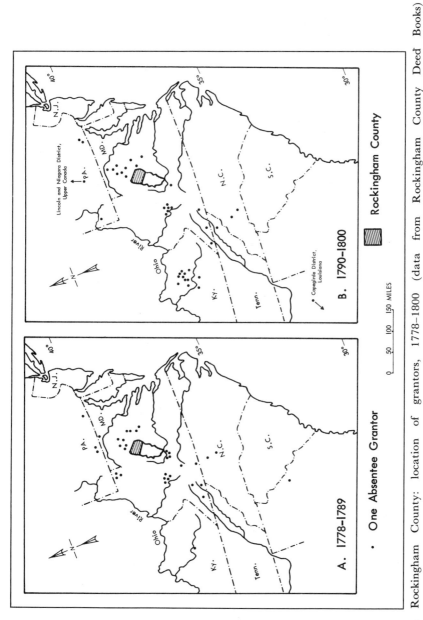

Fig. 16. Rockingham County: location of grantors, 1778–1800 (data from Rockingham County Deed Books)

and the lower valley, the Virginia Piedmont, and to a lesser
degree, southeastern Pennsylvania remained significant until well into
the 1770s.

Motivations for and Implications of Migration

For men of above-average ability and motivation, short-range migrations,
following the frontiers of settlement and county formation, could be
financially and politically remunerative. The surviving records of the
Prestons, Campbells, and Breckenridges, families which had settled
in Beverly Manor during the early 1740s, indicate that by 1775 members
of these familial groups were to be found in Botetourt and Fincastle
counties in southwest Virginia and as far south as the Holston
River.[67]

The career of William Preston exemplifies the activities that could be
associated with the processes of migration in frontier areas. Brought by his
father from Northern Ireland to Beverley Manor in 1740, Preston
had become deputy surveyor of Augusta County by 1752. Through his
surveying activities he became familiar with the southern part of
the Valley of Virginia. In the late 1760s he moved with his family
to the vicinity of Looney's Mill Creek, a south-bank tributary of the
James, and established his Greenfield Estate there. When Botetourt
County was established in 1770, he assumed five public offices (justice,
first surveyor, escheator, coroner, and colonel of the militia), and
he represented the county in the House of Burgesses for two and
a half years. In 1774 he moved farther south to that part of Fincastle
County which three years later became Montgomery County, where
he fulfilled many of the same functions, and died there in 1781.
Each stage of Preston's migration was facilitated by the profitable
sale of land and the acquisition of cheaper land in his new area
of residence.[68] Preston's moves and levels of operation certainly were
exceptional, but they highlight the opportunities that were available both

67. Collections of Preston Papers in Draper Mss., Wis. State Hist. Soc., and Va. Hist.
Soc.; Campbell-Preston Papers and Breckenridge Family Papers, Manuscript Div., Lib.
Cong. See also Kegley, *Kegley's Virginia Frontier,* pp. 53–135; Lewis P. Summers, *Annals
of Southwest Virginia, 1769–1800* (Abingdon, Va., 1929).

68. For information on William Preston, see Kegley, *Kegley's Virginia Frontier,* pp. 383–85,
401, and the map of Greenfield Estate opposite p. 500. His will is in vol. 2
of the Campbell-Preston Papers, Lib. Cong. For some general comments on the roles
of the gentry and the small farmer in county affairs, see D. Alan Williams, "The Small
Farmer in Eighteenth Century Virginia Politics," *Ag. Hist.* 43 (1969): 91–101.

to men of initiative and to men of caution. The failure of frontier situations to meet the economic and social expectations of many settlers probably encouraged some to migrate to other potentially attractive areas. The abundance of land was certainly a prime factor in facilitating periodic migration. At the same time, the migration corridor function of the valley provided a fairly constant supply of potential buyers of land and farms, so that property owners who sold their property and moved on were often able to do so at considerable profit. Conversely, settlers who held no land and little personal property were only loosely tied to any particular locale. For many of them, moving to a new area provided new opportunities for economic improvement with a minimum amount of difficulty. It was pioneer settlers like Preston who were the real frontier risk takers. Their occupance frequently paved the way for the bulk of frontier migrants, the second wave of settlement, comprising those who were extremely reluctant to be the first occupants of an area but were quite willing to move in once the initial risks had been taken and the area made secure for their way of life. In turn, when the economic potential of an area had been proved and the higher density of settlement had reduced the degree of risk, many pioneers sold out at a profit and moved on to new frontiers, better equipped psychologically and financially to repeat their original performance. This fact suggests that the sequential occupancy of trans-Applachian frontiers by financially able populations familiar with American environments reduced the degree of risk and speeded up the establishment of a commercially oriented society.

It has been argued that periodic moves to new frontier areas shattered the social structure of the settlers, particularly the unity of the family and primary group ties.[69] There appears to be a good deal of truth in this assertion; yet relatively little is known about the actual relationships between geographical mobility and such critical variables as social structure and mobility, changing economic conditions, general opportunities, and ethnicity in eighteenth-century rural America. In terms of social relationships, the whole process of frontier migration was based initially on the movement of nuclear families, extended families, and groups of families; but the selective mechanisms at work in the migration process meant that extended families in particular were broken up and dispersed. The movement of individual males was also a persistent feature of migration, but of relatively minor significance

69. Allan G. Bogue, "Social Theory and the Pioneer," *Ag. Hist.* 34 (1960): 30–31. See also Lemon, *Best Poor Man's Country*, pp. 3, 71–97.

within the total picture. At the same time, migration was frequently associated with certain phases of the life cycle, especially marriage and the death of the family head. Families often migrated or gradually broke up after the death of the father or his widow. In some instances only after an estate was disposed of could sons obtain enough money to buy land elsewhere.[70]

In southeastern Pennsylvania, with increasing population densities and farm subdivisions, the practice of impartible inheritance generally superseded division after 1760, and more and more younger sons had to move out on to the frontiers to find reasonably priced land and establish families. The will books for Shenandoah Valley counties indicate that if such a definite shift to impartible inheritance also took place there, it must have occurred some time during the nineteenth century. Throughout the eighteenth century both partible and impartible practices were widely used by valley settlers, and there was no obvious trend toward a greater emphasis on impartible inheritance during the final decades of the century.

There is some evidence of cultural variations in emigration patterns. Although the majority of settlers in the southern part of the Valley of Virginia by 1770 were primarily of Scotch-Irish background, German settlers were also involved in the processes of emigration from, and migration through, the upper valley. Because of linguistic and religious barriers to initial assimilation, migrations of German settlers were distinguished by two features. The basic migration pattern, one of small family groups or extended families, seems to have persisted longer among Germans than among other ethnic groups that retained some degree of distinct identity. Second, Germans tended to move to two specific localities, which thereafter became important centers of German settlement. A group of German settlers moved from the valley to the west bank of the New River about 1743 and were followed by others during the next twenty years. Most of these families were Moravians and Dunkards.[71] A second focus for German settlement,

70. Ramsey, *Carolina Cradle*, p. 22; Lemon, *Best Poor Man's Country,* pp. 92–94.

71. Wust, *Virginia Germans*, p. 39; Hinke and Kemper, "Moravian Diaries of Travels through Virginia," *Va. Mag. Hist. Biog.* 11 (1904):113–31; Augusta Co. Deed Book 6:31–120; Ramsey, *Carolina Cradle*, pp. 59–60, 63–79, 83–85, 91–92, 96, 101–7, 111, 123, 143–51. James Patton sold many tracts in his New River lands to Germans. See also John Buchanan, "Memorandums Relating Sundrey Passages with Respect to My Journey to Wood's River Commencing the 4 of Octobr. 1745," Preston Papers, IQQ38–56, Draper Mss., Wis. State Hist. Soc., and Dr. Thomas Walker's description of the New River settlers in March 1750 in Journal of Dr. Thomas Walker, 1750, Thomas and Francis Walker Papers, William C. Rives Collection, Manuscript Div., Lib. Cong.

which emerged during the late 1750s, was the south fork of the
Potomac River in Hampshire County.[72]

German settlers were also to be found on the frontiers of settlement
in western Virginia during the last ten years of the colonial
period. In November 1766 the House of Burgesses received a petition from
some settlers in Augusta County which stated that "great Numbers
of People from the interior Parts of this Colony are desirous of
settling on the Waters of the Ohio, and many German Emigrants
are desirous of doing the same."[73] It was argued that the establishment
of such settlements would minimize the dangers of Indian incursions
and would encourage the commercial production of hemp and flax
for export to the mother country. But since the king's Proclamation
of 1763 had banned any settlement beyond the Applachians to prevent
conflicts with the Indians, the House of Burgesses tabled the petition.
This request is indicative of the desires of settlers of all national-culture
groups west of the Blue Ridge to move farther westward and to open
up any new lands for settlement, despite decrees from London.

Post-Revolutionary Migration Patterns

During the Revolutionary War the Shenandoah Valley was not seriously
affected by military activities. Because of the relative safety afforded
by the region, Staunton and Winchester were used as prisoner-of-war
barracks and supply centers. As had been the case during the French
and Indian War, the free play of migration was interrupted until 1783.
By that time, however, the nature of the migration processes associated
with the Shenandoah Valley had changed considerably.

After the late 1770s immigration was reduced to a trickle except
for the very important movement of eastern Virginians to the lower
valley. Few Northern Neck settlers of English origin who owned land
in Frederick County had contemplated moving there before the 1750s.
In a sense, Lord Fairfax led the way for such a movement. He took
the extraordinary step of leaving England permanently in 1747 and in
1752 settled in the valley at Greenway Court near Winchester, thus
becoming the only resident peer in the American colonies. From there he
supervised the allocation of his western lands to northern settlers

72. See Augusta Co. Deed Books 5–10, 16:477–79.

73. *Journals of the House of Burgesses of Virginia, 1619–1777*, ed. H. R. McIlwaine and
J. P. Kennedy, 13 vols. (Richmond, 1905–15), 11:37. See also Wust, *Virginia Germans*,
pp. 39, 68–69, 95–97, 193.

and Virginia planters. At the same time, the young George Washington, who surveyed some of these lands for Fairfax, settled in Frederick County briefly and represented it in the House of Burgesses until 1765 when he was elected from Fairfax County. Thereafter he maintained his links with the lower valley and became an active absentee landowner.[74] These two individuals symbolize the emerging connections between the lower valley and eastern Virginian planter society.

The financial difficulties of the tobacco industry during the early 1760s produced an increasing awareness among many smaller eastern planters of the potentialities of lower valley lands. Between 1765 and the outbreak of the Revolution about one hundred small-planter families from the Northern Neck emigrated to eastern Berkeley and Frederick counties. They were the vanguard of several hundred families who migrated to the region during the last two decades of the century.[75] It was these settlers, latecomers to a relatively long settled postfrontier area, who were instrumental in completing the transfer of the socioeconomic traits and aspirations of eastern Virginian planter life to the lower valley: membership in the Anglican church, a predisposition to tobacco cultivation and slavery, more conspicuous consumption habits than those displayed by valley small holders, and long-standing commercial contacts with eastern Virginian merchants. Despite their small numbers and their late appearance in the valley, they were to influence patterns of development within the region out of all proportion to their size.

Emigration patterns in the post-Revolutionary period were oriented away from the Carolinas and Georgia toward Kentucky, with Tennessee, southwestern Virginia, and the New River settlements as secondary focuses (see figs. 14–16). The delinquent and insolvent tax reports for the 1780s record the destinations of many of the valley emigrants. From Augusta County, which has by far the most comprehensive set of these records, almost 40% of those shown to have left the county whose destination was known had gone to Kentucky, 20% had moved to nearby counties in present-day Virginia, 10% had moved to other counties in the Shenandoah Valley, and the remainder had scattered between Pennsylvania, Georgia, and Tennessee. Similar trends were apparent in other valley counties, with a tendency for more Berkeley and Frederick

74. Hart, *Valley of Virginia*, p. 59; Bliss, "Rise of Tenancy," *Va. Mag. Hist. Biog.* 58 (1950): 427–41.

75. Bliss, "Tuckahoe in New Virginia," *Va. Mag. Hist. Biog.* 59 (1951): 387–96.

County migrants to move to Pennsylvania and eastern Virginia than was evident in other valley counties.[76]

Thus, mapping the range of emigration from the upper valley between 1745 and 1800 clearly shows the region's changing relative importance within the early westward movement. During the colonial period, the major focus for emigration was the Piedmont of the Carolinas, an area whose economic geography was only partially linked to that of the Shenandoah Valley. After 1775, the emergence of a western migration focus in Kentucky opened up an area whose commercial development was later to become competitive with that of the valley.

The advent of large-scale migrations of settlers from the Atlantic seaboard to Kentucky and Tennessee after the Revolution revitalized the function of the Shenandoah Valley as a migration corridor. Jacques Pierre Brissot de Warville, a French traveler who did not actually visit the valley, gave this advice to the land-seeking immigrant in 1788: "If he is interested mainly in the fertility of the soil, the beauty of the trees, the opportunities for hunting and fishing, he will surely choose Kentucky. If he is looking for large crops, inexpensive land, a more temperate climate, and the promise of good transportation by water, he will settle in the Shenandoah Valley. But if he clings to his European ways and wishes to satisfy his European tastes and needs society, his best choice will be Pennsylvania."[77]

Even if Brissot de Warville's book had been read widely at the time, few would have heeded his advice. Just as the Shenandoah Valley had been the new frontier from 1740 to 1765, so Kentucky was the promised land after 1775. Isaac Weld and the duc de La Rochefoucauld-Liancourt, on their visits to the Shenandoah Valley during the 1790s, were more cognizant of the settlement processes operative in the westward movement and the patterns of circulation they generated. Weld remarked on the great numbers of people from Kentucky and Tennessee traveling to

76. Delinquents and Insolvents: Land and Property Taxes, Va. State Auditor's Item No. 148, Va. State Lib. I am indebted to Peter Albert for bringing these records to my attention. They contain addenda to the land and personal property taxes established in 1782. The three lists for Augusta County in 1784, for example, indicate that 50 tithables were omitted from the 1783 tax lists, 36 tithables were insolvent, 72 had moved out of the county, 8 had died, 12 were not known, and some 90 tithables had their property recorded wrongly (out of a total of 2,069 tithables listed for 1783). Those moving out of Augusta County had a destination recorded at least 60% of the time while only about 30% were so recorded for other counties.

77. Brissot de Warville, *New Travels in the United States of America, 1788* (Cambridge, Mass.: Harvard University Press, Belknap Press, 1964), p. 361.

Philadelphia and Baltimore, "and with many others going in a contrary direction . . . to search for lands conveniently situated for new settlements in the western country. . . . formerly it used to be a very serious undertaking to go by this route to Kentucky. . . . now if five or six travel together they are perfectly secure."[78] La Rochefoucauld-Liancourt described the migration history of the Shenandoah Valley in these words: "The inhabitants are most of them emigrants from the county of Lancaster, from Maryland, and the environs of Reading and Carlisle. They purchase land in these back parts of Virginia at a cheaper rate than they sold that which they quitted. They are the main points of direction for the emigration from Virginia, where most of the families from Pennsylvania and Maryland settle only for a certain time."[79]

In his final estimation, La Rochefoucauld-Liancourt was not impressed by the results of the settlement processes in the Shenandoah Valley. "It is but thinly inhabited in proportion to its extent, and to the length of time since it first began to be settled. . . . It has . . . been more extolled, in my opinion, than it deserves."[80] It bore no comparison in his mind with the Mohawk Valley, which he had recently visited. What he had observed, however, were two different phases of the westward expansion of settlement during the eighteenth century. The Shenandoah Valley had functioned, at various times during the century, as a settlement focus, migration corridor, and migration source. The Mohawk Valley, and its extension westward to Lake Erie, only began to perform these functions after the Revolutionary War. The development of upstate New York had been delayed by Indian occupance and land engrossment, and that of central Kentucky by its distance from source areas of population, but both these regions eventually provided energy to the westward movement because of their attractiveness as areas of desirable land, offering agricultural potentialities, speculative possibilities, and property legacies for later generations, just as the Shenandoah Valley had done earlier. In short, the key element in early expansion and development was the availability of land and the timing of its acquisition.

78. Weld. *Travels through the States of North America*, pp. 134–35.
79. La Rochefoucauld-Liancourt, *Travels through the United States of North America*, 2:89.
80. Ibid.

3 Land Acquisition and Speculation

THE disposal of land west of the Blue Ridge by colonial authorities and its acquisition by immigrant settlers was the major element in opening up western Virginia to permanent settlement. Many observations have been made on the role of the land speculator in western development, but they generally have emphasized the activities of prominent, well-established individuals or land companies that made conscious efforts to acquire lands for speculative purposes from their home bases in the tidewater.[1] Yet the economic motivations of frontier settlers, the widespread availability of land, the eagerness of colonial governments to settle their interiors effectively, and the liberal land-granting policies that were put into practice provided a context within which the acquisition of land by actual settlers far beyond the needs of immediate sustenance was facilitated. The residual land that they acquired could be used for speculative purposes, or it could be held for transfer to the next generation, and the relative significance of these two kinds of decisions must be clearly defined. Alternatively, residual land could be sold on the death of the owner in order to provide a sound financial legacy for his children. In terms of land speculation itself, it is important to examine the degree to which areal and temporal changes took place in land values in the Shenandoah Valley and the relationships between these changes and the various levels of speculative activity in western Virginia during the eighteenth century.

Land in the valley was the prime tool used by colonial administrations to achieve their settlement goals. Strategic considerations demanded that

1. Ray A. Billington, "The Origin of the Land Speculator as a Frontier Type," *Ag. Hist.* 19 (1945): 204-12, and Paul W. Gates, "Role of the Land Speculator in Western Development," *Pa. Mag. Hist. Biog.* 66 (1942):314-33, focused on an aspect of frontier America neglected by Turner. For more recent contributions, see Aubrey C. Land, "A Land Speculator in the Opening of Western Maryland," *Md. Hist. Mag.* 48 (1953): 191–203; Charles S. Grant, "Land Speculation and the Settlement of Kent, 1738–1760," *New England Quarterly* 28 (1955): 1–71; Grant, "A History of Kent, 1738–1796: Democracy on Connecticut's Frontier" (Ph.D. diss., Columbia University, 1957), which was in large part published as *Democracy in the Connecticut Frontier Town of Kent* (New York: Columbia University Press, 1961); Allan G. Bogue, *From Prairie to Corn Belt* (Chicago: University of Chicago Press, 1963); Robert P. Swierenga, "Land Speculator 'Profits' Reconsidered: Central Iowa as a Test Case," *Journal of Economic History* 26 (1966): 1–28, and Swierenga, *Pioneers and Profits: Land Speculation on the Iowa Frontier* (Ames: Iowa State University Press, 1968).

the backcountry be inhabited by settlers loyal to the political and economic premises of the British cause. Virginia and its neighboring colonies attempted to protect their settled areas by the development of buffer settlements which were neither simply westward continuations of previously settled areas nor necessarily communities that were economically integrated into existing colonial patterns.[2]

Although the land grant policies of eighteenth-century Virginia governments were largely fashioned by the act of 1701, "for the better strengthening of the frontiers," the first practical applications of the more liberal policy came from Governor Alexander Spotswood after he took office in 1710.[3] The establishment in 1721 of the two new frontier counties of Spotsylvania in the west and Brunswick in the south set an important precedent for later western land policies. Quitrents were remitted for seven years on new grants in these counties. More important, both Spotswood and the Virginia Council believed that the original limit of 1,000 acres per grantee would discourage potential patentees, especially since those patentees would be mainly from leading Tidewater landholders. The cancellation of this limitation opened the way for a more liberal policy by the Virginia government, but one which, in terms of the opportunities it provided for land aggregation by a few favored individuals, distinctly supported the prominent, well-established landed classes.[4]

Through these settlement procedures the Virginia government promoted the westward expansion of land control by Tidewater families in areas which were often to become settled by non-Virginians. Conversely, the scale on which this land policy was administered and the acreages placed at the disposal of the distributing agencies encouraged widespread land speculation not only among the original patentees but also among the actual settlers who obtained grants from these patentees. This speculation was, therefore, largely a result of the rather extensive planning of land distribution and settlement by the Virginia authorities. In Upper Canada, by way of comparison, widespread land speculation occurred at all levels despite official attempts by the British to discourage it, which makes it

2. Lemon, *Best Poor Man's Country*, pp. 59–60; Meriwether, *Expansion of South Carolina*, pp. 17–20.

3. See Spotwood, *The Official Letters of Alexander Spotswood, Lieutenant Governor of the Colony of Virginia, 1710–1722*, 2 vols. (Richmond: Virginia Historical Society, 1882–85), 2:70, 95, 196; Couper, *History of the Shenandoah Valley*, 1: 123–47. For evaluation of Spotswood's interests in westward expansion, see Leonidas Dodson, *Alexander Spotswood, Governor of Virginia, 1710–1722* (Philadelphia: University of Pennsylvania Press, 1932); Morton, *Colonial Virginia*, 2:444–53, 472–85.

4. Faye B. Reeder, "The Evolution of the Virginia Land Grant System in the Eighteenth Century" (Ph.D. diss., Ohio State University, 1937), pp. 67–69.

difficult to refute the conclusion that speculation was almost inevitable within the milieu of the North American land situation during the second half of the eighteenth century.[5]

The geographic and economic results of the land grant policy of Virginia were perhaps most evident in the Shenandoah Valley. It was through the generous and largely indiscriminate land granting of Lieutenant Governor William Gooch between 1727 and 1749 that the valley was first settled, and it was during the same administration that the family settlement policy was put into operation. Gooch went beyond a simple buffer zone concept in his granting of western lands, for it is clear that he was using his land policy as a means of counteracting the land claims of Lord Fairfax west of the Blue Ridge.

The implementation and timing of the family settlement policy has been the subject of some dispute. Faye B. Reeder was of the opinion that "by the time of the occupation of the Shenandoah Valley the custom had become established in this part of Virginia [the Piedmont] of making grants of one thousand acres for each family settled within a certain time."[6] Manning C. Voorhis, however, believed that the pattern of settling one family for every 1,000 acres of a land grant within two years was a special policy originally introduced in the Shenandoah Valley.[7] Clearly a thorough study of land acquisition in the Piedmont is needed, but the low priority for a buffer zone on the Piedmont and the high degree of continuity of land appropriation by Tidewater landowners on the Piedmont north of the James suggest that a family settlement policy would not have been required there.

Methods of Acquiring Land

The method of land granting in the Shenandoah Valley stimulated the interest of both eastern Virginians and settlers from the Middle Colonies. William Beverley and Benjamin Borden exemplify both of these trends. Despite the differences in their social and economic backgrounds, both men had one interest in common—land acquisition and speculation. Both men were active land seekers before their ventures in the Shenandoah

5. Lilliam F. Gates, *Land Policies of Upper Canada,* Canadian Studies in History and Government no. 9 (Toronto: University of Toronto Press, 1968), pp. 303–7.

6. Reeder, "Evolution of Virginia Land Grant System," p. 69.

7. Voohris, "Land Grant Policy of Colonial Virginia," pp. 160–62. See also Voorhis, "Crown versus Council in the Virginia Land Policy," *Wm. and Mary Qtly.,* 3d ser. 3 (1946): 499–514; David Alan Williams, "Political Alignments in Colonial Virginia, 1698–1750" (Ph.D. diss., Northwestern University, 1959), pp. 239–40.

Valley; their grants in this region were the culmination of their speculative activities; and both were absentee landowners.

Though Borden's activities were all located west of the Blue Ridge, Beverley had already acquired considerable holdings in Spotsylvania County in the Piedmont before he showed any interest in the Shenandoah Valley. In June 1730 he applied unsuccessfully with his father, the planter and historian Robert Beverley, for 50,000 acres on the Shenandoah River.[8] However, between 1730 and October 1734, Beverley and various friends acquired six land grants totaling 169,000 acres on the upper Potomac River, the forks of Opequon Creek, the south fork of the Shenandoah River, and a 60,000-acre tract in Augusta County beginning just south of Jacob Stover's upper tract in Rockingham and Augusta Counties.[9]

Between 1734 and June 1739 Borden had accumulated interests in four land grants totaling 5,250 acres in the lower valley.[10] His land acquisitions up to this point, all located within the Northern Neck and all from Lord Fairfax, did not require him to pursue actively any land settlement policy. Beverley's requests for valley lands were all made to the Virginia Council, however, and he believed he could get Pennsylvania settlers to settle his lands since they could buy 100 acres from him at £6 to£7 Va. less than in Pennsylvania.[11]

Beverley concentrated his efforts on the 60,000-acre tract in Augusta County for which he requested patents with John Tayloe and Thomas Lee in October 1734.[12] This tract, the forerunner of Beverley Manor, was found to include a much larger area than originally intended when it was surveyed in 1736. It contained, among other things, some 18,000 acres of "mountain and barrens." The processes by which Beverley expanded this tract into the 118,491-acre Beverley Manor by August 1736 under a separate partnership still remain unclear.[13] His three new partners, Sir John

8. *Calendar of Virginia State Papers,* ed. Palmer, 1:216.

9. *Executive Journals,* ed. McIlwaine, 4:223–29, 244–45, 270, 325, 336, 346.

10. See Land Office Records, County Abstracts, no. 29, Orange Co., Book 15:326ff.

11. Beverley initially charged £3 Va. for 100 acres. For a similar acreage in Pennsylvania, on Beverley's calculation, a settler would have paid between £9 and £10 Virginia money. Unless otherwise stated all further prices are in Virginia money.

12. *Executive Journals,* ed. McIlwaine, 4:336.

13. The entire Beverley Manor acquisition is an excellent example of the kind of intrigue which was involved in the accumulation of western lands. In April of 1735 the three men were given leave to begin their survey any place not exceeding 20 miles from Stover's upper tract (*Executive Journals,* ed. McIlwaine, 4:346). On Aug. 23, 1736 the survey was finally reported to the Virginia Council, but the surveyor (Robert Brooke, sheriff of Essex County, Beverley's home county) pointed out that it was for much more than 60,000 acres (ibid., 4:375–76). Tayloe and Lee had by this time relinquished their claims to Beverley, who said he had imported 67 families to settle the tract. Beverley then requested permission

Randolph of Williamsburg, Richard Randolph of Henrico County, and John Robinson of King and Queen County, each had considerable power in his own right. Their names and their influence were probably used to obtain a new patent for this huge acreage. Similar, though less complex, mystery surrounds the patent issued to Borden for his tract in Augusta and Rockbridge counties.[14] Holders of such large patents did not have to pay the crown any money for the land, their only expenses being for the land surveys.[15]

Settlers could acquire land in the valley either from holders of large patents or directly from the crown. In the former case, the amount of land that settlers obtained was limited only by the amount of money they had or by the generosity of the grantor. In the latter case, they could obtain land in one of three ways: by headright, treasury right, or military right. Land

from the Virginia Council to take out a patent for the "surplus land" with Sir John Randolph and John Robinson (a member of the Council), with some exemption for quitrents. Richard Randolph was then brought into the partnership. On Sept. 6 the four men received a patent signed by Governor Gooch for 118,491 acres, presumably the original 60,000 acres plus 58,491 acres of "surplus land," a surveying "error" the magnitude of which suggests deliberate planning. On Sept. 17 the three other members relinquished their deed poll to Beverley (Orange Co. Deed Book 3:425–27). All three were related to the Beverley family by marriage and they apparently were used to facilitate the passage of the petition. However, Beverley's sole possession of the Manor was still not assured. An article of agreement between Beverley, Robert Brooke, and William Russell (also of Essex County) dated July 10, 1741, reveals that when the other three grantees had relinquished their rights to Beverley in 1736, he had held them in trust for himself, Russell, and Brooke, in the respective proportions of 40%, 40%, and 20% of the entire Manor grant. What the final agreement, signed on Nov. 26, 1741, seems to have done was to give Beverley sole possession of the Manor (Orange Co. Deed Book 6:311–13). I have found no reference in any Beverley materials to the 67 families he claimed to have imported by 1736. In the Beverley Manor Accounts 19 names are entered for 1737. It was in August of that year that Beverley asked Patton to obtain settlers for him. The first land grants were not officially recorded until September 1738.

14. In May 1735 he petitioned with a William Robertson of East Jersey on behalf of other Jersey families for a grant of 100,000 acres beginning at or near the south branch of the James River. Borden seems to have had the claim surveyed in 1737, and in November he and Robertson were granted an additional year in which to obtain settlers. However, when the patent was finally issued in November 1739, it was only to Borden, for 92,100 acres, and on the north branches of the James River in the upper Shenandoah Valley. The partnership seems to have been dissolved and the East Jersey families were not immediately forthcoming. See *Executive Journals,* ed. McIlwaine, 4:351, 408–9; Land Office Patent Book 18:360.

15. It is instructive to note how Beverley rewarded John Lewis for his services as a "lokator" for incoming settlers in the Manor. In the Beverley Manor Accounts (Va. Hist. Soc.) 2,071 acres is entered under Lewis's name for £14. No charges were made for the deeds or surveys for this land and Beverley returned Lewis's bond for £14 because of the latter's efforts to aid settlers who came to the Manor.

so acquired was subject to actual settlement and to the payment of an annual quitrent of 1s. per fifty acres. By means of the headright system each adult immigrant male who could prove that he had paid his own passage to America was entitled to apply for fifty acres of land free. Indentured or other imported servants could also apply for land on this basis after their term of service was completed. But the headright was rapidly being superseded by the treasury right by 1715, and gradually ceased to be an important source of land grants. It was seldom used in the Shenandoah Valley, although many early Ulster immigrants applied for it.[16] The treasury right was the most widely used method of securing a grant of crown land in the valley. A settler chose a piece of vacant land, had it surveyed by the county surveyor, and then applied to the colony's receiver general for the required number of treasury rights at 5s. 10d. current money for every fifty acres.[17] The military right system was not fully established until the French and Indian War. A member of the county militia could apply for a land warrant for an acreage which was commensurate with his rank, as payment for his military services. In addition, settlers could also lease land for an agreed period of time from landowners. Under a leaseholding system, the landholder was a tenant who had to pay a stipulated annual rent to the landowner, including quitrent.

Settlers who owned their land in the Shenandoah Valley held it as freehold (in free and common socage), that is, by paying a certain service such as quitrent annually to the ultimate owners of the land, be it the crown or the proprietor of the Northern Neck. Such freehold tenure did not subject these lands to escheat or to forfeiture if they were inherited by minors or widows, and the immediate owners could freely sell them. William Beverley employed both freehold and leasehold tenures on his lands. Except for his own 2,050-acre Mill Tract in Beverley Manor, Beverley and his heirs granted lands in the upper valley by means of "Deeds of Lease and Release," that is, as freehold. On his Piedmont lands and on his Mill Tract, his deeds to settlers were all for "Lease of Land for Lives,"

16. Harrison, *Virginia Land Grants,* pp. 11–12, 42, and Robert E. and B. Katherine Brown, *Virginia, 1705–1786: Democracy or Aristocracy?* (East Lansing: Michigan State University Press, 1964), pp. 11–12. John Preston's petition of his importation, dated May 6, 1746, stated that he had imported himself and his family directly from Ireland at his own cost, and requested the right to take up a land bounty (Preston Papers, Va. Hist. Soc.; Augusta Co. Order Book 1:44). The only land entries recorded for Preston were two tracts in Beverley Manor totaling 1,557 acres, for which he was charged over £46 quitrents (Beverley Manor Accounts, Va. Hist. Soc.)

17. Harrison, *Virginia Land Grants,* p. 48, and R. E. and B. K. Brown, *Virginia, 1705–1786,* p. 12. Because the boundaries of surveys were often ill-defined and temporary, the practice of processioning developed whereby representatives of the county were officially authorized to retrace and verify cadastral boundaries.

whereby the recipients could transfer their lands to their heirs only for a stipulated number of lives before land titles had to be sanctioned again by the heirs of the original grantor. This distinction suggests that Beverley wished to retain control of his Piedmont lands, on which there were no mandatory family settlement stipulations, while selling off his valley lands as quickly as possible.

Early Landholding Patterns in the Shenandoah Valley

The forms of land alienation are clearly reflected in the size of original landholdings in the upper valley shown in Table 1, which indicates the size of land grants patented from the crown between 1736 and 1779, including the grants to Beverley and Borden. Over 93% of all land patents granted in the upper valley before 1780 were for 400 acres or fewer. The reason for this is not difficult to find. Treasury rights for up to 400 acres could be purchased from any commissioned surveyor in the area; for larger amounts settlers had to petition the governor and Council in Williamsburg at a fee of 10s. 9d.

In order to publicize the terms on which western lands were granted, Governor Robert Dinwiddie and the Council issued a report in May 1754 describing how lands were held in fee simple, subject to an annual quitrent of 1s. for every 50 acres patented, and had to be cultivated within three years from the date of the patent.[18] The securing of land patents was often delayed by the necessity to pay these quitrents, which had to be paid only after patents had been secured. In 1754 between 900,000 and 1,000,000 acres of land in Virginia east of the Alleghenies were held by people who had not completed the process of securing a patent.[19]

Table 1 only shows patents of upper valley lands made by the crown, including the large grants to men like Beverley, Borden, and James Patton. In examining early landholding, grants made by these patentees must also be taken into account, as well as the activities of Jacob Stover and Jost Hite and associates. By 1760 about 1,800 grants and sales had been made in the upper Shenandoah and James valleys by the crown, the

18. Voorhis, "Land Grant Policy of Colonial Virginia," pp. 158, 173; Virginia Council, May 20, 1754, "Terms on Which Lands Are Granted in Virginia and the Encouragement to Settle Westward of the Allegenny," Loudoun Papers, Huntington Lib.

19. Voorhis, "Land Grant Policy of Colonial Virginia," p. 177. In Maryland a common device used by land speculators to avoid quitrent payments was to transfer land warrants from one individual to another without taking out patents.

Table 1. Crown land grants in Augusta County, 1736–79

Acres	1736–49			1750–59			1760–69			1770–79		
	No.	%	Accumu-lated%	No.	%	Accumu-lated%	No.	%	Accumu-lated%	No.	%	Accumu-lated%
10,000 +	4	0.9	100.0	0	—	—	0	—	—	0	—	—
5,001–9,999	1	0.2	99.1	2	0.3	100.1	0	—	—	0	—	—
2,001–5,000	4	0.9	98.9	11	1.7	99.8	2	0.3	100.3	1	0.1	99.9
1,001–2,000	5	1.1	98.0	13	2.0	98.1	6	0.8	100.0	3	0.4	99.8
901–1,000	0	0.0	96.9	11	1.7	96.1	2	0.3	99.2	7	1.0	99.4
801–900	1	0.2	96.9	5	0.8	94.4	0	0	98.9	1	0.1	98.4
701–800	4	0.9	96.7	5	0.8	93.6	0	0	98.9	4	0.6	98.3
601–700	4	0.9	95.8	14	2.2	92.8	8	1.1	98.9	2	0.3	97.7
501–600	1	0.2	94.9	9	1.4	90.6	8	1.1	97.8	8	1.1	97.4
401–500	1	0.2	94.7	10	1.6	89.2	12	1.6	96.7	5	0.7	96.3
301–400	207	45.7	94.5	85	13.2	87.6	67	9.0	95.1	61	8.7	95.6
201–300	76	16.8	48.8	122	19.0	74.4	141	19.0	86.1	85	12.1	86.9
101–200	111	24.5	32.0	183	28.5	55.4	242	32.6	67.1	209	29.9	74.8
1–100	34	7.5	7.5	173	26.9	26.9	255	34.5	34.5	314	44.9	44.9
Total	453			643			743			700		

SOURCES: Land Office Records, County Abstracts, Orange County, Books 15–24; Augusta County, Books 18–42 and Commonwealth Books A-B.

large grantees, and Lord Fairfax (before the redrawing of the Fairfax Line.)[20]

There was no limit on the amount of land the patentees could sell to individual settlers, and individual grants of more than 400 acres were therefore made more frequently by these landowners than by the Virginia governor and Council. By 1769, 78 of Beverley's 260 grants (30%) and 42 of Borden's 218 (19%) had been for more than 400 acres (table 2). Some early settlers also acquired more than one piece of land, and thus could accumulate land well in excess of 400 acres.

The earliest account of landholding for Augusta County as a whole occurs in the county rent rolls for the period 1760 to 1762 (table 3).[21] There is some correlation between the pattern of original land patents issued before 1760 and the pattern of landholdings by individual settlers in the early 1760s. By this time 72.2% of the 1,188 landholders recorded had 400 acres or fewer and 69.6% held between 100 and 400 acres. In the original patents up to 1760, where accumulations of grants by single individuals were not indicated, 91.9% of the grants were for 400 acres or fewer and 73.9% were for acreages of between 100 and 400 acres. By 1762 landholders who owned 400 acres or fewer (76.5% of the grants) controlled 45.3% of the total recorded acreage of 459,200 acres, while the 40 persons who owned more than 1,000 acres each (3.3% of the grants) controlled 23.5% of the total acreage. A further breakdown of the rent rolls is possible to show, to some degree, the areal variations in land ownership that existed (table 4). Twenty-seven percent of the landowners in Beverley Manor and 26% of those in Borden's Tract held more than 400 acres of land, compared with only 17% and 20% in the areas immediately north and south of these tracts, respectively. Thirty-five percent of the landowners on the Calfpasture and Cowpasture Rivers held more than 400 acres.[22]

Two other aspects of landholding must be taken into account, the presence of tenancy and, one that is more difficult to assess, the ratio of landowning to landless settlers. In terms of leaseholding, Beverley began

20. Information on land grants to 1760 was gleaned from the same data as used to compile table 1 together with Grants by Proprietor of Northern Neck in Augusta County, 1747/48–56, Land Office Records, Books E, G, H, and S; Orange Co. Deed Books 1–10; Augusta Co. Deed Books 1–8.

21. Compare R. E. and B. K. Brown, *Virginia, 1705–1786*, table B, p. 14, which is derived from the same data as table 3; their source is mistakenly given as being in the Va. State Lib.

22. The largest acreage owned was 7,930 acres by Thomas Walker, probably Dr. Thomas Walker of Albemarle County who was a deputy surveyor for Augusta County 1752–55 and later commissary general for George Washington during the French and Indian War (see Thomas and Francis Walker Papers, Rives Coll., Lib. Cong.). No settler owned more than 1,838 acres within Beverley Manor itself.

Table 2. Land grants made by the Beverleys and Bordens, 1738–79

Acres	Beverleys			Bordens		
	No.	%	Accumu-lated %	No.	%	Accumu-lated %
2,001–3,000	2	0.6	99.7	0	—	—
1,001–2,000	7	1.7	99.1	1	0.3	100.1
901–1,000	0	0	97.4	1	0.3	99.8
801–900	4	1.2	97.4	1	0.3	99.5
701–800	6	1.7	96.2	6	1.9	99.2
601–700	10	3.0	94.5	9	3.0	97.3
501–600	23	7.0	91.5	10	3.2	94.3
401–500	38	11.2	84.5	23	7.4	91.1
301–400	60	17.7	73.3	57	18.4	83.7
201–300	58	17.1	55.6	80	26.0	65.3
101–200	74	21.5	38.5	86	28.0	39.3
1–100	57	17.0	17.0	35	11.3	11.3
Total	339			309		

SOURCES: Orange County Deed Books 3–8, and Augusta County Deed Books, 1–22.

Table 3. Landholders in Augusta County, 1760–62

Acres	No. of landholders	Landholders		Acreage	
		%	Accumu-lated %	%	Accumu-lated %
5,001–8,000	6	0.6	99.9	8.7	100.1
2,001–5,000	8	0.6	99.3	6.3	91.4
1,001–2,000	26	2.1	98.7	8.5	85.1
901–1,000	13	1.0	96.6	2.7	76.6
801–900	13	1.0	95.6	2.5	73.9
701–800	23	1.9	94.6	3.7	71.4
601–700	34	2.9	92.7	5.0	57.7
501–600	65	5.5	89.8	7.8	62.7
401–500	96	8.1	84.3	9.6	54.9
301–400	250	21.0	76.2	19.2	45.3
201–300	288	24.3	55.2	15.7	26.1
101–200	288	24.3	30.9	9.4	10.4
1–100	78	6.6	6.6	1.0	1.0
Total	1,188				

SOURCE: Augusta County Rent Rolls, 1760–62, Preston Papers, Virginia Historical Society.

Table 4. Distribution of landholders in Shenandoah Valley section of Augusta
County, 1760–62

	Crown land, north of Beverley Manor		Beverley Manor		Borden's Tract		Calf pasture and Cowpasture Rivers	
Acres	No.	%	No.	%	No.	%	No.	%
5,000–8,000	3	1.5	0	—	1	0.4	0	—
2,000–5,000	4	2.0	0	—	1	0.4	0	—
1,001–2,000	4	2.0	5	1.9	5	2.1	2	3.3
901–1,000	2	1.0	1	0.4	2	0.8	1	1.6
801–900	1	0.5	3	1.1	1	0.4	2	3.3
701–800	2	1.0	3	1.1	5	2.1	1	1.6
601–700	5	2.6	9	3.3	8	3.3	4	6.6
501–600	6	3.0	21	8.0	11	4.6	8	10.2
401–500	6	3.0	32	11.9	28	11.7	4	6.6
301–400	54	27.0	51	19.0	44	18.3	10	16.4
201–300	42	21.9	82	30.4	73	30.4	16	26.2
101–200	44	22.8	53	19.7	53	22.8	13	21.3
1–100	20	10.3	10	3.7	8	3.3	0	—
Total	193		270		240		61	

SOURCE: Augusta County Rent Rolls, 1760–62.

renting out part of his Mill Tract within the Manor in 1754 for terms of
fifty-seven to eighty-nine years at annual rents of 20s. to 45s. per holding.
By 1762 he had leased 1,367 acres to six tenants.[23] Otherwise,
recorded tenancy was virtually absent in the upper valley before the mid-
1760s, although there was probably a large number of unrecorded leases
made between local settlers, particularly short-term leases of less than
twenty-one years between neighbors. Leasing extra land was more likely
than selling it if the owner had no desire to emigrate.

If there were few tenants among the first generation of landholders,
there were certainly many settlers who held no land at all. It has been
argued, on the basis of membership in the Tinkling Spring Church in
Beverley Manor during the 1740s, that many settlers did not acquire land
until there was a reasonable assurance that a regular minister had been
established in the community.[24] There may be some truth in this ob-

23. A cadastral map of the Mill Tract and adjacent woodlots can be found in
Augusta Co. Deed Book 2:461.
24. Wilson, *Tinkling Spring*, p. 69. This observation suggests a possible relationship between

servation, but the proportion of landless settlers appears to have increased steadily during the 1750s. While there were at least 1,188 landholders in the upper Shenandoah and James valleys by 1762, almost all of whom were residents, 2,287 tithables were reported for Augusta county. Tithables included all males, white and black, of sixteen years and over; in Augusta county at this time almost all were white. Even if one allows for the possibility that a quarter of the approximately 1,100 landless tithables were sons under twenty-five years of age living at home, white servants, and male boarders, this would still leave at least 36% of Augusta tithables in 1762 holding no land.

Some additional data are available to make possible a comparison of early landholding patterns in the upper valley (Augusta County), the lower valley (Frederick County), and Southside Virginia (Lunenburg County). Records of Frederick County rentals are available for 1746, 1750, and 1764, although the 1750 rentals in particular are far from complete. Table 5 summarizes the rentals for 1746 and 1764. Of the 171 landholders recorded for 1746, 117 (67.7%) held 400 acres or fewer; but they controlled only 29.5% of the total recorded acreage of 73,750, while the 15 largest possessed 37% of total acreage. This highly concentrated pattern of landholding had been reduced by 1764, but it remained, at most levels, more pronounced than in the upper valley.[25] The 400-acre level was relatively insignificant as a threshold of land ownership in the lower valley. Nearly one-fifth of all recorded landholders in 1764 had between 400 and 500 acres, which illustrates the contrasting land grant policies of the crown and the proprietary. Indeed, by the early 1760s, the average size of a holding in Frederick County (473 acres) was almost one-fifth larger than the average holding in Augusta County (386 acres). It is difficult to estimate the importance of tenancy in the lower valley at this period, but it was probably only slightly higher than in the upper valley until the influx of eastern planters after 1765.

In 1764, of the 983 families or individuals holding land in Lunenburg County, 64.0% held less than 400 acres, 26.5% held between 400 and 1,000 acres, and 9.5% held more than 1,000 acres.[26] The respective ratios for

the intent to establish churches and the locational stability of the various religious groups in the backcountry.

25. According to the 1750 rentals George Washington owned 422 acres in the lower valley and Lawrence Washington had 935 acres. George Washington had acquired 662 acres by 1759, by which time another prominent eastern Virginian, Lewis Burwell, was shown to possess 3,173 acres. Washington was seven years in arrears with his quitrents, which was not unusual since almost two-thirds of those landholders recorded were delinquent.

26. Landon C. Bell, *Sunlight on the Southside: List of Tithes: Lunenburg County, Virginia, 1748-1783* (Philadelphia: George S. Ferguson and Co., 1933), pp. 212-68. Variations in

Table 5. Landholders in Frederick County, 1746 and 1764

Acres	No. of landholders 1746	No. of landholders 1764	Landholders 1746 %	Landholders 1746 Accumulated %	Landholders 1764 %	Landholders 1764 Accumulated %	Acreage 1746 %	Acreage 1746 Accumulated %	Acreage 1764 %	Acreage 1764 Accumulated %
over 1,000	15	70	8.8	99.2	7.5	100.5	37.0	100.0	22.5	99.2
901–1,000	3	15	1.7	90.4	1.6	93.0	3.9	63.0	3.2	77.7
801–900	3	23	1.7	88.7	2.5	91.4	3.5	59.1	4.6	74.5
701–800	5	28	2.9	87.0	3.0	88.9	5.0	55.6	5.0	69.9
601–700	7	44	4.1	84.1	4.7	85.9	6.2	50.6	6.9	64.9
501–600	15	61	8.1	80.0	6.4	81.2	11.2	44.4	9.8	58.0
401–500	6	183	3.5	71.9	20.0	74.8	3.7	33.2	19.0	48.2
301–400	19	155	11.0	68.4	16.5	54.8	9.5	29.5	12.6	29.2
201–300	46	208	27.0	57.4	22.2	38.3	11.3	20.0	12.0	16.6
101–200	37	120	21.6	30.4	12.8	16.1	7.4	8.7	4.1	4.6
1–100	15	31	8.8	8.8	3.3	3.3	1.2	1.2	0.5	0.5

SOURCE: Frederick County Rentals, 1746 and 1764, Fairfax Papers VII, Brock Collection, Huntington Library, San Marino.

Augusta County were 76.2%, 20.4%, and 3.3%, and for Frederick County 54.8%, 38.2%, and 7.5%. Although there were fewer large grantors in Southside Virginia than in Augusta County, a larger proportion of settlers held over 400 acres, a much greater range of acreages was held, and a much larger proportion of settlers owned more than 1,000 acres. All of these characteristics tended to place Lunenburg County in an intermediate position with respect to Augusta and Frederick counties.

Areal Variations in Land Prices

For settlers planning to stay in the Shenandoah Valley, however temporarily, and establish farms or acquire profitable pieces of land, a prime factor in their land appraisal was the price they had to pay for their land. Few attempts have been made to analyze the variations that occurred in land prices either within an area over a particular period of time or at selected periods throughout the eighteenth century. In terms of land occupance, the problem of land prices and their areal variations becomes crucial, particularly when competitive systems of land settlement and land use are under consideration. These problems are also closely related to the whole question of land speculation as a formative element in westward expansion and the use of land as a commodity worth commercial exploitation.

Any attempt to examine the changing patterns of land prices and transfers through time is clearly fraught with difficulties. A major problem is the fluctuations that occurred in the value of money during the late colonial period.[27] Moreover, the American colonies lacked a common currency and a centrally maintained value system. Most colonies had their own currency systems, which necessitated the need for rates of exchange

---

Southside Virginia in terms of the percentage of acreages held were not calculated in the published statistics.

27. Until very recently the only published works on the problem of prices during the later colonial period were Anne Bezanson, Robert D. Gray, and Miriam Hussey, *Prices in Colonial Pennsylvania* (Philadelphia: University of Pennsylvania Press, 1935), and Anne Bezanson, *Prices and Inflation during. the American Revolution, Pennsylvania, 1770–1790* (Philadelphia: University of Pennsylvania Press, 1951), both concerned mainly with commodity and sterling prices. For more recent efforts to solve some of these transformational problems, see Alice Hanson Jones, "Wealth Estimates for the American Middle Colonies, 1774," *Economic Development and Cultural Change* 18, no. 4, pt. 2 (1970): 1–172; Jones, "Wealth Estimates for the New England Colonies about 1770," *Jour. Econ. Hist.* 32 (1972):98–127; Joseph A. Ernst, *Money and Politics in America, 1755–1775: A Study in the Currency Act of 1764 and the Political Economy of Revolution* (Chapel Hill: University of North Carolina Press, 1973).

not only with respect to sterling but also between each colony. Both Virginia and Pennsylvania money were circulating in western Virginia before 1776.[28] In addition, after about 1750, when emigrations from the Shenandoah Valley began to occur with greater frequency, it becomes increasingly difficult to ascertain whether prices were for virgin unimproved lands or for farms and partially improved lands. Although most land sales were made directly between the buyer and the seller, instances of increasing prices accruing simply from the transfer of land through a number of intermediaries cannot be ruled out. Family land transactions further complicate the situation. Land and farm sales between members of the same family were frequently made for nominal sums of 5s. to £1 rather than for the higher sums that would have reflected the real negotiable price for the property more accurately. Land was often mortgaged by valley settlers involved in trade with or purchases from outside the area, and there were instances here also of land being transferred to creditors at prices that bore more direct relationship to the size of the debt than to the negotiable value of the land.[29]

Perhaps the most difficult problem of all is identifying motives for acquiring, retaining, and transferring unimproved land; such motives can alter substantially one's definition of speculation. If one labels as "speculative" a resident who, in his will, requests that an unimproved portion of his land, which he has held for some years, be sold on the open market and the income received be distributed as inheritance to his children, then many examples of such procedures exist. However, the concern here is with landowners who sold land for profit during their active lifetimes, although this is not to deny that some of these sales may have been motivated by the desire to provide for their children during their own lifetimes.

Despite these problems, I have attempted to discern areal variations in land prices through time with the purpose of defining the extent to which land speculation was a prevailing commercial factor in the upper valley be-

28. Land prices expressed in Pennsylvania money have been converted here to Virginia money at the rate of £1 of Pennsylvania money equal to 17s. of Virginia money. There were considerable fluctuations in the rates of exchange between the two currencies and between each and sterling. Guidelines have been derived from occasional references to rates of exchange in the ledger of Mathew Read and Hugh Johnston, merchants, Staunton, Va., 1761–1770 (Library, College of William and Mary, Williamsburg), and Augusta Co. Deed Books 1–4 (1745–52). See also Ernst, *Money and Politics in America*, pp. 44–68, 193–96, 350–54.

29. Where land prices are quoted in unround numbers, such as £5 7s. 4d., the chances of credit considerations being involved are high. Such transactions, which were often mentioned in debt payments, began to occur with more frequency after about 1760. See also the discussion of Augusta County debtors and creditors between 1745 and 1773 in R. E. and B. K. Brown, *Virginia, 1705–1786*, pp. 102–8.

fore 1776. Figure 17 locates the seven areas into which this region has been divided for this investigation. Beverley Manor and Borden's Tract have been retained intact. The remaining area of the upper valley has been divided into five watershed districts, each containing one or two major streams. The original sale prices made by the six largest landowners to incoming settlers at intervals of approximately six years up to 1780 are shown in table 6; table 7 indicates prices for land resold within the seven designated areas at ten-year intervals up to 1774.

The most noticeable feature of these tables is the general upward trend of land prices. This trend is most evident in the prices charged by the Beverleys for their land, which can be assumed to have been vacant unimproved land; the trend is less marked and more fluctuating in Borden's Tract. A second point to note is that the price of £3 per 100 acres for which Beverley and Borden have long been reputed to have sold their lands was partly true only before 1745; thereafter there was a gradual increase in the sale price well beyond the £3 level. This increase was particularly felt in Borden's Tract, where by the early 1750s vacant land was selling for half as much again as it was in Beverley Manor. The largest percentage increases in Beverley's prices occurred during the 1770s; in Borden's prices, the increase came a decade earlier. Even so, table 6 shows that other large landowners operating in the upper Shenandoah and James valleys were generally charging much higher prices between 1734 and 1754 than either Beverley or the Bordens. Both Hite and Patton charged twice as much as Beverley, while Stover charged three times as much. Only John Lewis and Patton, on their relatively isolated Calfpasture River tract, were asking prices as low as Beverley's. One of the most striking features revealed in table 6 is the apparent lack of response that Beverley's son, Robert, and the Borden executors made toward the price inflation of the Revolutionary War period. Between 1775 and 1780, when general commodity prices were rising tenfold, the average price of vacant land in Beverley Manor remained unchanged, and it rose by less than 25% in Borden's Tract. This suggests that most of the vacant land being sold at this time was probably poor quality scrubland.

But table 7 shows that average resale prices by settlers owning land in Beverley Manor were almost ten times the original prices for unimproved land and in Borden's Tract were three times the original sale prices. This suggests that substantial improvements were made in the land—by both cultivation and building—in the Manor, or that settlers were indulging in considerable speculation themselves, or both. The period 1745 to 1754 provides at least a partial answer. While the average price of unimproved land in Beverley Manor was 8d. or 9d. per acre, land was being resold

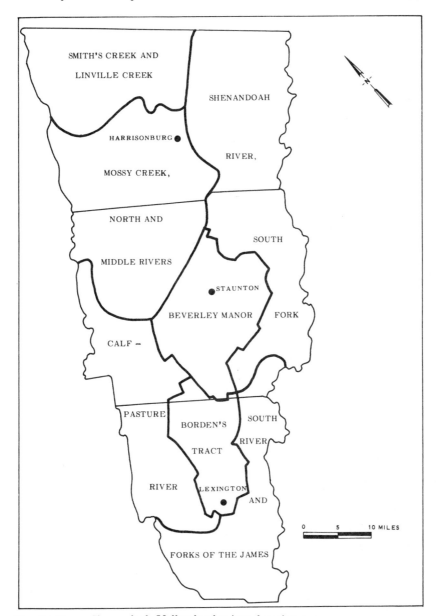

Fig. 17. Upper Shenandoah Valley land prices: location map

Table 6. Original sale prices made by large landowners

Grantee	Period	No. of grants[1]	Total price	Acreage	Average Price	
					Per acre	Per 100 acres
William Beverley and Robert Beverley	1738–44	84	£1,206. 9.9	42,119	7d.	£2.18. 4
	1745–50	108	1,228. 8.2	37,762	8d.	3. 6. 6
	1751–56	27	212. 7.6	5,574	9d.	3.15. 0
	1762–69	19	244.13.6	4,567	1s. 1d.	5. 8. 4
	1770–74	67	1,133.10.4	9,071	2s. 6d.	12.10. 0
	1775–80	12	200.18.0	1,584	2s. 6d.	12.10. 0
	1785–93	13	199. 1.5	1,258	3s. 2d.	15.16. 8
Benjamin Borden, Sr., Jr., and executors	1741–44	49	475. 7. 5	16,091	7d.	2.18. 4
	1745–50	72	791. 5.10	23,251	8d.	3. 6. 6
	1751–56	72	1,241.11. 4	20,499	1s. 2½d.	6. 0.10
	1757–61	17	93.10. 0	4,628	5d.	2. 1. 8
	1762–69	49	1,139. 0. 0	11,021	2s. 1d.	10. 8. 4
	1770–74	12	295. 0. 0	2,281	2s. 7d.	12.18. 4
	1775–80	15	406. 0. 0	2,550	3s. 2d.	15.16. 8
	1791–95	6	186. 0. 0	1,748	2s. 1½d.	10.12. 6
Jost Hite	1734–44	44	1,302.10. 0	19,182	1s. 4d.	6.13. 4
Jacob Stover	1735–41	16	1,023. 0. 0	11,470	1s. 9½d.	8.19. 2
Lewis and Patton	1745–50	21	324.11. 4	9,463	8d.	3. 6. 6
James Patton	1750–54	106	2,141. 7.10	28,399	1s. 6d.	7.10. 0

SOURCES: Orange County Deed Books 1–10, and Augusta County Deed Books, 1–27.

NOTE: Prices are in Virginia currency.

[1] This column only includes fully recorded grants which gave acreage, location, and price. There were 17 incomplete Beverley grants entered in the deed books, totaling 4,860 acres, and 11 incomplete Borden grants, totaling 1,654 acres. Lewis and Patton had 2 incomplete grants totaling 1,064 acres, and Patton had 3 incomplete grants totaling 498 acres.

Table 7. Average resale prices in the upper Shenandoah Valley, 1745–74

	1745–54			1755–64			1765–74		
	No. of entries	Average price		No. of entries	Average price		No. of entries	Average price	
		Per acre	Per 100 acres		Per acre	Per 100 acres		Per acre	Per 100 acres
Linville Creek/ Smith's Creek	39	2s. 10d.	£14.3.4	62	5s.	£25. 0.0	99	8s. 7d.	£42.18.4
South Fork of Shenandoah	64	3s.	15.0.0	66	4s. 6d.	22.10.0	134	9s.	45. 0.0
North River/ Middle River	69	3s. 4d.	16.3.3	130	4s. 3d.	21. 5.0	211	6s. 11d.	34.11.8
Beverley Manor	102	4s. 3d.	21.5.0	128	5s. 5d.	27. 1.8	165	10s. 5d.	52. 1.8
Calfpasture River	17	1s. 10d.	9.3.4	41	4s. 7d.	22.18.4	65	5s. 5d.	27. 1.8
Borden's Tract	50	3s. 8d.	18.6.6	68	4s. 1d.	20. 8.4	103	6s. 10d.	34. 3.4
Forks of the James	73	3s.	15.0.0	80	5s.	25. 0.0	98	7s. 6d.	37.10.0

SOURCE: Augusta County Deed Books 1–20.
NOTE: Prices are in Virginia currency.

at an average price of 4s. 3d. per acre—about a sixfold increase. In Borden's Tract the increase was about fourfold. These high resale prices within a relatively short period of time indicate that there was considerable and widespread interest in the profitable sale of land itself.

Table 7 indicates how valuable resold land in Beverley Manor proved to be during the colonial period. Average prices were consistently higher than in other areas of the upper valley, and the rate of price increase in the Manor was progressively higher than elsewhere.[30] In three other areas, Linville-Smith creeks, South Fork of the Shenandoah, and Calfpasture River, average land prices tripled between the early 1750s and the early 1770s. The increase was least in Borden's tract, where prices only doubled over the same period. The relatively small increase in the North-Middle River area is also revealing, and may be the result of the wide variety of terrain to be found within the area and of its proximity to the more attractive Beverley Manor; there is some indication that areas farthest from the Manor had higher resale prices than areas adjacent to it.

A Typology of Land Speculation

The changing patterns and prices of land transfers in the upper valley before 1776 add a new dimension to the study of land accumulation and its commercial significance in the settled interior of eighteenth-century America. The evidence available for this region indicates that the question of land speculation as an element in westward expansion is much more complex than is generally stated, but it appears that Robert E. and B. Katherine Brown were correct in maintaining that although the large land speculator was present, he was not oppressive and that lands were comparatively cheap.[31] The experiences of the upper Shenandoah Valley are relatively similar to those found in the North Carolina Piedmont. H. Roy Merrens concluded that there "the practice of using land for speculation had little effect on the progress of the settlement. Not only did squatters tend to ignore, and even resist, the protestations of speculators, but the speculators themselves were concerned to sell their properties in small parcels as quickly as possible."[32] In the valley, large land speculators seldom had to deal with squatters. To the degree that they sold off most

30. It is difficult to judge to what extent this higher rate was a result of the functional significance of Staunton. Within the Manor itself there was no clear relationship between land prices and distance from the town.

31. Compare Abernethy, "The First Transmountain Advance," *Humanistic Studies*, pp. 137–38, and R. E. and B. K. Brown, *Virginia, 1705–1786*, p. 16.

32. Merrens, *Colonial North Carolina*, p. 26.

of their lands rapidly, they helped to speed up the settling of the area while making relatively little impression on the patterns of land subdivision or rural settlement.

In general, writers have discussed colonial land speculation in the Valley of Virginia only in terms of the largest landowners. However, among the upper valley residents and absentee owners interested in western lands, there were at least six different types of land speculators: (1) small landholders, (2) large landholders, (3) valley settlers speculating in lands to the west and south, (4) land companies, (5) holders of military land warrants, and (6) residents and nonresidents speculating in Staunton town lots.

The relatively large amounts of land which were acquired by so-called small farmers in the upper valley provided the basis for the smallest scale of speculation. The small-scale speculator has largely been overlooked. Yet he was an important element in the patterns and levels of land transfer in all areas of the upper valley. He often charged high prices for land because of his desire to make as much profit as possible from the relatively few acres he had at his disposal. Notable examples of this can be found in Beverley Manor, where the disparity between original sale prices and resale prices is particularly evident. John Lewis, Beverley's "lokator" in the early years of settlement, received 2,071 acres free for his services. In 1746 he sold 274 acres of this land for £30.[33] William Preston sold 1,334 acres of land to his son in January 1746 for £20, perhaps a nominal, within-the-family price. The son sold 675 acres of this for £105 six months later, thus making about 1,000% profit.[34]

The small holder was also adept at land negotiations and selling land and real property to newcomers, and then moving on to new locations. Land disputes seem to have been a constant topic of conversation and legal action. The Reverend Robert Rose, on his visit to Augusta Courthouse in 1751, noted the litigious predisposition of the settlers and their general ignorance of the law.[35] The early court records bear out this observation. However, other colonial travelers to the upper valley rarely mentioned land activities, and it is not until the RevolutionaryWar period that some information becomes available about the manner in which valley settlers conducted commercial ventures in land and real property. In 1782 the marquis de Chastellux, on his return journey from Natural Bridge, met an innkeeper named Grigsby who "showed me two plantations which he

33. See note 15 above, and Augusta Co. Deed Book 1:78–82.

34. Orange Co. Deed Book 10:29–32, 209–12.

35. Diary of the Reverend Robert Rose, p. 101, Research Dept., Colonial Williamsburg, Inc., Williamsburg, Va.

had successively owned, before he settled on the one he at present cultivates. He had left them in rather good shape, and had sold them at the rate of twelve or thirteen shillings [Virginia currency] an acre."[36]

Commercial activity in land and farm sales had been an integral part of valley settlement at the small-holder level since the early 1740s. Early in 1746 a former settler of Beverley Manor who had moved to South Carolina sold 731 acres which were partially improved for £110, or 3s. per acre.[37] The more substantial the improvements, the higher the price that could be asked for the land. In November 1750, 416½ acres on Mill Creek in Beverley Manor were sold for £260, or 12s. 6d. per acre. This price included the gristmill that had been built on the tract.[38] By 1760 a few parcels of farmland in the upper valley were beginning to fetch prices of over £1 per acre. During the 1760s, 5% of all deed transfers involved land valued at £1 or more per acre. Between 1770 and 1775 this ratio had risen to 15%, and occasionally land sold for as much as £5 per acre.[39] Thus, throughout the late colonial period the small-scale speculator was able to take advantage of considerable price increases, at least within the bounds of the valley itself.

An inordinate amount of attention has been given to the large speculators who owned or were granted land in the Shenandoah Valley, such men as Lord Fairfax, a landed sovereign in his own right; Jost Hite and his associates; William Beverley; and Benjamin Borden, Sr. Although they did have control of a substantial amount of land in the Shenandoah Valley, the general image of these men as rather greedy, profit-seeking speculators is in need of some revision. Lord Fairfax seems to have dealt reasonably with settlers on his lands in the lower valley. Furthermore, there were considerable variations in the prices which the large speculators in the upper valley charged for their lands. William Beverley in particular charged relatively low prices. To some degree, the greater the amount of land an individual had at his disposal, the less extortionate were his prices.

The Hite-Fairfax controversy, although legally won by Hite's descendants, does not indicate Hite to have been a very enlightened landowner. Jacob Stover did not have the reputation of being an honest man, and part of his estate was eventually confiscated by the crown.[40] Similarly, Benjamin Borden, Sr., brought some disrepute upon the large speculator because of

36. Chastellux, *Travels in North America*, 1:410. This rate was considerably above the average resale prices for the decade immediately preceding the Revolutionary War.

37. Augusta Co. Deed Book 1:42.

38. Ibid., 3:67–70, 9:128–31.

39. See, for example, ibid, 14:217–20, 292–93, 18:253–55, 20:80–82.

40. Wust, *Virginia Germans*, p. 32.

his conduct in the upper valley, and this was further complicated by the problem of the Borden family succession. Borden not only had difficulty in obtaining the initial settlers for his large tract, he also perpetrated some misinformation in this regard and was posthumously charged with having falsified his quitrents.[41] Whereas Beverley's son continued to conduct the Manor affairs smoothly after his father's death, Borden's son, although he settled in Rockbridge County, expressed a desire to sell the whole tract off to someone who would take the responsibility for the quitrents.[42] After he died in 1753, family succession and the inheritance of land titles in Borden's Tract were thrown into confusion and prolonged litigation for the remainder of the century.

Writers who have questioned the wisdom of the large land grant, family settlement policy seem to have been particularly concerned about such prolonged situations as the Hite-Fairfax controversy and the Borden litigations. "Looked at in hindsight the practice of handling the large grants seems unjustified. It provided a monopoly and incited seemingly endless lawsuits. The heirs, with the exception of Benjamin Borden, Jr., were non-residents and it appears that more satisfactory results would have been obtained if patents had been issued by the Virginia government for individual purchases."[43] Yet it seems doubtful that the Virginia government would have found enough dedicated land officers to carry out the policy this writer suggests. There would have been no guarantee that litigation would have been diminished, and there might have been considerably more illegal land engrossment, falsifying of records, and bribery. The distribution of population might have been denser and less fragmented, but the upper valley might not have been settled so rapidly nor perhaps developed so much as it was by 1776.

A third level of land speculation is that involving upper valley settlers whose profit-seeking ventures carried them beyond the Shenandoah Valley itself. Although this type of speculation was not common among local settlers, it did help to enhance the status of a few individuals. Benjamin Borden, Sr., had land interests south of the James River, and William Preston moved with the formation of new western counties. By 1777 he owned over 8,000 acres of land in Augusta, Botetourt, and Montgomery counties and more than 1,000 acres in Kentucky.[44]

41. *Executive Journals*, ed. McIlwaine, 3:408–9; Kegley, *Kegley's Virginia Frontier*, pp. 148–50; Couper, *Shenandoah Valley*, 1:265–84; Augusta Co. Order Book 1:257.

42. Virginia Papers, 4ZZ4, Draper Mss., Wis. State Hist. Soc. The Bordens charged 2s. 6d. annual quitrent for every 100 acres a settler held. William Beverley charged 2s. 8d.

43. Couper, *Shenandoah Valley*, 1:306.

44. William Preston's will, Mar. 29, 1777, Preston Papers, Va. Hist. Soc. See also Montgomery Co. Will Book B:55; the Will of William Preston, Montgomery County, Feb. 11,

By far the most prominent resident of upper valley who accumulated western lands was James Patton. As early as 1743 Patton petitioned the Virginia government for 200,000 acres on the Holston and New rivers in southwestern Virginia, on which he proposed to settle one family for every 1,000 acres.[45] The petition was refused at that time because Virginia did not wish to get involved in a dispute with the French, but in 1745 he and some associates were granted 100,000 acres in western Virginia. However, lawsuits were soon begun against him by the Ohio Company, which had a petition for 500,000 acres, and by the Greenbrier Company, which had petitioned for 800,000 acres, both of which were interested in lands north of the New River. By the time he died Patton owned 17,007 acres in his own name, including his 1,390-acre farm at Springhill in Beverley Manor. In addition, the Roanoke and James River groups for whom he had been a land agent in southwestern Virginia had assigned their shares totaling several thousand acres of "the great grant on the Waters of the Mississippi" to Patton.[46]

Conflict between the land companies and land seekers such as Patton and Preston often occurred. The large land grants which the Virginia government permitted to be established in the Shenandoah Valley set the pattern for competitive western land projects. For one thing, the government was obviously concerned about control of the Ohio Valley. For another, many eastern Virginia planters, having observed the successful ventures of the Fairfaxes, the Beverleys, and others, came to realize by the mid-1740s the commercial possibilities of western land speculation. The increasing scale of land speculation that resulted from the fusion of these two motivations was the culmination of land policies in Virginia going back to the 1720s, rather than a specific policy of successive Virginia governments.[47] As the British Board of Trade emphasized, the strategy against the French was to be land control and settlement. Those who were in a position to profit from this strategy were large Virginia planters

---

1781, Campbell-Preston Papers, vol. 2, Manuscript Div., Lib. Cong.

45. See James Patton to John Blair, Jan. 1752, Preston Papers, 1QQ75-77, Draper Mss., Wis. State Hist. Soc.

46. Ibid., 1QQ63–66.

47. Voorhis, "Land Grant Policy of Colonial Virginia," pp. 166–68. I agree with Voorhis's argument that there was no planned policy of land speculation. However, since influential members of the Virginia government were themselves involved in western land speculation, there was always a strong lobby for a liberal land policy which allowed for ample opportunity by eastern Virginia planters to obtain western lands for speculation or for agricultural activities which supplemented the output from their eastern plantations. For some insights into Virginia government, see Jack P. Greene, "Foundations of Political Power in the Virginia House of Burgesses, 1720–1776," *Wm. and Mary Qtly.*, 3d ser. 16 (1959): 485–506.

and a few Shenandoah Valley residents whose knowledge of terrain and surveying proved useful. Thus, William Beverley was one of the original members of the Greenbrier Company when it received a 100,000-acre grant on the Greenbrier River in 1745, and the agents and surveyors for the company were John and Andrew Lewis of Beverley Manor.[48] Similar relationships with western residents were set up by the other two major Virginia land companies engaged in western land speculation after 1749, the Ohio Company of Virginia and the Loyal Land Company. John Lewis was also a member of the latter company.[49]

To some degree, these land companies were a westward extension of the speculative activities of various planter cliques in eastern Virginia. Their activities were conducted at a socioeconomic level and on an areal scale which went far beyond the activities of any western settlers themselves, with the notable exception of Lord Fairfax. But their impact on the westward expansion of settlement in Virginia was diminished both by the poor accessibility and rugged topography of their lands and by London's prohibition of settlement beyond the Appalachians. Moreover, it was diminished by another form of western land acquisition which eventually led not only to competition with the land companies but also to another form of land speculation.

This fifth type of speculation was encouraged through the Virginia government's policy of granting military land warrants to veterans of the French and Indian War and later to Revolutionary War veterans. These warrants were granted without fee and without payment of quitrents for ten years, but they were otherwise subject to the same conditions of cultivation and improvement as other grants. The amount of land granted varied according to rank, with field officers receiving 5,000 each, captains 3,000 acres each, down to privates with 50 acres each.[50] This procedure further encouraged the accumulation of demands for land by eastern Virginia planters and western settlers who attained high military rank. Men of the lowest military ranks from Augusta County do not seem to have exercised their bounty rights to any great extent at this time, but the use of military land warrants was an important feature of the early settlement of Kentucky.

The establishment of, and speculation in, the town lots of Staunton was of more direct significance to the settlement of the upper Shenandoah Valley

48. *Executive Journals*, ed. McIlwaine, 5:172–73; Williams, "Political Alignments in Colonial Virginia, 1698–1750," pp. 327–37.

49. See Kenneth P. Bailey, *The Ohio Company of Virginia and the Westward Movement, 1748–1792* (Glendale, Calif.: Arthur H. Clarke Co., 1939).

50. See the discussion in Reeder, "Evolution of Virginia Land Grant System," pp. 111–12.

before 1776. When Beverley granted twenty-five acres of his Mill Tract to the county in 1746, the land was to be laid off in half-acre lots with one and a half acres for the courthouse and prison. Town lots that remained unsold were to be rented out for a period of twenty-one years.[51] During 1750, the first year of transactions, seven lots (with a fifty-acre woodlot assigned to each) were sold for an average price of £5 17s. each. Two of the lots were bought by Alex Wright, a merchant in Fredericksburg. This purchase marked the beginning of a growing interest by Fredericksburg people in the town lots of Staunton both as speculative land ventures and as a means of tapping the trading potentialities of the Virginia back-country.[52]

Prices for lots increased very rapidly. Wright bought four additional lots from Beverley in 1755 for £10 and five years later sold them for £100 and his two original lots for £200.[53] The great variations that occurred in the prices for vacant and built-on lots during the 1760s was further compli-cated by the apparently inexplicable fact that both Robert Beverley and the Augusta County justices were selling lots at very low prices. This situation produced the same opportunities for speculation as occurred in lands transferred by the Beverleys to settlers in the Manor. The county justices were selling vacant lots at approximately £5 each, and Beverley continued to sell vacant lots for as little as £2 10s. each, while vacant half-lots were reselling for £20, and half-lots with a house or store on them for as much as £170. The inflation of the early 1770s also showed up in the sale of lots, with vacant half-lots selling for £40. Half of lot 12, which was bought for £16 15s. in November 1773, sold for £100 six months later.[54] By and large, price rises in town lots were higher and increased at a faster rate than prices for agricultural land.

Post-Revolutionary Changes in Land Ownership

The Revolutionary War and the political changes that ensued had sig-nificant effects on the land situation in the upper valley. In the first place, land prices soared during the period 1777 to 1782, with lingering effects occurring through 1784. By July 1778 land in Augusta County was selling

51. Augusta Co. Order Book 2:313, 351, 413, 437. See also City of Staunton, Virginia (microfilm reel 14, Va. State Lib.), pp. 1–2.

52. Augusta Co. Order Book 2:470–71. Other Fredericksburg residents began to take an interest in Staunton and vicinity from the mid-1750s on. See Augusta Co. Deed Books 6:488–89, 7:28–30, 8:366, 9:60–63, 11: 859–60.

53. Augusta Co. Deed Books 7:28–30, 9:60–63.

54. Ibid., 19:99–101, 212–15, 20:302–4.

for anywhere between £1 and £3 per acre; by August 1779 prices had tripled. A year later land prices were as high as £60 to £65 per acre and remained at that level until the beginning of 1782. The period of peak land prices occurred during the fall of 1780. In August of that year 150 acres of farmland on Moffett's Branch in Rockbridge county sold for £10,000, and lot 13 in Staunton, which had sold for £2,000 five months earlier, was purchased for £40,000.[55] During this period, it should be recalled, Robert Beverley was still selling vacant land in Beverley Manor for only 2s. 6d. to an upper limit of 10s. per acre, and Borden's executors were selling vacant land for 2s. to 10s. 6d. per acre!

The change from colony to commonwealth brought significant changes in the systems of land tenure in Virginia, at least on paper. In 1776 all feudal forms of land tenure were abolished in Virginia except in the Northern Neck, where Lord Fairfax retained his lands as a private owner. A year later all quitrents in Virginia were abolished except in the Northern Neck.[56] During the years 1779 through 1782 additional acts were passed for tax purposes which affected the commercial nature of landholding. At local discretion, lands were to be divided into classes, up to a maximum of six, for tax purposes and to be assessed without regard to the building on them.

In 1785 the Virginia Assembly finally passed an act which transferred all land records for the Northern neck to the state land office. All unappropriated lands in the proprietary were to be disposed of by the state.[57] However, from 1786 to 1793 agents for the new proprietor, Denny Martin Fairfax, as well as the Commonwealth of Virginia, granted land titles in the Northern Neck including the lower Shenandoah Valley. It was only in the late 1790s that private owners began to buy up large parcels of Northern Neck lands, including the Winchester town lots, and land control was finally diverted from the possessions of one man.[58]

The new Commonwealth Assembly passed another important act in 1780 whereby new tax laws had to be implemented by each county. Thus, in 1782, for the first time the counties of Virginia reported ownership of land and personal property in a relatively comprehensive, systematic manner. Table 8 provides a comparison of the distribution of landholding in 1782 and 1800 for four of the valley's six existing counties. The total number of landholders in both Frederick and Augusta counties in 1782 is

55. Ibid., 23:297–300, 359–60.

56. Hening, *Statutes*, 9:226ff., 359. See also C. Ray Klein, "Primogeniture and Entail in Colonial Virginia," *Wm. and Mary Qtly.*, 3d ser. 25 (1968): 545–86.

57. Hening, *Statutes*, 12:111.

58. Reeder, "Evolution of Virginia Land Grant System," pp. 190–93; Dickinson, *Fairfax Proprietary*, pp. 20ff.

Table 8. Landholders, 1782 and 1800

Acres	Augusta County				Rockbridge County				Rockingham County				Frederick County			
	1782		1800		1782		1800		1782		1800		1782		1800	
	No.	%	No.	%	No.	%	No.	%	No.	%	No.	%	No.	%	No.	%
10,000+	0	—	7	0.6	0	—	3	0.3	0	—	6	0.6	1	0.1	2	0.2
5,001–9,000	0	—	3	0.3	0	—	1	0.1	0	—	0	—	2	0.3	0	—
1,001–5,000	17	2.2	37	3.6	8	1.4	14	1.5	12	1.8	24	2.3	27	4.2	27	2.2
901–1,000	5	0.6	12	1.7	3	0.5	7	0.8	5	0.8	7	0.7	7	1.1	11	0.9
801–900	4	0.6	11	1.7	6	1.0	7	0.8	6	0.9	10	1.0	6	0.9	13	1.1
701–800	20	2.6	21	2.0	4	0.7	8	0.9	7	1.1	17	1.7	10	1.6	19	1.5
601–700	16	2.1	21	2.0	8	1.4	18	1.9	13	2.0	19	1.9	8	1.2	19	1.5
501–600	33	4.3	42	4.1	28	4.8	18	1.9	27	4.1	42	4.1	15	2.3	38	3.0
401–500	58	7.5	80	7.8	43	7.4	45	4.9	32	5.0	50	4.9	42	6.8	57	4.6
301–400	120	15.6	131	12.7	67	11.6	90	9.7	67	10.1	90	8.9	88	13.7	127	10.3
201–300	187	24.3	203	19.7	131	22.6	176	19.0	179	27.2	186	18.1	143	22.2	212	17.1
101–200	283	30.9	294	28.5	180	31.0	282	30.5	218	33.3	298	29.3	195	30.9	418	33.8
1–100	73	9.4	170	16.5	102	17.6	255	27.6	93	14.1	264	25.8	99	15.4	294	23.8
Total	771		1,032		580		924		659		1,025		643		1,237	

SOURCE: County Land Tax Books, 1782 and 1800, Virginia State Library.

NOTE: Figures for the number of landholders in 1782 in Augusta and Frederick counties are incomplete.

incompletely recorded. Of the 787 holders listed for Augusta, 80.2% owned 400 acres or fewer. This is a slight increase from the pattern of landholding in the upper valley in 1760, when 76.2% held 400 acres or fewer (see table 3). The comparative 1782 figures for Rockingham and Rockbridge counties were 82.8% and 84.8%, respectively. By the end of the colonial period about 35% of the land in the upper valley was owned by only 10% of the land-owners. The great majority of the residents in the area, therefore, remained relatively small-scale landholders. A similar situation prevailed in Frederick County by 1782, despite the establishment of a few large plantation quarters by absentee planters, because of the influx of small planters from eastern Virginia eager to acquire land. The proportion of landholders in Frederick with 400 acres or fewer had increased to 82.2% by 1782 from 54.8% in 1764 when Frederick encompassed the entire lower valley (see table 5). However, 500 acres was a more critical breaking point in Frederick's landholding structure in 1764 than 400 acres. In that year 74.8% of landholders in the lower valley had 500 acres or fewer, compared with 84.3% of landholders in the upper valley. By 1782 the respective proportions for the much-reduced Frederick and Augusta counties were 89% and 87.7%, a shift in the margin of difference which reflected the small-planter influx.

In Augusta County 35% of the landholders had more than one tract of land in 1782, but no landholder in the upper valley held more than 4,402 acres.[59] Only three men held more than 2,000 acres (compared with seven in Frederick County alone). Concentration of ownership in Staunton town lots was well developed by this time. Two people held thirteen and a half lots between them, or 27% of the total lots. There is very little evidence of a growth of tenancy in the upper valley, but the increasing proportion of landless settlers makes it probable that there were many unrecorded leases.

Freeman H. Hart has provided some comparative data on patterns of landholding for the period 1786 to 1788.[60] Within the entire Valley of Virginia, from Berkeley County to Botetourt County, there was a definite contrast in landholding patterns between the upper Shenandoah Valley, on the one hand, and the lower Shenandoah Valley and Botetourt County, on the other. Hart's tables show only one landowner in

59. Henry Miller owned 3,827 acres in Augusta and 575 acres in Rockingham. Compare the table on p. 162 in Hart, *Valley of Virginia*. Although it is understandable on the scale at which Hart was working, he made no attempt to correlate individual landowners who held land in more than one county. Hence, he omitted Henry Miller and also Isaac Zane, Jr., who held over 20,000 acres in Frederick and Shenandoah counties.

60. Hart, *Valley of Virginia*, p. 162. Because Bath County was not formed from Augusta County until 1790, the Augusta figures are somewhat inflated.

the upper valley with more than 2,500 acres, but there were actually two. Even so, a figure of two large landholders out of some 3,720 in the upper valley counties is considerably smaller than the thirteen out of 3,193 owner in the lower Shenandoah Valley counties and the seven out of 662 owners in Botetourt County south of Rockbridge. Conversely, 95% of all landholders in the upper valley held less than 500 acres, while the corresponding figures for the lower valley and the area south of the James River were 93% and 87%, respectively. The relatively high ratio of large landholders in Botetourt County reflects a relatively unadjusted frontier type of landownership pattern of the kind that had occurred in the upper Shenandoah Valley some twenty years previously.

There were other significant changes in the patterns of land acquisition and ownership during the last two decades of the eighteenth century. The first is the changing ratio of landless settlers to landowners. In 1782, in relation to the total number of tithables recorded, between 35% and 40% of Augusta's taxable population did not own land. The figures for Rockingham and Rockbridge were considerably smaller, 28% and 23%, respectively, while Frederick's was much larger at 52%. During the next eighteen years, with the growth of a nonagricultural and nonrural population, the number of landless taxables markedly increased in the upper valley. By 1800 55% of Augusta's tithables and 51% of Rockingham's were landless. Frederick's remained almost the same, at 51%, but Rockbridge's rose only to 38%. This would suggest that Rockbridge County remained more rural and more agriculturally oriented than the Shenandoah valley as a whole.

A second form of change took place in the upper echelons of the landholding structure by 1800. While the ratio of those holding 400 acres or fewer by the end of the century remained relatively unchanged in all three upper valley counties—77.3% in Augusta, 81.8% in Rockingham, and 86.9% in Rockbridge—a noticeable shift occurred in the number of persons holding over 1,000 acres. Seventy-five persons held more than 1,000 acres by 1800 compared with only thirty-seven in 1782 (see Table 8). More significantly, twenty persons held over 5,000 acres, where no one had held that amount in 1782. These changes reflect a new wave of land speculation which occurred near the end of the century.

Of the 2,850 new grants made in the upper valley between 1780 and 1800, 92% were for acreages of 400 or fewer.[61] But many Revolutionary soldiers from the upper valley who received warrants for less than 500 acres seem to have sold their land rights to speculators. In addition,

61. See Land Office Records, 1780–1800, for Augusta, Rockbridge, and Rockingham counties.

between 1795 and 1799 a number of very substantial grants were made for unappropriated lands in the three counties to nonresident land speculators. Most of these grants were located in the mountainous margins of the valley or among the headstreams of the Shenandoah and James rivers. The largest land-grabbers were John Berkeley, who amassed the enormous total of 143,000 acres in three grants in Rockingham and Rockbridge counties, and Levi Hollingsworth, who accumulated 92,757 acres in two grants in Rockingham and Augusta counties.[62] Both men were members of influential families in Virginia and Maryland, respectively, in the early post-Revolutionary period. The Berkeley family was perhaps the most powerful landed family of eastern Virginia, while Hollingsworth, a member of the Baltimore merchant family, was the leading flour merchant in Philadelphia during amd immediately following the Revolutionary War.[63] All of the individuals or partnerships filing for large land patents during this period of land acquisition were, with one exception, absentee merchants and planters whose names did not appear in the county tithables. Most had disappeared from local tax lists by 1805.[64]

Why did these huge land acquisitions in the upper valley during the 1790s occur? More valuable agricultural lands could have been found in Kentucky, where some of these speculators probably had other land investments. One possible explanation lies in the transportation improvements being carried out by the Potomac Company and the James River

62. See the 1800 land tax books for the three counties. Others with large acreages were recorded as Haveland and Coleman with 79,910 acres; Shafer and Shipman with 61,148 acres; John Fleming with 47,900 acres, and Major Dowel, a Rockbridge County tithable, with 26,740 acres. The wealthy Richmond lawyer Henry Banks acquired 12,989 acres in Rockbridge County, and Richard Adams, probably the prominent Richmond resident, obtained 4,781 acres in Augusta County. For the land deeds and locations of these grants, see Virginia Land Office Records for the three counties for the years 1795 to 1799; Rockingham Co. Survey Books A and B, and Survey Entry Book A; and Rockbridge Co. Surveys 1779–1806, especially pp. 7–10. For documentation of earlier interest by eastern Virginians in the lands of the Shenandoah Valley, see Jackson T. Main, "The One Hundred," *Wm. and Mary Qtly.*, 3d ser. 11 (1954): 354–84. The Benjamin Harrison who held 1,024 acres in Rockingham County in 1788 was not from Charles City County as Main tentatively suggests (p. 384n) but was a resident of Rockingham County.

63. It is not clear which John Berkeley this was and how he fitted into the Berkeley family structure. Levi Hollingsworth was placed in charge of the government's flour exports from Philadelphia in 1782. With the profits he made in the flour trade, he not only speculated in Virginia military land bounty warrants but also acquired large holdings in western Pennsylvania (see Robert A. East, *Business Enterprise in the American Revolutionary Era*, Columbia University Studies in History no. 439 [New York, 1938], pp. 151, 154, 316). A number of Hollingsworth families resided in Frederick County at this time, but no Levi existed among male Hollingsworth tithables.

64. Both Berkeley and Hollingsworth still had all their holdings in 1805.

Company in Western Virginia.[65] Renewed attempts were being made during the 1790s to improve the navigability of the lower Shenandoah and upper James rivers. On the other hand, no land acquisitions on such a scale occurred in the lower valley. In 1800 no new names with large acreages of land appeared in the records of that area, and only two men held more than 5,000 acres and neither exceeded 19,000 acres.

Small-scale land acquisitions, one of the most common processes in any community, took place during the last two decades of the century among a considerable number of upper valley settlers. When Henry Miller, an important ironmaker, died in 1796, he left some 7,742 acres of land, or over 3,300 acres more than he had possessed in 1782. Gabriel Jones, a prominent and long-established lawyer in Rockingham County, had expanded his holdings from 704 acres in the county in 1782 to 1,064 by 1800 largely as a result of the generosity of some of his clients. Possibilities of obtaining unappropriated lands still existed after 1800, although most of the remaining lands were of little agricultural value. More than 130,000 acres in Augusta County remained unappropriated in 1800, over 100,000 acres in Rockingham County, and more than 50,000 acres in Rockbridge County. By 1800 land agglomeration had gone furthest in Augusta County, where almost half of all landowners held more than one tract of land. In Rockingham County the number was less than one-third, and in Rockbridge only one-fifth.

Speculation in town lots developed an entirely new phase after 1780. Not only were the last twenty years of the century the most active in terms of the growth and physical expansion of Staunton, but a whole series of newly established settlements created their own patterns of land activity. The first major addition to Staunton's original twenty-five acres came in 1787, when another twenty-five acres on the west side of the town were incorporated.[66] The half-acre lots were sold both by the original landowner, Alex St. Clair, and by the county justices. Yet, while the latter were selling the new lots at £5 each, St. Clair was charging prices of £30 to £50 each. By the early 1790s some of the built-up lots in this new extension were selling for over £800 each. By 1791 a total of 70⅓ lots were owned and occupied in Staunton. No individual owned more than 5 lots, and only three persons owned more than 3. By 1800 speculation and accumulation had increased to the extent that seven individuals each owned 4 or more lots out of a total of 128.

65. See Cora Bacon-Foster, *Early Chapters in the Development of the Potomac Route to the West* (Washington, D.C.: Columbia Historical Society, 1912); Wayland F. Dunaway, *History of the James River and Kanawha Company*, Columbia University Studies in History, Economics, and Public Law, nos. 104, 236 (New York, 1922).

66. Augusta Co. Deed Book 25:293.

Elsewhere in Augusta County interest was focused on the lots of the new settlements of Waynesboro and Greenville.[67] Both villages were beginning to develop some shape by 1800. In Rockingham County active trading took place in the lots of Harrisonburg, the county seat, in the nearby village of Keisell'stown (Keezletown) and by the turn of the century in Port Republic. Interest was also being shown in the rapidly growing settlement of New-market, just across the county line in Shenandoah County. In Rockbridge County, there was considerable participation in the sale of lots in the county town of Lexington, despite a disastrous fire in 1796. The villages of Browns-burgh, Springfield, and Fairfield were also established by 1800. Lots in these new settlements generally sold for £5 to £10 each, although they frequently fetched prices of up to £100 by the late 1790s. The county towns generated the highest prices of all the new settlements. Prices of up to £500 were being asked for built-up half-acre lots in Harrisonburg and Lexington by the end of the century.

The inflationary effects of the Revolutionary War lingered on in land prices until the beginning of 1785, and by 1793 prices were beginning to be recorded in dollars as well as in the still-customary Virginia currency. These phenomena make it difficult to analyze land value patterns at the end of the century. In comparative terms, however, the comments made by travelers passing through the Shenandoah Valley throw some light on how the region fared in relation to the rest of Virginia. The more astute travelers observed that variations in land prices reflected variations in soil quality and in location. Moreover, they reported with some surprise that land values in the Shenandoah Valley tended to be higher than in the plantation areas of eastern Virginia. La Rochefoucauld-Liancourt, for example, found land prices in Augusta County higher than in Albemarle County, on the eastern side of the Blue Ridge; and Isaac Weld discovered land prices in the upper James Valley to be almost as high as in southeastern Pennsylvania.[68] La Rochefoucauld-Liancourt also observed that, on the whole, prices for good alluvial land tended to increase the farther north one went in the Shenandoah Valley.[69]

These observations were borne out by the findings of William Strickland's general survey of agriculture in Virginia in 1796.[70] He found that the best river bottomlands in the Tidewater were valued at between 30s. and 40s.

67. For the establishment of the post-Revolutionary settlements in the upper valley and the sale of lots, see Augusta Co. Deed Books 28–31; Rockbridge Co. Deed Books A–D; Rockingham Co. Deed Books 0 and 00.

68. La Rochefoucauld-Liancourt, *Travels*, 2:89; Weld, *Travels*, p. 123.

69. La Rochefoucauld-Liancourt, *Travels*, 2:93, 100, 110–11.

70. "Report of William Strickland to the [British] Board of Agriculture 1796," reprinted in *Farmer's Register* 3 (1835): 201–11, 262–69.

per acre. In the Piedmont such lands were worth 90s. per acre, and some of the better wheat lands were selling for as little as 18s. to 20s. per acre. In the northern Piedmont, in Loudoun County, the leading agricultural county in Virginia, the best farmlands were selling from 60s. to over 100s. per acre. Within the Shenandoah Valley, while he found the usual price of land along the Shenandoah River to be about 31s. 6d. per acre, good land in the upper valley was selling for over 90s. per acre. In the lower valley average prices for good land were around 90s., but in the vicinity of Winchester the best land was selling for up to 150s. per acre.

Thus, by the end of the eighteenth century, land values and the interest in land acquisition in the Shenandoah Valley as a whole were among the highest in Virginia. Interest in the lands of the valley remained high after the Revolutionary War despite the attractions of Kentucky and the region's relative disadvantage in relation to agricultural markets. Unquestionably, the high values placed on farmland also reflected a high level of agricultural enterprise.

4 Population Change and
Social Stratification

A FUNDAMENTAL FEATURE of any frontier occupance is the growth of
population and its organization into new communities. Settlers who
remained in one location for long periods contributed most to the initial
demographic and socioeconomic characteristics of frontier settlements.
Their influence on later transformations was sometimes preempted,
however, by newer immigrants who were able to enter local society
at levels of authority and influence. Over the long term frontier
areas were transformed from sparsely settled zones of population that
exhibited low levels of social differentiation to more densely settled
regions occupied by more complex, multifaceted, stratified societies
that had integrated in unique fashion the socioeconomic characteristics
of their population source areas.

The distributional and migrational aspects of the valley's population
examined in the previous chapters demonstrate some clear trends over
time and space. Population growth was heavily dependent on
immigration from initial settlement in the late 1720s until the mid-1750s,
when natural increase and emigration became more significant
factors in population change. Most of the valley's best agricultural
lands had passed into private ownership by the outbreak of the
Revolution. How did these shifts in demographic processes affect rates
of population change, and what evidence is there to indicate the timing
of the transition from a frontier to a postfrontier pattern of demographic
behavior? From the point of view of socioeconomic evolution, the
examination also revealed early evidence of commercialism in land
activities and population movements. What changes should be expected,
therefore, in a society undergoing such commercialization? And to what
degree and in what ways might the socioeconomic transformation of the
valley's population be influenced by the cultural and social traditions
of its settlers and the timing of their appearance in the region?

Population Growth and Demographic Change

No census of Virginia's population was taken in the eighteenth century
until the first federal census of 1790. For the earlier years population

reconstruction depends mainly upon county tithable lists, enumerating all adult (over sixteen) males and adult Negro, mulatto and Indian women for tax purposes.[1] The conversion of tithables and other population indicators into figures for total population is a long-standing problem. Using Herman Friis's multiplier of 5 for militia lists, for example, the approximately 615 men in the Augusta County militia in 1742 would indicate about 3,075 pioneer settlers in the upper valley, the product of fourteen years of continuous settlement with an average annual growth rate of almost 20%.[2] In 1756 Governor Dinwiddie used a multiplier of 4 for white tithables and a multiplier of 2 for Negro tithables in reporting Virginia's total population as 293,472.[3] The study of such a relatively small area as the Shenandoah Valley requires a more flexible approach to the conversion problem than is found in more general studies. Before the mid-1760s a multiplier of slightly more than 4 would seem to be a realistic one for the white tithables, considering that the average size of a family immigrating to the valley was five and that fewer than one in five families appears to have had more than one adult male member. After about 1765 a multiplier of 4 appears realistic for whites until 1780. During the 1780s, when the tithable age for whites rose from sixteen to twenty-one years, a multiplier of 5 expresses the total'

1. Hening, *Statutes*, 3:258–61, 4:133. Four main problems arise from the use of these lists: their accuracy and reliability from year to year, the changing definition of a tithable, the effects of political devolution on the size and location of the data units, and the designing of conversion ratios that best reflect the translation of tithables into total population figures. These problems of raw population data must be kept in mind when using printed sources of eighteenth-century population figures: Stella H. Sutherland, *Population Distribution in Colonial America* (New York: Columbia University Press, 1936); Evarts B. Greene and Virginia D. Harrington, *American Population before the Federal Census of 1790* (New York: Columbia University Press, 1932); U.S., Bureau of the Census, *Heads of Families at the First Census of the United States Taken in the Year 1790* (Washington, D.C., 1908); U.S., Bureau of the Census, *A Century of Population Growth in the United States, 1790–1900*, ed. W. S. Rossiter (Washington, D.C., 1909). James H. Cassedy, *Demography in Early America: Beginnings of the Statistical Mind, 1600–1800* (Cambridge, Mass.: Harvard University Press, 1969) provides valuable insights into the demographic ideas current during the colonial period.

2. Friis, *Series of Population Maps*, pp. 6–7, and Preston Papers, 1QQ10–17, Draper Mss., Wis. State Hist. Soc. See also Merrens, *Colonial North Carolina*, pp. 194–201; Herbert A. Whitney, "Estimating Precensus Populations: A Method Suggested and Applied to the Towns of Rhode Island and Plymouth Colonies in 1689," *Annals Assoc. Amer. Geog.* 55 (1965): 178–89.

3. "Great Britain. Board of Trade—Report on His Majesty's [George II] Colonies and Plantations in America. May 11, 1756, Whitehall," Loudoun Papers, Huntington Lib. In this report the tithable age for whites was 18; the black tithable age remained 16.

white population more accurately. A multiplier of 2 for Negro tithables probably reflects their numbers reasonably well for the colonial period; after the Revolution the large increase in the number of imported slaves in the valley makes a multiplier of 2.3 a more accurate conversion figure.[4]

Compilations from tithable records provide only an estimate of total population, and few tithable records for the valley before 1782 have been preserved intact. Moreover, the annual tithable report in the county court order books simply gives the total number of tithables without any information on composition. Figure 18 indicates the trend of tithable returns for the upper Shenandoah Valley from 1745 to 1800. The general pattern is a highly fluctuating one, reflecting the numerous boundary changes of the century. But between 1745 and 1754, when the redefining of the southern Northern Neck border reduced the number of Augusta tithables, there was a steady rate of growth of population in the upper valley of some 5% to 6% annually.[5]

The 1745 tithable returns for Augusta and Frederick counties totaled 2,479, with Augusta reporting 1,196 to Frederick's 1,283. Using a multiplier of 4.1, this would give a total of almost 10,200 settlers living in Virginia west of the Blue Ridge by 1745, some 8% of Virginia's total population of approximately 120,000 at this date.[6] The difference of 235 tithables between the Augusta records for 1745 and 1746, if accurate, would suggest that in 1745 there were already about 1,000 people settled south of the upper James River in western Virginia. By 1750 the number of tithables recorded west of the Blue Ridge had increased to around 4,100, or approximately 17,000 settlers.[7] In 1755 the total estimated population of western

4. Hening, *Statutes*, 10:241. Adam Stephen's inventory of 1791 provides a rare insight into the age of slaves. His 53 Negroes ranged in age from 2 to 80, with 30 identified as 16 years or over and 23 below that age (Frederick Co. Superior Court Will Book 1:142–54).

5. The failure to return a list of tithables south of the James River caused a decline in the number of tithables from 1,196 in 1745 to 961 in 1746.

6. Greene and Harrington, *American Population before the Federal Census of 1790*, p. 140.

7. There are conflicting statements about the population of western Virginia at mid-century. There were 2,124 tithables recorded in Augusta County for 1750 (Augusta Co. Order Book 2:489–90), and a seemingly incomplete total of 1,721 for Frederick County (Frederick Co. Order Book 3:368). In Greene and Harrington, for 1749 the total number of tithables is given as 3,004, with Frederick County numbering 1,581 tithables and Augusta 1,423. For 1750, R. E. and B. K. Brown, *Virginia, 1705–1786*, p. 79, n. 59, use the figures given in "A General List of Tithables Taken in 1750, as far as Returns Were Then Made," Chalmers Collection, New York Public Library, which indicates a total population of 6,680 in Augusta County, based on a tithable figure of 1,670.

Virginia was reported as 20,800, of which Augusta County's folk now comprised 9,172 and Frederick's 9,372.[8]

The impact of the French and Indian War on population distribution and the recording of tithables has already been discussed.[9] Only after the war with the resumption of more peaceful conditions were tithables more accurately taken. Moreover, the years 1764 to 1770 saw the most rapid growth of population during the eighteenth century after the 1730s. Much of this growth came in areas farther to the west and south, particularly in the Valley of Virginia south of the James River and in its headstreams. As a result, Botetourt County was formed south of the James in 1770, and it included some 1,570 tithables formerly of Augusta. However, what this rate of growth (about 9% annually) suggests is that, not the French and Indian War, but the early 1770s just before the outbreak of the Revolution marked the transition from a frontier to a postfrontier growth pattern in the upper valley. By this time, annual growth rates in the upper valley had dipped permanently below 4% (see fig. 18). Available tithable figures suggest that during the last two decades of the century average annual growth rates in the upper valley were no more than 2%.[10] Stabilization in growth rates, a feature of postfrontier societies, had thus set in at the very end of the colonial period.

8. "A List of Tithables in the Dominion of Virginia, 1755," Public Record Office, C.O.5/1338, p. 364, cited in R. E. and B. K. Brown, *Virginia, 1705–1786*, p. 79, n. 59. See also Louis K. Koontz, *Robert Dinwiddie: His Career in American Colonial Government and Westward Expansion* (Glendale, Calif.: Arthur H. Clarke Co., 1941), p. 160. The remaining 2,256 tithables for western Virginia were in the newly formed Hampshire County.

9. For further commentary, see Chester R. Young, "The Effects of the French and Indian War on Civilian Life in the Frontier Counties of Virginia, 1754–1763" (Ph.D. diss., Vanderbilt University, 1969).

10. The induction of males into the militia throws the tithable records into disarray for the war period. The formation of Rockingham and Rockbridge counties in 1778 subsequently produced three sets of relatively incomplete tithable returns instead of one reasonably consistent set; the records for Rockbridge were reported so haphazardly as to be of little value, and the Rockingham tithables recorded in the Minute Books, Judgments, and Orders are lower than those contained in the Minute Book, Overseers of the Poor, 1782–1863. Such difficulties are compounded by considerable errors in reporting individual tithable returns. For example, in March 1785, an Augusta settler reported that he had been charged in the 1783 tithable returns for 1 tithable, 20 cattle, and 8 horses which he had not possessed (Augusta Co. Order Book 19:7); another settler was indicated as having 1 slave in the Augusta County tax lists for 1785 when in fact she possessed 20 (Virginia State Auditor's Item No. 148, Box B, Augusta County, 1784–86, Va. State Lib.).

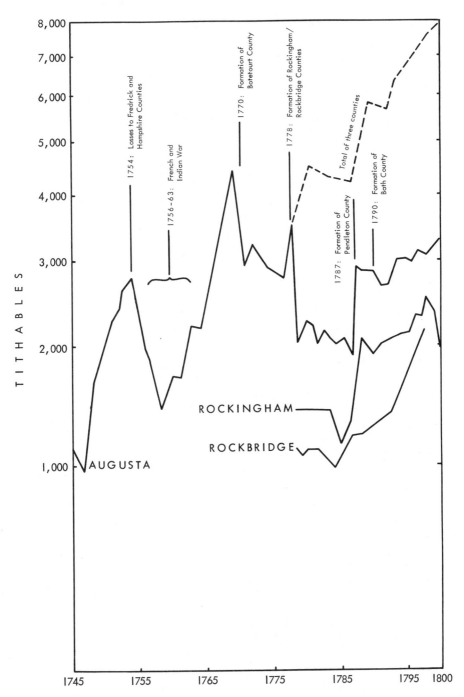

Fig. 18. Upper Shenandoah Valley tithables, 1745–1800 (data from Preston
Papers, IQQ29–30, and Augusta County Order Books, 1746–1800; Rockingham
County Minute Books, Judgments and Orders, 1788–1800; Rockbridge
County Order Books, 1778–1800, and Rockbridge County Tithables, 1778–88)

The federal census figures for 1790 and 1800 indicate a higher annual average rate of increase for the upper valley of 2.4% and a very low one of 0.7% for the lower valley (table 9).[11] For the entire Shenandoah Valley the annual rate was only 1.1%. Great variations existed from county to county, with Berkeley County losing over 6% of its population between 1790 and 1800, which actually included over 11% of its white population. The most rapid rates of growth occurred in the counties with the smallest populations, Rockingham and Rockbridge. The imbalance of population between upper and lower valleys, apparent by 1775, seems to have reached a peak around 1790, when the lower valley contained 66% of the region's total population, and was gradually reduced thereafter as rates of increase continued higher in the upper valley. Thus the lag in population growth in the upper valley, to be expected by reason of its more limited accessibility, remained consistent until almost the end of the century. The influx of small planters into Berkeley and Frederick counties after 1780 was clearly insufficient to offset high rates of emigration in their white populations. Here perhaps are the effects of a more constricted land ownership structure, discouraging landless settlers from remaining in the lower valley.

The slave population of the valley during the second half of the century reveals trends similar to those displayed by the white population—increasing rates of growth, particularly in the lower valley before 1790, and with a trend toward more rapid rates of increase in the upper valley by 1800 (table 10). The most rapid growth of the slave population undoubtedly occurred between 1765 and 1780 with the increasing influx of small planters to the lower valley. The increase is most striking in Frederick and Berkeley counties, which contained 72% of all the slaves in the valley by 1790. All six counties increased their slave numbers substantially between 1782 and 1800, but in markedly different proportions: 92.6% in Berkeley (1,910 to 3,679), 114.5%

11. Since the 1790 census returns for 41 Virginia counties were burned when the British took Washington in 1814, there has been considerable confusion over the alternative sources available for the reconstruction of Virginia's population in 1790. The Bureau of Census stated that it used the county tithable records for the years 1782 to 1785 as the bases for reconstructing the 1790 population (U.S. Bureau of the Census, *Heads of Families, 1790: Virginia*, p. 1). On page 3 of this volume the total population of Virginia is given as 747,160. On page 9, however, it is totaled as 747,610. But this latter total and the county figures enumerated on page 9 are taken from the official returns, *Return of the Whole Number of Persons within the Several Districts of the United States, according to "An Act providing for the Enumeration of the Inhabitants of the United States"* (Philadelphia, 1791), pp. 48–50 (Virginia returns), copy at Lib. Cong. For some highly critical comments on the methods used by the Bureau, see Bell, *Sunlight on the Southside*, pp. 39–41.

Table 9. Population of the Shenandoah Valley, 1790 and 1800

	White males		White females		Others: nontaxable		Slaves		Totals		% of change, 1790-1800	Mean annual % of increase/decrease[1]
	1790	1800	1790	1800	1790	1800	1790	1800	1790	1800		
Berkeley	8,800	7,667	7,850	7,071	131	156	2,932	3,679	19,713	18,573	− 6.1	− 0.6
Frederick	8,005	8,172	7,310	7,665	116	420	4,250	5,118	19,681	12,375	+ 8.6	+ 0.8
Shenandoah	5,188	6,027	4,791	5,698	19	84	512	738	10,510	12,547	+19.4	+ 1.8
Rockingham	3,468	4,759	3,209	4,507	—	56	772	1,052	7,449	10,374	+39.2	+ 3.4
Augusta	4,836	5,012	4,424	4,658	59	95	1,567	1,946	10,886	11,711	+ 7.6	+ 0.7
Rockbridge	3,049	3,822	2,756	3,956	41	97	682	1,070	6,528	8,945	+37.0	+ 3.2
Total	33,346	35,459	30,340	33,555	366	908	10,715	13,603	74,767	83,525	+11.7	+ 1.1

SOURCES: First and Second Census of the United States, 1790 and 1800.

[1] Calculated on a logarithmic scale.

Table 10. Slave population of the Shenandoah Valley, 1755–1800

	No. of slaves			% increase, 1782-90	No. of slaves	% increase, 1790-1800
	1755	1782	1790		1800	
Lower valley	680	4,429	7,694	73.7	9,535	23.9
Upper valley	80	2,315	3,021	30.5	4,068	34.6
Total	760	6,744	10,715	58.8	13,603	26.9

SOURCES: A List of Tithables in the Dominion of Virginia, 1755, P.R.O., C.O.5/1338; County Personal Property Tax Books, 1782 (1783 for Berkeley County); Federal Census of U.S., 1790 and 1800.

in Frederick (2,386 to 5,118), 454.9% in Shenandoah (133 to 738), 70.0% in Rockingham (621 to 1,052), 63.4% in Augusta (1,191 to 1,946), and 112.7% in Rockbridge (503 to 1,070). What these figures reveal, by the end of the century, is that the increase of slaves was responsible for most of the population growth in Frederick and Augusta counties, where the white populations remained virtually unchanged, and for preventing a more drastic reduction in Berkeley's population. Only in Shenandoah, Rockingham, and Rockbridge counties were there substantial increases in both white and black populations. In addition, the evidence now begins to raise doubts about including Shenandoah County in the lower valley section, for it is clear in terms of population growth, density, and composition, as well as in land ownership structure, that Berkeley and Frederick counties differed from the other valley counties by the outbreak of the Revolution. Shenandoah County, despite its location within the Northern Neck, seldom attracted attention from eastern Virginians and displayed many socioeconomic traits that were more typical of the counties to the south.

More than half of the valley's 1800 population had been added since 1775. The frontier phase of the region's population growth, which had lasted for some forty years, had ended by the outbreak of the Revolution. By 1775 a thin veneer of settlement had emerged west of the valley's overwhelmingly (over 90%) rural population, growth rates had begun to slow down substantially, and population densities were on the increase. The overall density for the valley by the end of the colonial period was just over five persons per square mile; the lower half of the valley had over eight persons per square mile and the upper valley less than four. In fact, in terms of density, the lower valley had probably passed through its frontier population phase during the 1760s, to be followed by the upper valley during the early 1770s. By 1800 the valley's overall density had reached more than thirteen persons per square mile. The lower valley remained the more densely settled, with an average of almost eighteen persons per square mile to half that for the upper valley. But the most striking contrast was between Berkeley and Frederick counties, with average densities of twenty to twenty-five persons, and the remaining four counties, with average densities of only eight to ten persons per square mile. How far were these contrasts reflected in the demographic structures of the counties?

It is difficult to answer this question fully, and indeed many questions about demographic change, because of the paucity of data. The question of birth and death rates, for example, is an extremely elusive one. Parish records provide little more information than county records.[12] It has been suggested that birth rates in the late colonial period probably ranged between forty-five and fifty per thousand of the population and death rates a moderate twenty to twenty-five per thousand, although more recent research in mid-eighteenth-century New England indicates a lower level of births of around forty per thousand.[13] With the reduction of immigration after the 1750s but the continuation of growth rates of 5% or more, birth rates in the valley must have been on the order of at least forty to forty-five per thousand until the end of the colonial period. In terms of death rates, one would expect frontier counties to have higher incidences of deaths than would occur in longer settled, more secure areas, especially during the French and Indian War. The effects of disease incidence on death rates is almost impossible to determine, but the valley was affected by several smallpox outbreaks between the 1750s and the 1780s.

Age and sex composition during the colonial period are equally difficult to determine.[14] In a colonial frontier area such as the valley,

12. See L. Henry, "The Verification of Data in Historical Demography," *Population Studies* 22 (1968): 61–81. See also *List of Baptisms by Rev. John Craig, Augusta County, Virginia, 1740–1749* (Richmond, n.d.), 38 pp., copy at Va. Hist. Soc.

13. J. Potter, "The Growth of Population in America, 1700–1860," in *Population in History*, eds. D. V. Glass and D. E. C. Eversley (Chicago: Aldine Publishing Co., 1965), p. 646; Robert Higgs and H. Louis Stettler, "Colonial New England Demography: A Sampling Approach," *Wm. and Mary Qtly.*, 3d ser. 27 (1970):287, 291.

14. This difficulty is underscored in Herbert Moller, "Sex Composition and Correlated Culture Patterns of Colonial America," *Wm. and Mary Qtly.*, 3d ser. 3 (1945): 113–53. See also Jack E. Eblen, "An Analysis of Nineteenth-Century Frontier Populations," *Demography* 2 (1965): 562–602.

one would expect the age structure of the population to be heavily weighted in favor of youth, with over half of the population being below thirty at any one time. The longer the area was settled, and the less attractive it became to backcountry migrants, the greater the tendency for the median age of its population to increase. After the Revolutionary War, therefore, one would expect the age pyramid of the valley's population to increase most noticeably in the thirty-to-fifty age bracket, and that a larger proportion of people over sixty would be present. Evidence in the county records to support these arguments is patchy and inconclusive. It is only with the detail of the county personal property records from 1782 to 1800 that some pattern of age structure is discernible. The 1790 census returns show that the number of free white males under sixteen years of age composed 45.5% of the free white male population of Augusta County, 47.6% in Rockingham County, and 50.2% in Rockbridge County. Augusta and Rockingham were the only counties in Virginia west of the Blue Ridge that had more whites over the age of sixteen than under, but these were still relatively young populations. Figure 19 is an attempt to suggest these trends. By 1800 only in Augusta County was a majority of the white population over the age of sixteen (51.3%); at the other extreme, in both Shenandoah and Rockingham counties 55% of the white population was under sixteen years of age.

The chronic shortage of brides in pioneer areas of colonial America is well known, and the situation in the Shenandoah Valley was probably no exception to this rule (see fig. 19). However, by the time of the 1790 census, which provides comprehensive information on the region, the female portion of the white population had long been increasing. In 1790 white male-female ratios throughout the valley ranged from 90 females for every 100 males in Berkeley County to 95 females for every 100 males in Shenandoah County. By 1800 every county had rations of 95 or 96 females for every 100 males except Rockbridge County, where the ration was 103 females for every 100 males in a total white population of 7,780. The facts that young and middle-aged widows soon remarried and that mulatto children were frequently born in the valley lend some credence to the supposition that white women were in short supply. Again evidence from southern New England, which suggests ages of marriage of twenty-one for females and twenty-four for males, seems to indicate that colonial settlers married later in life than was hitherto thought to have been the case.[15] This

15. Higgs and Stettler, "Colonial New England Demography," *Wm. and Mary Qtly.*, 3d ser. 27 (1970): 284–86.

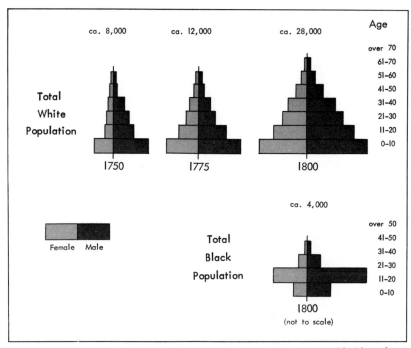

Fig. 19. Upper Shenandoah Valley: hypothetical population pyramids (data from County Tithable Lists, 1750–1800; County Will Books, 1750–1800; Personal Property Tax Books, 1782–1800)

was probably no more true than in colonial frontier areas, where much effort had to be expended during the first generation to provide a secure basis for the second and where sons had often to wait for the death of their fathers in order to obtain the wherewithal to acquire their own farm and to think about raising a family.

Information on the age and sex composition of Negro slaves is even more difficult to find than for whites. The personal property tax records from 1782 on, however, do reveal some characteristics of the black population. During the 1780s the number of Negro slaves under sixteen years of age composed between 50% and 60% of all slaves reported in the upper valley.[16] This would have produced a hypothetical

16. See the personal property records for the three counties for the years 1782 to 1788. From 1789 on, estimating the number of blacks in each county becomes more difficult because the only categories of blacks reported were those above 16 years of age and those between 12 and 16. In Berkeley and Frederick counties, where slaveholding

age pyramid similar to that indicated in figure 19, with a highly inflated eleven-to-twenty age bracket, and a virtual truncation above fifty, especially for females. In terms of sex composition, the reports of black children and adults that occur in the records for the upper valley indicate that during the second half of the eighteenth century, black males outnumbered black females in the approximate ration of 3:2, and among young Negro slaves under sixteen years of age males outnumbered females about 9:5.

Ethnicity and Cultural Change

Cultural pluralism, an important quality of colonial American popula-tions, was spread to the interior with the expansion of settlement. In Chapter 2 the selective importance of cultural heritage has been demon-strated in the case of German-speaking settlers, who tended to immigrate and emigrate less frequently but more consistently in family groups than English-speaking settlers and who were inclined to sell lands to fellow Germans and move on to frontier areas previously characterized by German settlement. On the other hand, the duration of ethnic identity throughout the entire eighteenth century was questioned.

The concentration of Scotch-Irish settlers in the three upper valley counties was one of the major regional differences within the Shenandoah Valley during the eighteenth century. Thus, a close correlation between national origins, church membership, and the development of region-alism might be expected. And indeed, by the end of the colonial period there were more than twenty Presbyterian churches in the upper valley but only one Anglican church and two small chapels. [17] Over the same period, at least twelve Anglican churches had been established in Berkeley and Frederick counties and three in Shenandoah, in contrast

was more prominent, the age structure of the slave population was probably more attenuated. None of the 17 slaves of Adam Stephens's total of 53 that were definitely identifiable as female was more than 40 years old (Frederick Co. Superior Court Will Book 1:142–54).

17. Augusta Parish Vestry Book (1746–80), pp. 1–4, 318; G. MacLaren Brydon, "List of Episcopal Colonial Churches and Sites of Churches in the Diocese of Virginia," Report of the Colonial Churches Commission, n.d., typescript photocopy, Va. State Lib.; Hart, *Valley of Virginia,* pp. 34–36, 40–51. See also Delemo L. Beard, "Origin and Early History of Presbyterianism in Virginia" (Ph.D. diss., University of Edinburgh, 1932, microfilm, Va. State Lib.), pp. 161–218; Robert F. Scott, "Colonial Presbyterianism in the Valley of Virginia, 1727–1775," *Journal of the Presbyterian Historical Society* 35 (1957): 71–92, 171–92; Robert D. Mitchell, "The Presbyterian Church as an Indicator of Westward Expansion in 18th Century America," *Professional Geographer* 28 (1966): 293–99.

to less than ten Presbyterian congregations.[18] On the basis of these figures, the numerical strength of settlers of English origin in the upper valley would have been very small. Two other factors reduce the value of church membership as an indicator of ethnicity. First, since one could not hold any political office without being a member of the Anglican church, some Scotch-Irish settlers found it politically astute or prestigious to join the official church while still maintaining their Presbyterian faith. Second, English and German communities contained settlers who were affiliated with sectarian denominations rather than with church-oriented groups. Both English and Welsh Quakers were prominent in the pioneer settlement of the lower valley. Hopewell Meetinghouse near Winchester was the most active center of valley Quakerism, but Quakers elsewhere in the valley usually conducted their meetings in the homes of local members, a procedure followed by later groups such as the Baptists, so that they cannot be pinpointed to one location.[19] While many Germans belonged to the Lutheran church or, less frequently, the German Reformed church, substantial numbers were members of the Mennonite, Dunker, or, less frequently, Moravian sects scattered throughout the valley.[20] Germans displayed the lowest correlation between national origins and church membership of any major ethnic group in the valley.

The socioevangelical movement of the 1750s known as the Great Awakening and the religious revivals of the Revolutionary period helped to break down the ethnic homogeneity of some immigrant groups to the valley.[21] Some settlers who had demonstrated no previous religious commitment were caught up in the revivalist trends of the late colonial period and joined former members of established churches in boosting the strength of the Baptists and Methodists during the last third of the century. This process further emphasized differences between national origins and religious affiliations and encouraged assimilation of some groups into the predominantly English-based culture. Sectarian influences were often critical in delimiting the effects of denominational

18. Frederick Parish Vestry Book (1764–1818); Malone, "Distribution of Population on the Virginia Frontier," p. 100; Bliss, "Tuckahoe in the Valley," pp. 147–48; and Hart, *Valley of Virginia*, pp. 36–62.

19. *Hopewell Meeting House Records*, ed. Walker McC. Bond (Winchester, Va., 1937), and Chalmer Papers, vol. 4, Manuscript Div., N.Y. Public Lib.

20. Wust, *Virginia Germans*, pp. 37–39, 44–49; Harry A. Brunk, *History of the Mennonites in Virginia, 1727–1900* (Staunton, Va.: McClure Printing Co., 1959), pp. 39–41.

21. Bliss, "Tuckahoe in the Valley," pp. 157–71; Hart, *Valley of Virginia*, chs. 2, 8; Wesley M. Gewehr, *The Great Awakening in Virginia, 1740–1750* (Durham, N.C.: Duke University Press, 1930), ch. 8.

trends; despite defections among sectarian groups, especially Mennonites, most persisted well into the nineteenth century. On the other hand, Scotch-Irish settlers, speaking English, lacking ethnic-sectarian identification, and some distance removed intellectually from their sparsely distributed, college-educated clergy, responded enthusiastically to the mood of the Great Awakening and were probably the ethnic group most thoroughly altered by religious change. They were so affected, in fact, that it is difficult to discuss them realistically as a group after the Revolution, when there were no reinforcements in the form of new immigrants. They were much more thoroughly assimilated than the German community, which exhibited a wider range of cultural responses.

German self-consciousness, especially among sectarian groups, remained a significant cultural force throughout the Shenandoah Valley at least into the early 1800s. The valley, with its approximately 23,000 settlers of German origins in 1790, remained the heart of German settlement in Virginia. The retention of the German language among a substantial number of settlers may be responsible for the relatively late appearance of German-speaking (or bilingual) participants in the political and mercantile affairs of the valley until after the Revolution.[22] Only gradually did they become familiar with English traditions of local government, merchandizing, and wholesale trade. Politically, their involvement took place at local and state levels. Local participation was encouraged by the increasing number of German lot owners in the main towns in the valley, especially Winchester and Staunton. In Staunton there had never been more than one German among the town's trustees during the colonial period; there were at least three by the end of the century. Only in Shenandoah County were Germans consistently prominent in local legislatures during the colonial period. It was the Revolutionary generation, a combination of second- and third-generation Germans, who began to move into local offices in Rockingham, Augusta, and Frederick counties in significant numbers during the 1780s and 1790s.[23] As late as 1792, almost two hundred German settlers in Augusta County successfully petitioned the Virginia House of Delegates for copies of the House proceedings to be printed in German and distributed to interested citizens.[24] The use of the standard German language (*Hochs-*

22. For a different view, see Lemon, *Best Poor Man's Country*, pp. 13–15.

23. Compare Marcus L. Hansen, "The Problems of the Third Generation Immigrant," *Augustana Historical Society Publications*, no. 8, pt. 1 (1938): 5–20.

24. Legislative Petitions, Augusta County, Oct. 16, 1792, Va. State Lib., printed in *Journal of the House of Delegates of the Commonwealth of Virginia* (1792), (Richmond: Thomas White, 1828), p. 53.

prache) remained strong in both church and public services among settlers of German origin until about 1830, when it began to be replaced rapidly by English.[25] The maintenance of the German language may have been the result in part of the establishment of formal German schooling for some members of the community, although it was not until the early 1760s that such parochial schools began to appear in Winchester, Strasburg, and Woodstock.[26] These schools appeared to flourish throughout the latter part of the century, and as late as 1807 a proposal was made to open an evening school in Staunton for the teaching of German.[27]

Although the processes of assimilation were certainly far from complete for many Germans and some settlers of English and Scotch-Irish heritage by the end of the eighteenth century, access to wealth, particularly in the form of land, transcended national origins and fostered easy entrance into the mainstream of Virginia life.[28] Absorption occurred more quickly among wealthy, long-established German families than among middling or poor Germans. The Hite family epitomizes this process. Despite his troubles with Lord Fairfax, Jost Hite was an active supporter of the Anglican church in Frederick County and entertained prominent Tidewater planters in his home. Of his five sons, the three eldest, John, Jacob, and Isaac, also became members of the Anglican church. John entered local administrative affairs in 1747 as Frederick County surveyor and worked his way up through justice of the peace and assemblyman to county lieutenant after Lord Fairfax's death in 1781. Jacob went to sea for a few years, brought back an Irish bride from Dublin, and settled down comfortably for a time in Berkeley County. Isaac was appointed sheriff of Frederick County in 1748 and held the post for over twenty years. The fourth son, Abraham, married a cousin, moved farther west to Hampshire County where he was a member of the House of Burgesses from 1769 to 1774, and finally migrated to Kentucky in 1782. In the third generation, Isaac Hite, Jr., attended the College of William and

25. John Stewart and Elmer L. Smith, "The Survival of German Dialects and Customs in the Shenandoah Valley," *Society for the History of the Germans in Maryland*, Report 31 (1963): 66–70. See also Wust, *Virginia Germans*, pp. 139, 175, and Wertenbaker, *The Old South*, pp. 188–91.

26. Wust, *Virginia Germans*, pp. 56, 66, 71.

27. *Staunton Eagle*, Aug. 28, 1807 (Huntington Lib.).

28. The notion of a "melting-pot" process in the formation of an American culture has been used by Bliss, "Tuckahoe in the Valley," especially abstract and pp. 202–32 and, more cautiously, by Wertenbaker, *Old South*, pp. 1–3, and ch. 5, and Bridenbaugh, *Myths and Realities*, ch. 3. The notion has been questioned by Wust, *Virginia Germans*, pp. 111–12. For a more recent perspective on the melting-pot concept, see Milton M. Gordon, *Assimilation in American Life: The Role of Race, Religion, and National Origins* (New York: Oxford University Press, 1964), ch. 5.

Mary after the Revolution, married a daughter of the Bishop James Madison family of Tidewater Virginia, and lived well as a member of the landed gentry near Middletown in Berkeley County.[29]

Socioeconomic motivations were principally responsible for the presence in the valley, as elsewhere in Virginia, of one group whose physical appearance, cultural heritage, mode of migration, and castelike status prevented them from participating fully in colonial life. The Negro and mulatto slave remained unassimilated despite the destruction of their traditional culture and, as property, operated as an important factor in the socioeconomic differentiation of the valley's white population.

Of the 760 recorded black tithables in the entire Shenandoah Valley in 1755, all but 80 were located in the lower valley. This contrast in the number and proportion of blacks was to remain one of the most salient differences between Berkeley and Frederick counties and the rest of the valley for the remainder of the century. It was one of the most significant repercussions of Tidewater influences on the valley, and to some degree it created similarities in slaveholding patterns between these two counties and the counties of the western Piedmont that were not to be found anywhere else west of the Blue Ridge.[30] By 1790 the percentage of Negroes in the counties of the southwestern Piedmont was no higher than in the lower Shenandoah Valley, and Frederick County had a Negro population proportionally as large as Loudoun County just east of the Blue Ridge. Within the Shenandoah Valley by 1790 there were marked contrasts in distribution. Frederick County, with 21.3% of its population Negro, was by far the leading slaveowning county, followed by Berkeley (14.9%) and Augusta (14.4%). In both Rockingham and Rockbridge 10.4% of the population was black, while in Shenandoah only 4.9% was black.[31] This situation remained basically the same in 1800, when there was a total of just over 13,600 slaves in the valley, representing 16.4% of the region's total population.

Slaves were used mainly as field hands and domestic servants, although

29. Wayland, *German Element of the Shenandoah Valley*, pp. 102–5; Bliss, "Tuckahoe in the Valley," pp. 202–6; Hillier, "The Hite Family in the Settlement of the West," pp. 41–51, 68–82.

30. For distribution maps of blacks in Virginia in 1750, 1775, and 1790, see Mitchell, "The Upper Shenandoah Valley," pp. 226–8.

31. In 1796 Isaac Weld made this comment about the distribution of slaves in the Shenandoah Valley: "About one sixth of the people, on an average, are slaves, but in some of the counties the proportion is much less, in Rockbridge the slaves do not amount to more than one eleventh, and in Shenandoah County not to more than a twentieth part of the whole" (*Travels*, p. 134). Perhaps he had seen the 1790 census returns.

skilled slaves were used by planters who owned more than about a dozen slaves. They were an expensive form of labor to buy and maintain, and they represented the single most valuable item in the personal inventories of valley settlers. As such they provided an element of economic selectivity, between slaveholder and nonslaveholder, that was to become an increasingly important factor in the stratification of the region's society with the rapid growth in the numbers of slaves after 1765.

Wealth and Social Stratification during the Colonial Period

Discussions of Virginia's population west of the Blue Ridge during the eighteenth century have generally emphasized the relatively high degree of economic equality and self-reliance and the lack of strong social distinctions. The relatively small size of individual landholdings, the small scale of agricultural enterprise, and the presence of few slaves have also been presented as indicative of a relatively undifferentiated society. At the same time, few scholars have suggested that all class divisions disappeared in recently settled frontier areas. The necessity for local social and political leadership has been particularly emphasized as a factor leading to distinctions.[32]

Several attempts have been made to devise basic typologies of the socioeconomic structure of eighteenth-century populations. Most have emphasized the familiar divisions of upper, middle, and lower classes, with slavery as the fourth and lowest level.[33] On the other hand, Jackson T. Main's attempt to categorize the social structure of the population of the Revolutionary period, despite its static approach and invalid assumptions, is of some relevance here.[34] He suggested four levels of stratification on a rather vague locational basis. "Frontier" areas were characterized

32. See especially Abernethy, "The Southern Frontier, an Interpretation," in *Frontier in Perspective*, eds. Wyman and Kroeber, pp. 133–37; Stanley M. Elkins and Eric McKitrick, "A Meaning for Turner's Frontier, Part II: The Southwest Frontier and New England," *Political Science Quarterly* 69 (1954): 565–602.

33. See, for example, R. E. and B. K. Brown, *Virginia, 1705–1786*, pp. 32–77; Ray Allen Billington, *America's Frontier Heritage* (New York: Holt, Rinehart and Winston, 1966), pp. 98–99. The Browns contend that the lower class in eighteenth-century Virginia was least well-defined because there were so few actual "poor" people in the colony, although they did include laborers, apprentices, indentured servants, and convict servants in this category.

34. Main, *Social Structure*, pp. 7–8, 277–78. This study is based on an analysis of selected county land and property tax lists for the period 1782–85. The germination of Main's classification can be seen in his article, "The Distribution of Property in Post-Revolutionary Virginia," *Miss. Valley Hist. Rev.* 41 (1954):256–58.

by middle-class small farmers owning less than 500 acres of land. Socio-economic distinctions were minimal, and property was relatively equally distributed among the members of the community. "Subsistence" areas were also predominantly middle class, consisting of small farmers in the process of entering into the commercial economy, plus some artisans and professional men. "Commercial" areas displayed increasingly socio-economic class distinctions in terms of wealth, land and personal property, and the use of slaves. "Urban" areas, although predominantly middle class, had the highest proportion of wealthy and nonagricultural men, and the greatest opportunities for social mobility. These ideas can certainly be tested in the Shenandoah Valley.

A critical factor in evaluating the changing socioeconomic character-istics of the valley's population is the conditions under which the first generation of settlers came to the region. It has often been assumed that the European immigrants and colonists who settled the interior frontier areas of eighteenth-century America were largely from the poorer, lower classes of European societies and that the presumed crudeness and simplicity of backcountry life merely reflected the attitudes and living standards these settlers brought with them. James T. Lemon has challenged this view, arguing that most settlers were upwardly mobile bearers of a liberal, individualistic ideology which they quickly put into practice by entering the ranks of landownership in colonies where land was plentiful.[35] In terms of land acquisition and geographical mobility, his description fits the behavior of the early settlers in the valley. Many pioneer settlers, particularly in the lower valley, had farmed elsewhere in the colonies and were better prepared psychologically and economi-cally than migrants who had arrived directly from Europe. In addition it has also been demonstrated that many of the migrants from Ulster were not the "optimistic poor" or the "peasant folk" so often described in the secondary literature.[36] Most of these immigrants did not emigrate because of famine, and a majority seem to have paid their own passage, ranging from £5 a person in the 1730s and 1740s to £3 5s. in the early 1770s.[37] Many settlers did find a better life and improved living stan-dards in the valley than what they had known and decided to stay; others

35. Lemon, *Best Poor Man's Country*, pp. xv–xvi, 1–13, 42–70.

36. See, for example, T. W. Moody, "The Ulster Scots in Colonial and Revolutionary America," *Studies, an Irish Quarterly Review* 34 (1945): 85–94, 211–21; James G. Leyburn, *The Scotch-Irish: A Social History* (Chapel Hill: University of North Carolina Press, 1962); E. Estyn Evans, "The Scotch-Irish in the New World: An Atlantic Heritage," *Journal of the Royal Society of Antiquaries of Ireland* 95 (1965): 39–49.

37. See R. J. Dickson, *Ulster Emigration to Colonial America, 1718–1755* (London: Routledge and Kegan Paul, 1966), pp. 50–53, 85–86.

did not and moved on or remained outside of the ranks of the landed proprietors. Surviving records tend to give evidence of the successful rather than those who failed, but these records must be used, with some caution, to ascertain how the first and later generations fared in their striving for a satisfactory material well-being.

Calculations of socioeconomic structure and wealth distribution during the eighteenth century have been made at a number of levels using a wide variety of source materials.[38] In the main, estimates have been made of land or portable wealth, or both, using probate inventories and tax lists supplemented with will testaments, family records, and newspaper advertisements. For the Shenandoah Valley probate records are by far the most useful for gauging trends over time, while land and personal property tax records exist only from 1782 on. County will books in Virginia provide up to four sets of information about the material possessions of individuals whose estates were probated: the testament, which contains in standard form a description of the individual's landed and household property and directions for its distribution or disposal; the inventory, which itemizes and evaluates all material possessions except land and was witnessed by three local settlers appointed by the county court; the accounts, which contain all outstanding debts owed to and by the deceased; and, if directed by the court, the sale of items from the estate.

There are two critical questions concerning the utility of the inventories. What proportion of property owners who died in a county over a given period of time left inventoried estates? And how representative are the recorded inventories of the county's surviving population as a whole? For the period 1740 through 1769, 1,021 extant inventories exist for the Shenandoah Valley, almost equally divided between the upper (509) and lower (512) halves of the region. For the 1770s Shenandoah County inventories have been added to those for Augusta and the now much-reduced Frederick, while those of the 1770s for Rockbridge have been carried over to the 1780s.[39] On this basis, an additional 369 in-

38. See Jones, "Wealth Estimates for the American Middle Colonies, 1774," *Econ. Develop. and Cult. Change* 18 (1970): 1–172, and Jones, "Wealth Estimates for the New England Colonies about 1770," *Jour. of Econ. Hist.* 32 (1972): 98–172; Aubrey C. Land, "Economic Base and Social Structure: The Northern Chesapeake in the Eighteenth Century," ibid., 25 (1965): 639–54; Main, *Social Structure of Revolutionary America*, pp. 68–220; Lemon and Nash, "The Distribution of Wealth in Eighteenth-Century America," *Jour. Soc. Hist.* 2 (1968): 1–24; Gloria L. Main, "Probate Records as a Source for Early American History," *Wm. and Mary Qtly.*, 3d ser. 32 (1975): 89–99; Daniel Scott Smith, "Underregistration and Bias in Probate Records: An Analysis of Data from Eighteenth-Century Hingham, Massachusetts," ibid. 32 (1975): 100–110.

39. The Berkeley County Will Books are located in the Archives Division of the State of

ventories have been examined for the region, making a total of 1,390 inventories for the four decades after 1740.

It is very difficult to estimate what proportion of deceased property owners these numbers represent, but for Augusta County during the 1740s the enormous extent of the county, the sparse population (about 8,500 by 1750), and the small number of recorded inventories (69) suggest that less than 20% of deceased property owners left inventories. For Frederick County, with 111 inventories, the proportion was probably about 25%. By the 1760s about one-third of the estates of deceased property owners appear to be recorded in the will books. Recorded estates clearly reflect conditions among land and personal property owners rather than among those who owned no land or little personal property. Drifters, laborers, young adults, and, to a lesser degree, tenants go largely unrecorded in the inventories. On the other hand, the variation in inventory evaluations is substantial, ranging within the valley before 1780 from £4,055 to 12s. And the proportion of inventories valued at less than £25 is large enough to indicate that property owners of small wealth, while certainly underrecorded, were by no means unrecorded.

Probate inventories also tend to have a strong age and sex bias. In general, the older the head of household and the longer he had settled in the valley, the more wealth he had accumulated as compared with younger men. Widows usually received between one-half and one-third of their husbands' estates. The inventories of widows, therefore, are invariably appraised at a much lower value than those of their deceased husbands and generally at less that £25. In some ways, the most intractable problem of all in analyzing inventories is the changing value of money, which becomes particularly acute from the Revolutionary War on. For comparisons with other colonies and states, it would be useful to convert the Virginia currency into sterling at least for the colonial period, but the Revolutionary inflation, changing currency base, and sterling fluctuations toward the end of the century preclude the use of one standard base for the entire eighteenth century.[40]

West Virginia in Charleston and were not examined for this study. No eighteenth-century will books have survived for Rockingham County.

40. Between 1777 and 1783 inventories were frequently evaluated in pre-Revolutionary monetary terms while others were adjusted in terms of the spiraling inflation. The values of the adjusted inventories for the period 1777–79 had to be reduced 10 times to make them comparable with unadjusted inventories. In several cases, some items in an inventory were evaluated at 1775 price levels while others were evaluated at 1779 prices. Between late 1780 and late 1782 many adjusted inventories had to be reduced as much as 40 times to make them comparable with unadjusted inventories. For example, an inventory evaluated at £1,728 in December 1780 would have been £43 4s.

Table 11 indicates that 64% (507) of all inventories recorded between 1740 and 1779 were evaluated at less than £100. Less than 5% (66) were for more than £500, while almost 18% (244) were for less than £25. These general figures probably fared well with inventories of personal property for settlers in the Virginia and Maryland Piedmont during the late colonial period.[41] Moreover, even allowing for a slight decline in the value of Virginia currency during the period, there is a clear trend toward an increasing accumulation of wealth over time, and also some indication of regional differences within the valley by the 1770s. The proportion of inventories valued at more than £100 consistently increased in Augusta County from 23% during the 1740s to 54% during the 1770s and in Frederick County from 26% to 59%. Not only was the proportion of inventories under £100 on the decrease over the period, but those under £25 took a sharp drop in Frederick County after the 1750s and in Augusta after the 1760s. For the entire period only 16 inventories in Augusta County (3%) were evaluated at more than £500, compared with 40 (6%) in Frederick County.

Regional differences in inventory evaluations do not appear sigificant until the 1770s, when the lower valley was subdivided into three counties. During the 1750s the median value of Augusta inventories was £56, compared with £42 in Frederick; during the 1760s the medians rose to £73 and £68, respectively. But during the 1770s, with the separation of Frederick, Berkeley, and Shenandoah counties, the reduced Frederick County demonstrated a substantial concentration of lower valley personal property with a median value of £165, compared with Shenandoah County's £70 and the still intact, much larger Augusta County's £114. Thus, once the internal variations in the lower valley are unmasked after 1772, the interest that eastern Virginia planters had already begun to demonstrate in settling in the lower valley begins to show up in the Frederick inventories.

Further insight into the valley's personal property structure during the colonial period can be obtained from an examination of selected

---

at prices "the usual old way" (Frederick Co. Will Book 4:549). Where the value of land was included in an inventory I excluded it from the total evaluation. See also Main, *Social Structure of Revolutionary America*, pp. 288–90, although his estimates of exchange rates are not sensitive enough to price fluctuations within individual colonies after the mid-1760s.

41. Land, "Economic Base and Social Structure," *Jour. of Econ. Hist.* 25 (1965): 653–54, indicates that almost 55% of Maryland inventories during the 1740s were for less than £100 sterling (£125 Va.), while the Browns, *Virginia, 1705–1786*, pp. 32–47, emphasize the "fluidity of social classes" in Virginia during the late colonial period but make little use of inventories.

Table 11. Value of Shenandoah Valley inventories, 1740–79

(Virginia £s) Value	No. of inventories								
	1740–49		1750–59		1760–69		1770–79		
	Au-gusta	Fred-erick	Au-gusta	Fred-erick	Au-gusta	Fred-erick	Au-gusta	Fred-erick	Shenan-doah[1]
over 1,000	0	0	1	1	2	1	4	8	0
901–1,000	0	0	0	0	0	0	1	2	0
801–900	0	0	0	1	1	0	0	1	1
701–800	0	1	0	0	0	1	3	2	0
601–700	0	0	1	2	1	1	4	5	3
501–600	0	0	0	1	1	4	4	9	2
401–500	0	2	0	1	1	4	6	6	1
301–400	1	1	1	1	8	6	11	13	4
201–300	5	1	10	7	23	13	20	11	4
101–200	9	24	36	30	63	40	50	16	9
51–100	23	25	52	36	63	65	46	22	13
25–50	17	29	49	46	50	51	23	15	10
0.1–24	10	28	38	63	39	26	18	14	8
Total	65	111	188	189	252	212	190	124	55

SOURCES: Orange County Will Books 1 and 2; Frederick County Will Books 1–4; Augusta County Will Books 1–6; Shenandoah County Will Book A.

[1] The dates for Shenandoah County are 1772–79.

inventory contents (table 12).[42] A general trend is evident toward owner-ship of a larger number and wider range of items over the period from 1740 to 1779, but this is not true of all items, nor should it be expected. The most striking inconsistency would appear to be in the Frederick County inventories during the 1770s, when the median inventory value had reached £165. Although there is a significant increase in the propor-tion of inventories containing references to wagons, plows, and slaves over previous decades, the proportion of inventories referring to slaves (23%) was not much greater than in Augusta County (20%). However, most of the Frederick County inventories referred to more than two slaves, while those in Augusta mainly mentioned one or two; and the use of indentured servants was more widespread in Frederick. Possession

42. The itemized value of an inventory of a settler during the late 1750s or early 1760s who owned the minimum amount of each of the items in table 12 totaled between £60 and £100. The impact of owning a slave (£25–£35) or a still (£15–£20) is obvious. Of the 24 valley inventories before 1760 that contained references to slaves, 19 were appraised at over £100.

Table 12. Shenandoah Valley inventories: ownership of selected items, 1740–79

| | 1740–49 | | | | 1750–59 | | | | 1760–69 | | | | 1770–79 | | | | | |
| | Augusta County | | Frederick County | | Augusta County | | Frederick County | | Augusta County | | Frederick County | | Augusta County | | Frederick County | | Shenandoah County | |
	No.	%	No.	%	No.	%	No.	%	No.	%	No.	%	No.	%	No.	%	No.	%
Total no. of inventories	69		105		186		175		225		192		183		120		52	
Horses —at least 1	67	97	96	91	170	91	160	91	206	91	181	94	159	87	95	80	45	87
—more than 5	44	64	45	43	94	50	64	37	121	54	60	31	60	33	31	26	6	11
Wagon or cart	5	7	18	17	23	12	33	19	47	21	58	30	48	26	50	42	24	46
Plow	23	33	41	40	54	30	61	35	78	35	92	48	90	47	75	63	41	80
Still	4	6	4	4	8	4	13	7	7	3	14	7	13	7	16	13	8	15
Furniture (3 or more items)	17	25	60	57	44	24	100	57	60	27	152	80	78	43	102	85	45	87
Servant	0	0	4	4	6	3	22	13	10	4	8	4	15	8	18	15	2	4
Slave	5	7	3	3	7	4	9	5	33	15	18	9	37	20	28	23	6	11
Book	25	36	49	47	70	38	78	45	93	41	86	45	93	48	52	43	23	44
Money (cash, debts owed to)	23	33	55	52	46	25	75	43	57	25	121	63	50	27	49	41	22	43

Sources: Orange County Will Books 1 and 2; Frederick County Will Books 1–6; Augusta County Will Books 1–4; Augusta County Will Books 1–6; Shenandoah County Will Book A.

of a horse was a major aspect of the valley's ownership structure, especially during the earliest years of settlement. Before the 1770s over 90% of all inventories contained references to at least one horse; during the 1770s over 80% referred to them. Although references to horses remained consistently higher in the upper valley, the lower valley was better equipped in terms of wagons, plows, and furniture by the end of the colonial period, and it also, perhaps surprisingly, had more stills.

Extensive debt networks were revealed by the inventories. Everyone seemed to owe everyone else. In most cases debt patterns seem to have been highly localized, with individuals of relatively great wealth or stature turning up frequently as creditors, such as Jost Hite, Gabriel Jones, James Patton, and Benjamin Borden, Jr. Borden's estate was owed almost £2,000 in 1754, and Patton's estate had £3,682 due to it in 1758.[43] Where both debts owed to and owed by a settler were recorded, in approximately one-fourth of the cases the value of the outstanding debts was greater than the total value of the inventory. Thus, when Thomas Anderson died in Frederick County in 1751 his entire inventory of £71 was owed to twenty-eight creditors, leaving nothing for funeral expenses or for his heirs.[44]

Wealth and Social Stratification, 1780-1800

For the last two decades of the century, property assessments from the inventories can be supplemented by county personal property and land tax returns. Tables 13 and 14 show the value and content of valley inventories for the period 1780 to 1800. Anomalies now begin to appear in the data which indicate that inventories are less useful indicators of wealth distribution toward the end of the century. The influx of small to middling planters, and a few really substantial ones, into Berkeley and Frederick counties during the 1770s and the end of the century is not reflected clearly in the inventories. During the 1780s and 1790s Frederick County had a much more impressive array of inventories over £1,000, both absolutely (26) and relatively (10%), than the other three counties, but the differences are less than one might have anticipated. This is clearly because many of the landowners who were responsible for transforming parts of the lower valley into commercial tobacco or wheat production after the 1760s were absentee owners whose inventories were recorded in their county of residence in eastern Virginia

43. Augusta Co. Will Book 2:22–26, 3:202–7.
44. Frederick Co. Will Book 1:272–74.

Table 13. Value of Shenandoah Valley inventories, 1780–1800

Value (Virginia £s)	Frederick County		Shenandoah County		Augusta County		Rockbridge County	
	1780-1789	1790-1800	1780-1789	1790-1800	1780-1789	1790-1800	1780-1789[1]	1790-1800
Over 3,000	1	4	0	0	0	4	0	0
2,001–3,000	0	4	0	0	2	1	0	0
1,001–2,000	5	12	2	3	3	1	2	4
901–1,000	1	4	0	1	0	1	0	0
801–900	1	2	0	2	3	2	1	0
701–800	0	1	1	1	2	2	1	1
601–700	1	3	2	0	4	4	2	0
501–600	2	10	2	3	2	6	1	5
401–500	3	10	2	9	2	4	6	2
301–400	4	7	13	12	5	6	10	5
201–300	12	11	12	24	21	13	11	19
101–200	26	19	24	31	39	21	18	25
51–100	27	23	38	29	19	25	16	13
25–50	19	15	25	24	10	9	12	18
0.1–24	15	12	31	22	9	13	11	10
Total	117	137	152	161	121	112	91	102

SOURCES: Frederick County Will Books 4–6 and Will Book 1 (Superior Court); Shenandoah County Will Books A-E; Augusta County Will Books 6-9 and Will Book 1-A (Superior Court); and Rockbridge County Will Books 1 and 2.
[1] The dates for Rockbridge County are 1778–89.

rather than in Berkeley or Frederick counties. A discrepancy therefore arises between what the inventories reveal and the actual development of the land use and economic patterns of the lower valley.

Median inventory values for the 1780s are also unrepresentatively low for Frederick and Shenandoah, but those for the 1790s are more accurate reflections of wealth distribution. Frederick County's £198 is considerably more substantial than that for Augusta (£137), Rockbridge (£130), or Shenandoah (£117). During the two decades slaves were reflected in a higher proportion of Augusta inventories (36%) than of Frederick's (31%), although the median number of slaves owned was three and five respectively. Though the proportion of inventories under £25 was about 10% in all counties except Shenandoah (17%), Augusta had a smaller proportion of inventories evaluated at £100 or less (37%) than Frederick (44%), Shenandoah (54%), or Rockbridge (55%). Yet

Table 14. Shenandoah Valley inventories: ownership of selected items, 1780–1800

	Frederick County				Shenandoah County				Augusta County				Rockbridge County			
	1780–89		1790–1800		1780–89		1790–1800		1780–89		1790–1800		1780–1789		1790–1800	
	No.	%	No.	%	No.	%	No.	%	No.	%	No.	%	No.	%	No.	%
Total no. of inventories	114		133		138		150		115		105		90		102	
Item																
Horses—																
—at least 1	99	87	113	85	110	80	118	80	92	80	85	81	73	81	81	80
—more than 5	20	17	34	26	20	15	20	13	50	44	39	37	36	40	34	33
Wagon or cart	33	29	65	48	36	26	55	37	30	26	42	40	21	23	25	25
Plow	53	46	92	69	84	61	88	60	49	43	46	44	42	47	53	52
Still	13	11	15	11	10	7	12	8	31	27	24	23	7	8	6	6
Furniture (3 or more items)	99	87	120	90	100	72	103	70	49	43	47	45	40	44	49	48
Servant	3	2	0	0	0	0	0	0	6	5	1	1	1	1	0	0
Slave	27	24	50	30	12	9	14	9	40	35	40	38	26	30	29	28
Book	50	44	64	48	58	42	67	45	52	45	48	46	35	40	50	50
Money (cash, debts owed to)	41	36	64	48	53	38	74	50	23	20	27	26	42	47	19	18

Sources: Frederick County Will Books 4–6 and Will Book 1 (Superior Court); Shenandoah County Will Books A–E; Augusta County Will Books 6–9 and Will Book 1-A (Superior Court); and Rockbridge County Will Books 1 and 2.
[1] The dates for Rockbridge County are 1778–89.

one of the more subtle measurers of Frederick's distinctiveness was the much greater range of the value and content of its inventories than anywhere else in the valley. Excluding Lord Fairfax's personal property, which may have been worth as much as £100,000,[45] Frederick's inventories ranged up to £12,000, while the top evaluation barely reached £5,000 elsewhere in the valley. In terms of slaves, the contrast between Frederick and Augusta counties, for example, is revealed by the facts that eighteen (24%) of the Frederick inventories which referred to slaves included totals of more than ten, compared to only five (6%) of the Augusta inventories, and up to ninety-seven slaves were mentioned in individual inventories in Frederick compared to a maximum of forty-two in Augusta.

Except for stills (mentioned in a remarkable 25% of Augusta's inventories) and horses, the lower valley counties exhibited a more impressive personal property structure than the upper valley by the end of the century, with more wagons and plows and seemingly better furnished homes. In general, the inventories reveal increasing accumulations of property over time and increasing differences between the upper and lower ends of the property ownership spectrum in all counties. These trends are even more evident in the land and personal property tax lists.

In terms of the ownership of land, it was demonstrated earlier that by the late colonial period, at least one-third of the taxable population of the upper valley and more than two-fifths of the taxables in the lower valley did not own land. Of those who did, just over three-quarters of the landholders in the upper valley held 400 acres or under, and fewer than one-tenth had under 100 acres; in the lower valley the respective proportions were just over one-half and fewer than one-twentieth. In the upper valley by 1782 almost one-third of the region's taxable population owned no land; by 1800 this figure had increased to almost one-half, and the proportion of settlers with 400 acres or fewer was now more than four-fifths. During the entire century, with the exception of the large land speculators, no local settler ever owed more than 10,000 acres, and only two owned more than 5,000 acres. In terms of landed property, therefore, there were few substantial landowners. By the end of the century, land alienation and dispersal had developed to such proportions that the ownership of land became a major differentiating factor among valley residents.

45. Fairfax's inventory was itemized but not evaluated. He left £47,837 in specie and paper money alone, together with 26 pounds of silver plate, 136 books, 97 slaves, 15 horses, 134 cattle, 154 pigs, 221 sheep, 10 hogsheads of tobacco, and 550 barrels of corn, among other items (Frederick Co. Will Book 4:583–95).

In the lower valley, trends toward increasing stratification had gone much further than elsewhere in the valley, if the Frederick County figures are any indication. In 1782 just over half of the taxable population in Frederick owned no land. By 1800 more and more of its settlers were at the lower end of the landholding structure, while the few owners with more than 1,000 acres were expanding their control over the county's land and transferring thousands of acres among themselves.[46] In 1783 only seventeen settlers in the entire Shenandoah Valley had more than 2,500 acres, and twelve of these (virtually all of eastern Virginia origins) were in Berkeley and Frederick counties.

The personal property tax returns corroborate the two opposing trends of the last quarter of the eighteenth century—a general improvement of living standards and accumulation of wealth, on the one hand, and a more restricted property ownership base and increasing socioeconomic stratification of the population, on the other. In 1782 less than 6% of the taxable households in the Shenandoah Valley (only 3% in the upper valley) were recorded as having no slaves, horses, or cattle.[47] By 1800 the proportion had risen to almost 25% in the lower valley and 17% in the upper valley. By this date in the upper valley only 17% (857 out of 4,948) of all taxable households owned slaves, and the slaveowners had been reduced to 12% of Rockingham's taxable households, 22% of Augusta's, and 18% of those in Rockbridge. In the lower valley, 26% (1,139 out of 4,802) of the taxable households owned slaves in 1782. Shenandoah's proportion (9%) bore little comparison with either Frederick's (38%) or Berkeley's (31%). By 1800, 23% (1,881 out of 8,235) of the taxable households possessed slaves, but only 10% in Shenandoah County compared with 27% in Berkeley and 32% in Frederick. No one south of Frederick County by the end of the century came close to owning 100 slaves, a status that was achieved by at least four individuals in Berkeley and five in Frederick (including Nathaniel Burwell with about 250). Similar contrasts were evident in the possession of horses and cattle.

In general, therefore, the evidence available on patterns of property ownership in the valley during the eighteenth century substantiates the belief that the majority of the population, or at least those who have

46. Frederick Co. Land Tax Lists, Alterations 1783–86, Va. State Lib.

47. The tithables, including young men living with their parents and white servants, were recorded under the name of the head of the household to which they belonged. For example, Augusta County personal property records for 1782 contained the names of 1,248 white individuals but 1,305 white tithables; for 1800, there were 1,813 names but 2,320 white tithables. Clearly a discussion of slaveowning is more meaningful in terms of the number of households than in terms of white tithables.

been preserved in the records, were of "the middling sort" owning between 100 and 400 acres of land and personal property evaluated at between £50 and £150. Only about a score of residents in both Berkeley and Frederick counties raised those areas above the general levels of wealth found throughout the rest of the region. Throughout the second half of the century, the richest 10% of the resident adult population owned approximately 40% of the valley's real and recorded personal property.[48] In 1760 the richest 10% of residents in the lower valley owned about 45% of that subregion's real and personal property, while the richest 10% in the upper valley owned about 36% of that subregion's property. By 1800, according to the detailed records which did not exist in 1760, the richest 10% owned 48% of the real and 58% of the personal property in the lower valley and 35% and 46% in the upper valley.

Land accumulations in the upper valley emphasize this concentration further. The twelve nonresidents who owned 10,000 acres or more controlled almost 40% of the entire taxable acreage of the upper valley. As the richest tenth of the resident population owned another 35% of the land, this meant that the remaining 89% of the landowners owned only about 25% of the total taxable real property. The overall average of 40% for the valley agrees with Main's estimates for the 1780s. He calculated that the richest 10% of the population in southern "frontier" and "subsistence" areas owned 40% of the total wealth in these regions and that, in contrast, the richest 10% of the population in southern cities and commercial agricultural areas owned between 55% and 60% of total wealth.[49] In these terms, the lower valley, and especially Berkeley and Frederick counties, had a more advanced distribution of wealth than the upper valley but had not reached the level Main requires for classification as a commercial agricultural area. However, in actual fact, both parts of the valley were commercial agricultural, not "subsistence," areas by the time of the Revolution. Moreover, because of his static schema, Main can provide no accommodation for the increasing concentration of wealth in the region over time.

48. The fact that the personal property tax lists itemized only slaves, horses, cattle, wheels, plate, and licenses (and cattle and wheels were omitted by 1790) makes it difficult to generalize about all property ownership, although it seems reasonable to assume that the lists do indicate wealth distribution fairly well. If the valley had been more urbanized by the end of the century, the representativeness of the items in the lists would have been more questionable.

49. Main, *Social Structure of Revolutionary America*, p. 276n.

Wealth Accumulation and Social Change

This survey of the distribution of wealth in the Shenandoah Valley adds more fuel to the present debate over social change in eighteenth-century America. Although the conclusions reached above must be used with caution in attempting to devise a broader level of generalization, the figures for the upper valley bear some comparison with those for Chester County, Pennsylvania, examined by James T. Lemon and Gary Nash. Their conclusions were based on the study of seven Chester County tax lists for the period 1693 to 1802, while this analysis of the upper valley has been derived from a variety of less comprehensive sources. Moreover, they conducted their study in greater depth by examining not only the role of the top 10% of resident taxpayers but also that of the remaining 90%, at three socioeconomic levels. Nevertheless, both studies agree on two major points: (1) there was a gradual concentration of wealth and an increasing gap between rich and poor during the eighteenth century; (2) socioeconomic differentiation was particularly acute during and immediately after the Revolutionary War.[50] A comparison of the 1782 figures for both areas indicates that the upper 10% of the upper valley's resident population owned a much larger share of the region's total assessed taxable wealth (41.5%) than the same group in Chester County (33.6%); in 1800 the contrast was less evident (40.5% to 38.3%).

Yet the results of debates of this kind can only be tentative, for still unanswered are such critical questions as how wealth was actually used and how valid such arbitrary categories as the top or bottom 10% or 25% of the property ownership scale are in determining conclusions about wealth distribution over time.[51] Only a few remarks can be made at the level of analysis of this study.

Evidence from the inventories indicates that wealth was acquired and used in a variety of ways and makes it possible to classify property into personal and capital goods. Of the sixty-five individuals in the valley during the eighteenth century who left personal property worth over £1,000, at least forty were primarily large landowners and farmers (many of whom also dabbled in land speculation), twelve were merchants, four were artisans (two ironmasters and two tanners), two were

50. Lemon and Nash, "The Distribution of Wealth in Eighteenth-Century America," *Jour. Soc. Hist.*, 2 (1968): 1–6.

51. Some useful perspectives on these issues are to be found in P. M. G. Harris and Lois Green Carr, "Social Stratification in Maryland, 1658–1705," St. Mary's City Commission project, mimeographed, 1971.

tavern owners, two were millers, one was a lawyer, and another a doctor (leaving three whose main occupation or activity was unknown). Large landowners who speculated in land frequently left large amounts of real property to be transferred to their heirs, much of which appears to have been unused during their lifetimes or, in some cases, may have been used as collateral in other investment transactions. Of James Patton's total personal estate of £4,055, £3,683 was in the form of bonds, bills, and promissory notes due him for land sales, money lent, and favors done. Debt networks built on such activities had reached enormous proportions by the end of the century, and in many instances the more wealthy the individual, the more extensive the debts. Isaac Zane, Jr., one of the leading ironmasters in Virginia, left a personal inventory evaluated at £3,869 in 1795, but accounts against him accumulated to £12,896, which had to be offset with land and other property sales over the next seventeen years.[52] Thomas Bryan Martin, who took over Greenway Court after Lord Fairfax's death, left a personal estate of £4,371 in 1794, but accounts and costs against him of over £60,500 were scattered through the record books for the next twenty years.[53]

Successful merchants frequently had money to invest in land and other ventures, but they also had large amounts of fixed capital in the form of store goods, and they were generally the principal lenders to the local population during the latter part of the century. One Augusta merchant, Thomas Stuart, left an inventory of about £3,690 in 1789, of which £1,640 comprised debts in bonds, bills, and notes owed by 289 individuals, while another £1,000 represented book debts owed by 580 customers.[54] The records of the Winchester merchant William Holliday in 1790 reveal the extent to which some merchants accumulated wealth. His personal property was evaluated at £480, but he had a huge store inventory of cloth, clothing, domestic goods, hardware, and farm equipment valued at £2,545. His will testament revealed that he owned over 2,700 acres of land (including 1,500 acres in Kentucky), seven lots in Winchester (including lot 1 on London Street, where his store was located), and a lot in the spa town of Bath in Berkeley County.[55] Artisans, such as the two ironmasters Isaac Zane, Jr., and Henry Miller, generally had heavy investments in raw materials, equipment, and labor.

Many of the region's wealthiest settlers, especially in the lower valley, indulged in very conspicuous consumption during the last quarter of the century, displaying their riches in visible form. Although such

52. Frederick Co. Superior Court Will Books 1:199–205, 224–85, 362–79, 2:76–82.
53. Ibid., 1:320–25, 442–47, 2: 2–7, 227–41, 305–25.
54. Augusta Co. Will Book 7:237–60.
55. Frederick Co. Superior Court Will Book 1:33–45, 52–98.

displays rarely compared with the larger plantations in eastern Virginia, the estates of Generals Adam Stephen and Horatio Gates in Berkeley County and those of the Fairfaxes and the Hites in Frederick County were widely known. The focuses of by far the most distinctive social group in the entire valley after the Revolution were the Fairfax estate at Greenway Court and the town of Winchester a few miles to the west. There the wealthy, Anglican planters were entertained, kept in touch with the outside world, and supported a number of formal social gatherings, theater entertainment, specialized crafts, and summer horse racing. At Berkeley Springs, the Hampshire town established as a spa, many of them vacationed during the summer and mingled with planters of similar status from eastern Virginia. These behavior patterns were the most patent social expression of eastern Virginia influences.[56]

One other aspect of wealth accumulation and use for which relatively good data exist and which provides both insight into the operations of the valley's social geography and additional perspectives on social stratification is the exploitation of labor. Although there were few really wealthy men in the region at any time, many individuals of middling status employed others as part of their property structure either for short periods or, in the case of slavery, during the slaves' stay in the valley.

The Lower Strata and Labor Supply

Many propertyless or small-propertied settlers never turn up in the records, making it difficult to assess their numbers and to identify their characteristics and activities. Nevertheless, it is necessary to try to determine to what extent the lower strata of society formed the labor supply and the extent to which control over their services helped to create social and economic inequalities between members of the middle and upper strata. Finally, were there any cultural factors which help to explain the differences in ownership and hiring of laborers, servants, and slaves?

Much of the agricultural labor that was required in the Shenandoah Valley, especially during the colonial period, was supplied by the farming families themselves. However, both Negro slavery and white servitude were introduced into the region at an early date, and early settlers made frequent provision in their wills for the purchase of servants or slaves for their families.

Most indentured servants in the valley were of British origins. Many

---

56. Bliss, "The Tuckahoe in New Virginia," pp. 387–96; Hart, *Valley of Virginia*, pp. 107–10, 164–69; and Mitchell, "Content and Context," *Md. Hist.* 5 (1974):86–87.

were skilled workers or learned a trade as part of their indenture; others were employed as field labor or as domestic servants. Unlike slaves, they were only in servitude temporarily, after which they obtained their freedom. Because only those servants who had not served out their indenture period were recorded in inventories, such references to servants are few. On the average, they were more expensive to maintain than slaves. It has been estimated that the average annual cost of keeping a male servant in the mid-eighteenth century was about £3;[57] female servants who produced children illegitimately were more costly to maintain, although such children were often hired out later by the county. But the services of indentured servants were cheaper to obtain than those of slaves. During the 1750s and 1760s a male servant was worth between £5 and £6 per annum for every year of indenture outstanding. The institution of indentured servitude was familiar to many of the valley settlers who arrived from Pennsylvania. It is not surprising, therefore, that settlers would first look toward that colony as a prime source of white indentured labor, a source that was only gradually replaced by eastern Virginia.

All ethnic groups used indentured servants. German names occur relatively frequently as masters, but most traders in indentured servants were English or Scotch-Irish. William Preston was the most prominent trader in servants in the upper valley before the Revolution. Between 1755 and 1774 he sold scores of servants in the backcountry either by himself or as agent for Edward Johnson, a merchant near Richmond.[58] By the early 1770s this trade had virtually stopped. When Preston wrote to his brother-in-law near Staunton in 1774 inquiring about the potential for selling more servants there, the reply was that there was none because of the scarcity of money, the abundance of local servants, and the amount of debt already produced by investment in servants.[59]

There were two other elements of white labor supply operating in the region. The most destitute elements of the region's population were at the two extremes of the age pyramid, the old, infirm, or maimed, and the young, orphaned, or abandoned. There is very little information

57. Thomas J. Wertenbaker, *The Planters of Colonial Virginia* (New York: Russell and Russell, 1959), pp. 126–28.

58. See "Statement of Account between William Preston and Israel Christian for Sale of Servants," Sept. 4, 1755, and Edward Johnson to William Preston, April 8 and May 30, 1774, Preston Papers, Va. Hist. Soc.

59. John Brown to William Preston, Aug. 22, 1774, Preston Papers, Draper Mss., Wisc. State Hist. Soc. Russell R. Menard, "From Servant to Freeholder: Status Mobility and Property Accumulation in Seventeenth-Century Maryland," *Wm. and Mary Qtly.*, 3d ser. 30 (1973): 37–64, demonstrates that indentured servitude served as a prime means of social mobility for whites without capital only before 1660 in Maryland.

on either of these groups in the county or parish records. The elderly and those physically incapable of work were usually exempted from paying taxes and were maintained by the local parish. It was only in 1762 that a poorhouse was planned for the upper valley, and five more years elapsed before an overseer of the poor was appointed. One can be sure that the parish wardens and the overseer of the poor tried to curtail the number of public charges as much as possible. The French and Indian and the Revolutionary wars produced a number of maimed and orphaned individuals in the valley. Orphans and children produced illegitimately were less of a burden on the public levy since they were bound out by the parish wardens, from the age of four or five upwards to the age of eighteen, to local respected residents in much the same way as indentured servants.[60] Many were placed as apprentices to learn a skill or trade; others were employed as servants. During the period from 1760 to 1780, about 250 children were bound out as apprentices or servants in Augusta County, and the number in Frederick County was even larger.[61] The apprenticeship system remained intact throughout the entire eighteenth century,[62] but it is difficult to assess to what extent trained apprentices contributed numerically and materially to the skilled labor force of the region.

Hired wage labor played an important function in the valley from the first generation of settlement. Wagoners (farmers primarily) were an important element in the transportation and economic patterns generated by valley settlers. During the French and Indian War and the years immediately before it, wagoners were paid an average of 4s. 6d. per day. By the time of the Revolutionary War wagoners were in great demand and were being paid up to 18s. per day per team. These wages seem most favorable when compared with those paid to field labor. In December 1775 Philip Vickers Fithian remarked that "provision and Living here is very Low. In the best Times . . . the whole Expence here p[e]r Annum of a Labourer for Diet, Washing and Lodging was only five Pounds—at most five Pounds, ten shillings—And yet the Price of Labour is high—two shillings p[e]r Day in common—And in Time of

60. See Augusta Parish Vestry Book (1746–80), pp. 35–49.

61. See Augusta Co. Order Books 6–17, and Frederick Co. Order Books 8–17.

62. R. E. and B. K. Brown, *Virginia, 1705–1786*, pp. 51–52, have maintained that the apprenticeship system made a considerable contribution to solving the problem of labor scarcity in Virginia. Hart, *Valley of Virginia*, p. 19, was of the opinion that the apprentice problem rivaled that of indentured servants, but does not go so far as to suggest that the apprenticeship system might have rivaled that of indentured servitude. It does seem probable that the presence of many mature, skilled apprentices prevented the number of indentured servants from being larger than it was by the end of the colonial period.

Hay and Harvest half a Crown 2/6d.—and forty shillings per Month— This, considering the Currency and the Price of Living, make it a good Place for Labouring Men."[63] If this report was accurate, it would partly explain the large number of landless wage laborers who appeared in the county tax books by 1782. However, the increasingly more constricted opportunities to acquire land and enter the ranks of freehold farming by the late 1770s helped to produce a growing rural proletariat by the end of the century. It appears that as much as one-third of the adult male labor force in the valley by 1800 was composed of wage laborers.[64]

In the lower valley the structure of the labor supply and of society, especially after the late 1760s, became distinguished by two institutions which were never as well established in the upper valley—tenancy and slavery. The nature of the land distribution system within this western part of Lord Fairfax's Northern Neck was such that tenancy appeared early and had reached considerable magnitude by the end of the century. In instances where eastern Virginia planters acquired quarters or plantations, in Frederick and Berkeley counties, the institutions of tenancy and slavery were functionally related. Absentee owners left the responsibility for the operations of the plantations to overseers with tenant status who worked the land with slaves supplied from eastern Virginia. This is well illustrated by the records of Robert Carter of Nomini Hall in the Northern Neck Tidewater. Carter first began to develop his holdings in eastern Frederick County during the 1770s with the help of twenty tenants. By the early 1790s he had six plantations in operation under six chief tenants, and probably numerous subtenants, who paid £490 in annual rents (22% of his total income from rents) and controlled 124 slaves (almost 23% of his total of 550 slaves).[65]

Lord Fairfax and George Washington were the most prominent tenant employers in the lower valley during the 1760s, and although they appear to have lost many tenants by migration or default during the Revolutionary War, they were soon joined by other eastern Virginian

63. Fithian, *Journal*, p. 147.

64. This figure might have been higher but for the opportunities for militiamen after the Revolutionary War to acquire land warrants for lands to the west or for sale to others interested in acquiring such lands. In this manner some potential laborers may have been able to move out of the laboring ranks, although few would have made enough money to be able to enter the ranks of the small landowner and may well have ended up, at best, as tenants.

65. Rent Book and Bonds (1793–97) and Day Book (1790–92), Robert Carter Papers, Manuscript Div., Lib. Cong. See also Louis Morton, *Robert Carter of Nomini Hall* (Williamsburg, Va.: Colonial Williamsburg, Inc., 1941).

landowners.[66] Most tenants were operating holdings much less substantial than those working for Carter—about 150 to 200 acres with one or two slaves and small numbers of livestock. Turnover rates at all times seem to have been high and rents always well in arrears. At least 44 (20%) of Lord Fairfax's Northern Neck tenants were located in the lower valley by 1772, and ten years after his death in 1781 there were still more than 220 tenants on the former Fairfax manor lands (Leeds and Potomac estates) in Berkeley and Frederick counties.[67] By the end of the century about one-fifth of the landholders in these counties appear to have been still in tenant status.

Slavery was in a category all its own, one which, despite some emancipation after 1781, did not lead to much social mobility for those whose labor was involved. As an institution it was unimportant even in the lower valley until the 1760s. The initial cost for slaves in comparison with other forms of available labor was prohibitive. During the 1750s, for example, an adult male slave cost between £25 and £35 (about £20 to £27 sterling) in the valley. Once purchased, however, slaves were long-term acquisitions, to which were added the children they produced. Moreover, slaves were cheaper to keep than indentured servants. A male slave cost between £1 and £1 10s. annually to keep—less than half the cost of maintaining a male servant.

The price of slaves rose rapidly after 1760. By 1762 the general range of prices (Virginia money) in the valley were: children, £10 to £20; teenage girls, £25 to £40; teenage boys, £30 to £50; women, £45 to £60; men, £55 to £70.[68] These prices remained typical until 1775, when prime field hands began to sell for £80 to £85 and the most valuable female slaves were fetching £75. After the Revolutionary War a good male slave could not be purchased for less than £100.

Slaveowning was not a socioeconomic trait brought by settlers from Pennsylvania. A few perhaps had been exposed to slavery in Maryland. It was eastern Virginia that provided the most obvious influence leading to the acceptance of slaveowning by a substantial minority of valley settlers. Some individuals, such as Benjamin Borden, Jr., had been

66. See Bliss, "Tuckahoe in the Valley," pp. 73–104; Bliss, "The Rise of Tenancy in Virginia," *Va. Mag. Hist. Biog.* 58 (1950): 427–41. See also the records of Frederick and Berkeley rentals in the Fairfax Papers, Huntington Lib.

67. Bliss, "Tuckahoe in the Valley," pp. 73–76; Bliss, "Rise of Tenancy," p. 429. By 1776 Fairfax was receiving over £600 annually in rent from his lower valley tenants.

68. Information on slave prices comes from two main sources, sales of personal property (which are recorded in the county deed books and will books) and appraisals made in will inventories. Two other sources are the *Virginia Gazette* and collections of family correspondence.

exposed to the early use of slave labor by eastern Virginians in the lower Shenandoah Valley and probably spread the trait to the upper valley. It was from eastern Virginia that slaveowners in the valley initially purchased their slaves, and the desire of a few settlers to own slaves led to one of the earliest communications with eastern Virginia. Throughout the century the most prominent slaveowners in the valley purchased their best slaves in the central Piedmont and Tidewater counties or had slaves transferred from eastern Virginia estates to their quarters in Berkeley and Frederick counties. In general, the reaction to slavery was largely on the basis of cost rather than ethics.

Concerning the impact of slavery on white society in Virginia, Robert E. and B. Katherine Brown concluded that "there was a great consensus among the population in general over the desirability of slavery in spite of occasional protests against the institution. If the rich were accumulating slaves, so also were the poorer sort, and the deeds amply substantiate this fact."[69] There is some truth to this statement when applied to the essentially nonplanter society which established itself throughout the upper valley and, to a lesser extent, in the lower valley. Most Augusta County inventories before 1780, as pointed out above, rarely mentioned more than three or four slaves. Although slaves composed only one of every eight inhabitants of the upper valley during the last two decades of the century, slaveowning households there composed just over one of every five households in 1782, and one of every six in 1800. Yet, despite this relative decline in slaveowning families between the two dates, the slaveowning base of the population remained surprisingly broad.

Not only was the social significance of slavery especially in the upper valley reflected in the large number of slaveowners who owned very few slaves (and who in some cases did not own any land), it also was expressed in two other practices. As previously noted, last wills and testaments made by valley settlers, whether they owned slaves or not, often provided for a means whereby slaves could be purchased for some member of the deceased's family.[70] Another facet of slavery in the upper valley, in contrast to the general practice in eastern Virginia and in the lower valley, was the fact that white masters frequently worked in the fields along with their slaves. In 1754, for example, it was recorded that Joseph Tees worked in his fields with three Negroes, who did most of

69. R. E. and B. K. Brown, *Virginia, 1705–1786*, pp. 74–76.
70. See, for example, the will of Charles Campbell of Beverley Manor in Campbell-Preston Papers, vol. 1, Mar. 17, 1767, Manuscript Div., Lib. Cong. Campbell's wife sold part of her estate to buy slaves, which were divided between her children. In addition she retained a family servant (ibid., Sept. 1769).

the grubbing and preparation of the ground.[71] Other references to this phenomenon are rare, but in 1796 La Rochefoucauld-Liancourt observed whites and Negroes working together in the fields to harvest wheat near Newmarket in Shenandoah County.[72] He noted that there were no rich planters in the upper part of the Shenandoah Valley and therefore relatively few Negroes; "yet all these petty planters, however poor and wretched they apparently are, have one slave who shares in their toils and distress."[73] In the lower Shenandoah Valley the social and economic pressures on many of the settlers of northern origins increased progressively from the early 1770s on with the influx of eastern planters or their overseers. In essence, however, the large planters, who comprised about 15% of the slaveowners in Berkeley and Frederick counties, operated at a different economic scale and in a different social world from the vast majority of lower valley slaveowners.

The most nagging question about slavery in the Shenandoah Valley has been the attitude of German settlers. Several writers have argued that one of their most distinctive features was an aversion to owning slaves. Richard Shryock found little evidence to support the belief that the Scotch-Irish opposed slavery but declared that the Germans were disinclined to use slaves and preferred to rely on their own labors.[74] John Wayland found that although some Germans owned slaves, as a rule they opposed slavery because of their religious teachings. He believed that most of the slaves in the Shenandoah Valley were owned by English and Scotch-Irish settlers and by absentee eastern Virginians.[75]

Although the Germans had little aversion to hiring indentured servants if they needed them, of the clearly identifiable German names in colonial inventories, fewer than 5% owned any slaves. Similarly, references to Germans as slaveowners are rare, and the most heavily settled German county, Shenandoah, consistently had the fewest number of slaves, the lowest proportion of slaveowners, and the highest proportion of owners with only one or two slaves (90% by 1800). It appears that, indeed, Germans were not so prone to slaveholding as other groups; this reluctance seems to have been especially characteristic of sectarian groups

71. Augusta Co. Order Book 4:140–41.

72. La Rochefoucauld-Liancourt, *Travels*, 2:89.

73. Ibid., p. 98.

74. Shryock, "British versus German Traditions in Colonial Agriculture," *Miss. Valley Hist. Rev.* 26 (1939):39–54.

75. Wayland, *German Element of the Shenandoah Valley*, pp. 179–81, and Wayland, *Twenty-Five Chapters on the Shenandoah Valley*, p. 83.

within the German community. At the same time, British Quakers were just as likely to avoid slaveowning as the Germans.[76]

Demographic and economic factors probably also played a part in this phenomenon. If it could be determined that Germans had larger families than the English or Scotch-Irish, one might speculate about the effect of differing fertility rates on the use of outside labor or on the intensity of land use. As will be demonstrated later, there is information suggesting that Germans were not heavily involved in the most labor-demanding crops grown in the valley, tobacco and hemp. It is possible that most of the settlers of German origin who grew these crops on a large scale had anglicized their names. It is more probable, however, that the reluctance of the average German family to acquire slaves prevented them from competing commercially in the cultivation of these crops, and that this reluctance persisted, even after they had become acculturated in other ways, as they found other sources of investment more meaningful to them.

With the exception of the Negro slave, there was ample opportunity for the various segments of the Shenandoah Valley's population to improve their socioeconomic condition during much of the eighteenth century. The individual's status was open-ended and social mobility was the rule, although how far and how fast members of the nonpropertied classes climbed the social ladder is another question. Most of the lowest elements of the white population, whether they were originally orphans or seasonal laborers, had the opportunity to acquire some money, a trade, a skill, and even some education. Social and economic opportunities to better oneself could come from long attachment to a particular area. Unlike the lower Shenandoah Valley, where wealthy eastern Virginians with such well-known names as Carter, Harrison, Lee, Page, Randolph, and Washington, moved easily into the highest socioeconomic levels after 1765, most of the relatively prosperous, prominent members of the community in the upper valley had long been established in the area and formed a cohesive group in terms of political power.[77] Local offices were filled with Breckenridges, Johnstons, Lewises,

76. There were, of course, some notable exceptions. The single most important employer of slave labor in the upper valley during the last 20 years of the century was the German ironmaster Henry Miller. He employed up to 35 slaves in his ironworks and papermill at one time, some of whom held important jobs such as forgemen and colliers. When he died in 1796 he left 42 Negroes (35 men and 7 women), including two forgemen, a blacksmith, and a wagoner. His industrial counterpart in the lower valley, Isaac Zane, Jr., a Quaker, left 21 slaves when he died in 1795.

77. See Hart, *Valley of Virginia*, chs. 3, 5, 6, 8, 9, 10.

132

McDowells, Prestons, and Stuarts. On the other hand, primarily because of the ease with which land could be obtained in the areas to the west and south of the Shenandoah Valley, both dissident and successful elements of society could often obtain, through geographical mobility, increased opportunities for personal attainment in more recently settled areas. This exodus, in turn, could allow other individuals remaining within the valley to move up in the social structure by taking over property or local political power the migrants left behind. But much of this process changed during the last quarter of the century. The presence of slavery, the persistence of tenancy in the lower valley, and the increasing number of landless and propertyless laborers and settlers attest to the fact that social and economic improvement was not automatic. As the region underwent economic development and population expansion, the processes of commercialism operated in an increasingly selective manner. As the region's economy was transformed from a fluid, competitive situation with high property access during the pioneer phase to postpioneer conditions of slower population growth, increasing competition, and restricted property access, increasing social stratification of the population was the predictable result.

5 Pioneer Economy and External Contacts

AGRICULTURE formed the economic backbone of almost every settled frontier of eighteenth-century America. Yet, as part of the Turnerian legacy, most models of pioneer development have relegated agriculture to the second or even third phase of occupance. The preagricultural phase was frequently viewed as an almost mandatory precursor to the establishment of permanent farming. Turner postulated that fur trading, cattle rearing, and sometimes mining were occupational patterns which emerged before the ascendancy of agriculture. Others, although acknowledging criticisms of Turner's notion of socio-economic evolution, have merely expanded the preagricultural phase to include exploration and missionary and military activities and have categorized the farming sequence, stating that squatters or backwoodsmen were located on the outer fringes of the agricultural zone; small propertied farmers occupied the core of the zone; and larger propertied farmers often moved in last of all and lived in close association with their less wealthy neighbors.[1]

These evolutionary approaches suffer from a number of critical flaws. In the first place, they adhere to a subsistence-commercial dichotomy which is unrealistic. Second, the idea of repetitive stages is too deterministic and schematic to account for the wide variations in occupance patterns that occurred in the settlement of new environments. Third, the notion of discrete sequences of occupational and land use patterns rests on the erroneous assumption that internal, site-related factors are mainly responsible for change; thus the zonal concept, especially, fails to take into account the importance of external market conditions.[2] It is more realistic to place permanent agriculture at the focus of any model of frontier economic development and to view other economic activities as supplemental to or, at best, temporarily competitive with commercial farming.

1. For a synthesis of these ideas, see Billington, *America's Frontier Heritage*, pp. 39-45.
2. For an alternative perspective, see J. Richard Peet, "The Spatial Expansion of Commercial Agriculture in the Nineteenth Century: A Von Thunen Interpretation," *Economic Geography* 45 (1969):283-301.

Hunting and the Indian Trade

Although the great majority of pioneer settlers arriving in the Shenandoah Valley were farmers with little experience outside of farming, some were quick to take advantage of supplemental opportunities in the local environment. Hunting and trapping and Indian trading were two such pursuits. In some instances and in some areas they were closely associated; elsewhere they were competitive and mutually detrimental.

The fur trade was not important in the region. It was the supply of skins and meat available in the Southern backcountry that encouraged the early appearance of hunting and trading. Some activity was encouraged by governmental policies. The destruction of agricultural "pests," particularly crows, squirrels, and wolves, was sanctioned by assessing each county annual quotas in proportion to its number of tithables. In Augusta County, for example, the collection of wolves' heads became an integral part of the county levy as early as 1735, and for the remainder of the colonial period prices of 5s. and 2s. 6d. usually were quoted for old and young wolf heads, respectively.[3] From 1750 until 1769 between 100 and 250 heads were collected annually, mainly from areas to the west and south of the upper valley, but the numbers declined drastically thereafter.

Hunting was insignificant in the lower valley, but farther south there is ample evidence that small-scale hunting and trapping was commercially important. A register book of skins kept for Augusta County between 1744 and mid-1749 shows that ten settlers were responsible for a total of 1,286 deerskins, 93 fox furs, 67 raccoon skins, 14 otter pelts, 3 elk hides, 1 wildcat skin, and 202 pounds of beaver pelts. The total value of these skins would have amounted to between £120 and £150 Va., with the deerskins alone worth over £100.[4] In two 1749 debt suits deerskins, fox furs, beaver pelts, and elk hides paid for the bulk of the debts; two estates in 1754 left 400 skins (all but 5 of which were deer) between them, which would have amounted to some £30 to £40.[5] In 1762 one Staunton merchant had in his possession 370 pounds of skins and 2 elk hides worth a total of £27 14s. 2d.[6] Such figures are revealing when one remembers that 100 acres of undeveloped land in Augusta County could be bought for £3 to £3 10s. in the late 1740s.[7] References to skins, guns, and trapping equipment in

3. Orange Co. Order Book 1:40–41; Augusta Co. Order Books 3:204–5, 4:68–69, 321–22; Preston Papers, 1QQ23–26, Draper Mss., Wis. State Hist. Soc.

4. Preston Papers, Jan. 23, 1744–April 5, 1749, Va. Hist. Soc. Deerskins were worth about 2s. each, raccoon skins 6d., otter pelts about 6d. per pound, beaver pelts 3d. per pound, and elk hides between 10s. and 15s. each.

5. Augusta Co. Order Books 2:111, 115, 4:125, 203.

6. Alexander Boyd to William Thompson, 1762, Preston Papers, Va. Hist. Soc.

7. For a similar observation, see R. E. and B. K. Brown, *Virginia, 1705–1786*, p. 21.

upper valley inventories for the 1740s and 1750s indicate that about one estate in every eight contained one or more of these items, compared with one in twelve in the lower valley. However, only in three or four inventories did the products of hunting and trapping contribute a significant amount to the total evaluation.

Professional hunters were only found on the margins of the valley. In 1749 two Moravian missionaries came upon several groups of frontier families living along the Cowpasture River and other western tributaries of the upper James and reported: "A kind of white people are found here, who live like savages. Hunting is their chief occupation."[8] These settlers were mainly clothed in deerskins and ate a diet consisting chiefly of johnnycakes and deer and bear meat. Hunters were also active at the southern end of the Valley of Virginia along the headquarters of the Holston and Clinch rivers, but here they came into conflict with Virginia's trade with Cherokees.[9] This trade was seldom as large as South Carolina's, but its objectives were as much strategic as economic, which was also true of Virginia's trade with Indian groups in the Ohio Valley. Although the Shenandoah valley was accessible to both these areas, participation by its settlers in this trade was minimal.[10] Some Augusta settlers did take advantage of any trading opportunities that came their way and helped to build a fort for the Cherokees in 1756, reporting that the Indians were eager to trade with Virginia settlers. However, there was always an ambivalent attitude toward such contacts, with requests for official help in establishing trading relations with friendly Indians combined with petitions for forts to protect traders from potentially hostile groups.[11]

The Components of Pioneer Agriculture

Though most farmers in the Shenandoah Valley during the first thirty years or so of its occupation owned between 100 and 400 acres of land, only a fraction of this acreage comprised the "family farm." Data on the land use

8. Hinke and Kemper, "Moravian Diaries of Travels through Virginia," *Va. Mag. Hist. Biog.* 11 (1903):123.

9. Augusta Co. Order Book 1:151; Preston Papers, 1QQ70–74, Draper Mss., Wis. State Hist. Soc.; *Calendar of Virginia State Papers,* ed. Palmer, 1:243.

10. W. Neil Franklin, "Virginia and the Cherokee Indian Trade, 1673–1752," *East Tennessee Historical Society Publications,* no. 4 (1932):3–21; Franklin, "Virginia and the Cherokee Indian Trade, 1753–1775," ibid., no. 5 (1933):22–23; Franklin, "Pennsylvania-Virginia Rivalry for the Indian Trade of the Ohio Valley," *Miss. Val. Hist. Rev.* 20 (1933–34): 463–80.

11. Compare Andrew Lewis to Governor Dinwiddie, July 23, 1756, Loudoun Papers, Huntington Lib., and *Journals of the House of Burgesses,* eds. McIlwaine and Kennedy, 9:349.

patterns of the average farm are scarce, but it appears that the average farm usually had no more than 10 to 12 acres of cleared land during the early years of settlement. Two farms advertised in the Williamsburg *Virginia Gazette* provide the best available commentary on the maximum state of land clearance by the end of the first generation. One 500-acre farm in northeastern Rockingham County had 50 acres of cleared land, over 300 acres of rich low grounds along the floodplain of Shenandoah River, and the remainder in well-wooded higher land; it also contained a farmhouse, an overseer's house, a large peach orchard, and "other conveniences."[12] The other farm, located a mile from Staunton, contained 800 acres made up of "a considerable quantity" of cleared land (apparently about 50 acres), 20 to 30 acres of additional bottomland, 12 to 14 acres of timothy meadow, a house, a kitchen, and fences in good repair.[13] Other references to arable acreage ranged generally from 4 to 18 acres, with at least two farmers recorded as sowing 30 acres in the valley. Although he was clearly an unusually active cultivator, Martin Kauffman's 1749 Augusta inventory provides one of the rare insights into the components of the arable acreage. He left 17¼ acres planted in crops, consisting of 8 acres of wheat and rye, 5 acres of corn, 3 acres of oats, ¾ acre of barley, and ½ acre of flax.[14]

By way of comparison, in western frontier Connecticut during the pioneer period a typical farm contained about 116 acres, of which 16 acres were cleared.[15] This ratio of cleared land (14%) was considerably higher than the ratio for most of the Shenandoah Valley before the mid-1760s (8% to 10%). In southeastern Pennsylvania tax returns indicate much higher ratios of cleared land per farm by 1759 (20% to 25%), although these ratios were probably exaggerated and the proportion of cleared land on a typical farm by 1790 was no more than 20%.[16]

A typical pioneer farm in the valley consisted of a few acres of cleared land for cultivation (often river bottomland), a meadow (natural or timothy), a small orchard (apple and peach), a large amount of woodland in which cattle browsed and mast was available for swine, and occasionally some hilly grazing land. The cultivated acreage was generally fenced, and adjacent to it was the one-story log farmhouse, and perhaps a small outbuilding. Over time both fences and houses were modified and improved. The earliest fences were mainly post and rail, but during the last quarter of

12. Hunter's *Virginia Gazette,* Feb. 28, 1755.
13. Rind's *Virginia Gazette,* Dec. 11, 1766.
14. Augusta Co. Will Book 1:195–97.
15. Grant, "History of Kent," pp. 76–79.
16. Lemon, *Best Poor Man's Country,* pp. 168–69. No references to fallow land were encountered in any valley records, although the practice surely existed.

the century the worm, or Virginia, fence of rails supported by crossed poles seems to have been more common.[17] More importantly, early log houses were quickly replaced by frame structures, especially among the more successful settlers.[18]

It has been widely assumed that the pioneer crop on eighteenth-century frontiers was Indian corn. Though European settlers in the American colonies demonstrated a remarkable acceptance of this New World crop, they were not about to cast off their Old World heritage. During the first thirty years of settlement in the Shenandoah Valley the most frequently mentioned crops in the records were wheat, rye, corn, and flax, in that order. These were the basic components of valley agriculture. They were supplemented by barley, oats, hemp, and tobacco. However, one can not infer from this evidence that wheat was more important than corn. Most corn was fed to animals rather than stored and used for human consumption and was thus less likely to be mentioned in inventories and sales than wheat or rye. Although a definite prevalence of wheat over corn has been found in frontier Connecticut, more information is available for that region than for the Shenandoah Valley.[19] Nevertheless, wheat and rye seem to have been at least as prevalent as corn in the pioneer Shenandoah agriculture. Wheat and rye were sown in the fall (usually September) and harvested in early summer. Corn usually was grown as a spring crop (April planting), although it occasionally was planted in late fall. Barley,

17. See Preston Papers, 1QQ83-1/2, Draper Mss., Wis. State Hist. Soc.; Weld, *Travels*, p. 133; Harry Toulmin, *The Western Country in 1793: Reports on Kentucky and Virginia*, ed. M. Tinling and G. Davies (San Marino, Calif.: Henry E. Huntington Library and Art Gallery, 1948), p. 56. Worm fences were common in the Middle Colonies by mid-century. See Esther Louise Larson, "Per Kalm's Observations on the Fences of North America," *Ag. Hist.* 21 (1947):75–78; Lemon, *Best Poor Man's Country*, p. 176.

18. In 1753 James Patton had two round-log houses made on his home farm, each with clapboard roofs, and two end chimneys both wattled and daubed outside and inside and squared off (Preston Papers, Feb. 12, 1753, Va. Hist. Soc.) A year later he had another house built of square logs 20 feet long, dovetailed and with the roof shingled and the gable ends covered with clapboard (ibid., Jan. 15, 1754). But within a year he had a large (32 x 18 x 8 feet) frame house built on one of his farms (Preston Papers, 1QQ83-1/2, Draper Mss., Wis. State Hist. Soc.). For comments on forms of log housing and corner timbering prevalent in the early Shenandoah Valley, see Fred Kniffen, "Folk Housing: Key to Diffusion," *Annals Assoc. Amer. Geog.* 55 (1965):561; Fred Kniffen and Henry Glassie, "Building in Wood in the Eastern United States: A Time-Place Perspective," *Goeg. Rev.* 56 (1966):59, 61.

19. Grant, "History of Kent," p. 65. Grant's evidence was derived largely from widows' dowers as prescribed in their husbands' will testaments. From the same source in the Pennsylvania records James T. Lemon has been able to make some useful suggestions about dietary and consumption patterns in that colony. See his "Household Consumption in Eighteenth-Century American and Its Relationship to Production and Trade: The Situation among Farmers in Southeastern Pennsylvania," *Ag. Hist.* 41 (1967):59–70.

oats, flax, hemp, and tobacco were planted in the spring and harvested in late summer.

Wheat was the principal bread grain of the early settlers, while rye was used as a bread grain and as a base for whiskey. Wheat and rye were sown together in the same field and ground to form maslin, an old Western European flour.[20] This practice appears to have been fairly common, and up to thirty acres were sown in this manner in Frederick County. Some corn may have been used to make cornbread or corn cakes, but most of it was probably used to feed pigs. Oats and hay were used principally to feed horses, while barley served as a livestock feed and in the production of beer and ale. Flax was the leading fiber crop in the pioneer period and the basis of local linen production. A small amount of flaxseed was also grown. Hemp was reported on several occasions, but it did not become a major crop until the 1760s. Ginseng, a medicinal root, was first recorded during the early 1750s, and it contributed in a small way to the region's early trade. A number of vegetables, notably peas, beans, potatoes, turnips, onions, and cabbage, were occasionally mentioned, as were hops for brewing, and they rounded out the subsistence foodstuffs cultivated within the valley.

Regional variations in crop production during the pioneer period are not easy to discern. Oats, hemp, and apples appear more frequently in the records of the upper valley, while barley is more noticeable in the lower valley. But two crops, buckwheat and tobacco, do have a more distinctive regional identification. Buckwheat does not appear in the records of Augusta County until 1770, but in the lower valley it was being cultivated in small amounts from the early 1740s on.[21] It never became a commercial crop and really failed to diffuse to the upper valley to any noticeable degree. Because tobacco functioned not only as the major export crop of colonial Virginia but also as a means of currency and tax payment, it is not surprising that attempts were made to grow it in the Shenandoah Valley at an early date. The plant was introduced into the lower valley during the early 1740s. Benjamin Borden, Sr., left 1,000 pounds of tobacco in 1744, and George Washington saw tobacco being grown while he was surveying for Lord Fairfax in 1748.[22] Benjamin Borden, Jr., having planted it in the

20. See B. H. Slicher Van Bath, *The Agrarian History of Western Europe, A.D. 500–1850,* trans. Olive Ordish (London: Edward Arnold, 1963), p. 263; G. E. Fussell and C. Goodman, "Crop Husbandry in Eighteenth-Century England," *Ag. Hist.* 16 (1942):49, 55.

21. See, for example, Frederick Co. Will Book 1:82, 276–77, 315, 418–19, 430.

22. Ibid., 1:39–40; George Washington, *Journal of My Journey over the Mountains . . . 1747–8,* ed. J. M. Toner (Albany, N.Y.: Joel Munsell's Sons, 1892), p. 24; Washington, *The Diaries of George Washington, 1748–1799,* ed. J. C. Fitzpatrick, 4 vols. (Boston and New York: Houghton Mifflin Co., 1925), 1:5.

lower valley, may have spread its cultivation to the upper valley. In 1745 he paid off part of a debt with one hogshead of tobacco weighing 913 pounds (excluding the cask), worth about £6 at current prices.[23] Tobacco was recorded in Augusta County primarily in debt suits, while it was frequently mentioned in Frederick County inventories in amounts up to 2,900 pounds.[24] Most tobacco was cultivated on only one or two acres of land, and the recorded yields of 1,000 to 1,500 pounds per man were about average for the period.[25] In 1755 in Augusta County commissioners were appointed to sell the tobacco due from taxes. However, probably only a small proportion of county taxes were ever actually paid in tobacco. The annual salary of Anglican clergy was set by law at 16,000 pounds of tobacco, but in 1753 the Virginia Assembly allowed these salaries in Augusta and Frederick parishes to be commuted in money instead, "because in both instances the parishes never make any tobacco."[26]

Another, though minor, example of the experimentation that occurred among early valley farmers was the cultivation of cotton. One Augusta settler left two and a half pounds of cotton in 1745, and in 1747 another farmer owned a small cotton patch on Linville Creek.[27] Although occasional references continued to be made to the plant during the colonial period, it never developed into an important crop.

The fact that the agricultural economy of the valley before the mid-1760s was largely one of general or mixed farming is attested to not only by the relative diversity of crops grown but also by the reports on livestock and livestock products. Horses and cattle were by far the most frequently mentioned farm animals. As pointed out earlier during the 1740s and 1750s, 94% of Augusta inventories and 91% of those for Frederick contained references to horses. Cattle were mentioned almost as frequently, in 80% of Augusta inventories and 83% of Frederick's. However, swine and sheep were more numerous in the lower valley, and this is reflected in livestock ratios for the 1740s and 1750s. In both parts of the valley cattle were the most numerous farm animals and sheep the least numerous, but in the lower valley swine far outnumbered horses, while the situation was

23. Benjamin Borden's account with Andrew Ross, July 1745, Augusta Judgments, 1745–46 (file 385); Gray, *History of Agriculture*, 1:272.

24. See, for example, William Pearce's account with Anthony Strothers, 1745–46, Augusta Judgments, 1747–48, (file 386), and Richard Cradock's account with James Bayard, 1740–42, Augusta Judgments, 1751 (file 389); and Frederick Co. Will Books 1: 405–8, 433–34, 2:78.

25. Augusta Co. Order Books 3:432, 6:356.

26. *Papers Relating to the History of the Church in Virginia, 1650–1776,* ed. W. S. Perry, 2 vols. (Richmond, 1870) 1:437.

27. Orange Co. Will Book 2:43, 67–68; Augusta Co. Survey Book 1:42.

reversed in the upper valley. Thus, in the upper valley cattle outnumbered horses by a ratio of 3:2, swine by 2:1, and sheep by 3:1, while in the lower valley the ratios were only 2:1, 1:1, and 2:1, respectively. Swine outnumbered sheep almost 2:1 in the lower valley and 4:3 in the upper valley; while sheep were a well-established component of lower valley agriculture by 1740, they only became significant in the upper valley during the 1750s.[28]

Livestock products, especially milk, butter, cheese, and wool, were frequently mentioned in early records, as was equipment associated with these products. Because the food products were all perishable, they rarely turned up in inventories. However, butter was often referred to in other records, and next to horses was the most frequently mentioned item in the early records for Beverley Manor. Other less recurrent livestock products included beef, tallow, bacon, pork, and lard; in view of Frederick County's many swine, it is surprising that the latter items did not appear more often in the records.

Two other livestock elements present in the valley throw some light on pioneer agriculture. Although most plows, wagons, and carts were pulled by horses, a few farmers owned a yoke of oxen; six Augusta inventories and three Frederick inventories mentioned oxen before 1760. A yoke was usually evaluated at £6 to £6 10s.[29] Beehives appeared in fifteen lower valley inventories but in only six in the upper valley; both honey and beeswax were produced in small quantities. Although rarely reported, chickens ("dunghill fowl") and geese were quite common, and ducks were also present.

Subsistence and Surplus on the Farm

On the whole, the diversified agriculture of the valley, with its emphasis on grain crops and flax, horses, cattle, and dairy products, does nothing to distract from the eighteenth-century pioneer stereotype. When the issue of agricultural surplus arises, however, the picture becomes much more complex, because it poses a whole series of questions about agricultural production and farm efficiency, dietary patterns, and household consumption levels for which there is little information.

28. Diary of the Reverend Robert Rose, June 1, 1751, p. 102, Colonial Williamsburg, Inc. Sheep were usually regarded as the least valuable of the major farm animals. During the 1750s, for example, a horse in Virginia was worth £4 to £8, a milk cow £1 10s. to £2, a pig 7s. to 10s., and a sheep 2s. 6d. to 4s.

29. Augusta Co. Will Books 1:208–9, 370–72, 527–28, 2:22–26, 333–34; Frederick Co. Will Books 1:10–13, 2:148–49, 208–10.

Actual data on household consumption patterns for the eighteenth century are rare, and conclusions must be tentative. From the calculations of Charles S. Grant and James T. Lemon, it would appear that the average annual consumption of a widow, as reflected in foodstuffs allotted to her in the family will, was about 150 pounds of meat (100 pounds of pork, 50 pounds of beef), 35 to 40 bushels of grain (about three times more wheat than corn), 4 or 5 bushels of vegetables, dairy production from 1 or 2 cows, fruit production from 6 or 7 trees, 3 or 4 barrels of cider and apple or peach brandy, the fleece of 2 sheep or 15 pounds of hackled flax or hemp.[30] For an average family of five persons, assuming a widow's share to be an adult's share, Lemon has calculated that the products of 4 horses, 5 cows, ½ steer, 5 pigs, and 8 sheep would be required annually. To support a family, 8 acres of arable land would be needed plus the output from an additional 35 acres for the support of livestock, together with 15 acres of pasture and between 15 and 20 acres of woodland pasture, for a total of 73 to 78 acres.[31] Grant has suggested that one person could be adequately supported from 9½ acres, including 2½ arable, which would add up to some 48 acres, with 12½ arable, for a family of five.[32] Lemon's estimates are based on relatively low yields per acre. He calculated on 10 bushels per acre for wheat and rye, 15 bushels for oats, and 20 bushels for corn, but these yields reflected an area that had been settled for two generations. Max G. Schumacher, in his study of northern farming during the late colonial period, estimated average wheat yields to be 10 to 15 bushels per acre, but reaching as high as 30 bushels per acre in newly cultivated areas.[33]

Areal variations in soil conditions, agricultural efficiency, and dietary preferences, as well as differences in the quality of available data, make it difficult to compare food production and consumption in different areas of eighteenth-century America. During the 1750s wheat was worth 2s. 6d. to 3s. per bushel in the valley, corn 1s. 6d. to 2s., rye 1s. 6d. to 1s. 8d., and barley and oats 1s. to 1s. 3d.[34] On the basis of these prices, some evaluation of

30. Lemon, "Household Consumption in Eighteenth-Century America," *Ag. Hist.* 41 (1967):68–69, and *Best Poor Man's Country*, pp. 155, 180–81; Grant, "History of Kent," pp. 62–65, 76–79. Lemon's conclusions were based on an analysis of 159 wills from Lancaster and Chester counties during the years 1740 to 1790. Grant used one 1757 will which he took to be representative. His estimate of pork and beef was 100 pounds higher than Lemon's and seems too high, especially since Pennsylvanians allegedly ate more meat than New Englanders or Southerners.

31. Lemon, "Household Consumption," *Ag. Hist.* 41 (1967):69.

32. Grant, "History of Kent," 62–69, 323–28.

33. Max G. Schumacher, "The Northern Farmer and His Markets during the Late Colonial Period" (Ph.D. diss., University of California, Berkeley, 1948), pp. 14–15.

34. Grain prices are derived from those quoted in Frederick Co. Will Books 1–2, Augusta Co. Will Books 1–2, and Augusta Judgments (files 388–402).

yields can be ascertained from the reports given in estate inventories. There is not enough information on barley and oats to make calculations worthwhile. For wheat, rye, and corn the available data suggest that yields in the valley were average to low for the period from 1740 to 1760. Wheat and rye yields ranged from 8 to 12 bushels per acre, averaging out to the same figure prevailing in the longer settled southeastern Pennsylvania. Corn yields varied from 12 to 17 bushels per acre, or an average of 5 bushels less than in southeastern Pennsylvania. Using these figures, plus a rough estimate of 12 bushels for oats and barley, Martin Kauffman's 17¾ acres of arable land in the upper valley in 1749 would have produced 80 bushels of wheat and rye, 75 bushels of corn, 36 bushels of oats, 9 bushels of barley, and about 200 to 250 pounds of flax. To keep an average family of five, he would have required 60 of his 80 bushels of wheat and rye, and his 27 horses, 19 cattle, 35 swine, and 17 sheep would have commanded his total output of corn, oats, and barley, as well as some 110 to 120 acres of pasture. His agricultural surplus would have consisted at most of about 20 bushels of wheat and rye, some of the flax, and the products of his livestock. Considering the fact that the average farmer during the 1750s was cultivating only about half of Kauffman's acreage and maintaining about one quarter of his livestock, there would seem to have been relatively little in the way of surplus livestock products and any specialized, non-feedstuff crop, such as flax, tobacco, or ginseng.[35]

Some modification of these calculations has to be made to fit the agricultural realities of the early Shenandoah Valley, especially with respect to livestock. The average sizes of the animals for which Lemon made calculations (600 to 700 pounds for cattle for example) are at least one-fifth larger than the typical animals being raised in the valley before 1760. Second, livestock raising in the region depended much more heavily on pasture, supplemented by hay, than on grain feedstuffs. Even if the largest recorded arable acreage of 30 acres had been sown entirely to oats and rye and yielded 15 bushels per acre, this would only have provided 450 bushels, sufficient to feed about half of Kauffman's stock. Moreover, yields and agricultural efficiency may have been higher in the lower valley during the pioneer period. The northern half of the valley was not only better endowed physically for agriculture, but its farmers appear to have been more progressive. Frederick and Augusta inventories frequently contained references to farm implements in addition to plows, especially hoes, mattocks, scythes, sickles, and grindstones, but references to the use of dung (about

---

35. The above calculations are based on Lemon's estimates for human food supply and a slightly reduced version of Grant's estimates of 3 acres annually per horse and 2 acres per cow, which may still be too high. See Grant, "History of Kent," pp. 76–79.

twenty-five inventories mentioned dung forks) or fertilizers were rare. The use of the cradle to harvest grain was evident in both parts of the valley by 1750, but it is more frequently mentioned in Frederick County during the 1750s and early 1760s.[36] The use of the windmill for cleaning grain was evident in Frederick County by the early 1750s, a decade before it is mentioned in the upper valley, and clover and timothy were being incorporated into improved pastures in the lower valley during the early 1750s, almost two decades before they were used widely in the rest of the valley.[37]

Differences in dietary patterns seem to have been of minor importance. In terms of meat consumption, pork and beef were by far the most significant items. Bacon was also important and deer meat (venison) was often used to supplement farm produce. Mutton was scarcely mentioned. There is no evidence to suggest that rye was cultivated more by Germans than by British settlers, nor that oats were most prevalent among the Scotch-Irish. Drinking habits seem to have been more excessive than in Pennsylvania or Connecticut, but evidence of cultural differentiation in the consumption of liquor is inconclusive. On his return from Staunton in 1751, the Reverend Robert Rose remarked that in the absence of claret he had consumed more whiskey than ever before in his life.[38] Philip Vickers Fithian expressed a similar sentiment almost twenty-five years later, giving the only good descriptions of dietary patterns in the valley for the late colonial period: "They have not, it is true, Coffee, Chocolate, nor many other of what is allow'd to be needful in polite Life—But they have Bread, Meat of many kinds, Milk, Butter, and Cheese, and all in great Plenty, and the best Quality . . . Large Platters covered with Meat of many Sorts; Beeff; Venison; Pork;—and with these Potatoes, Turnips, Cabbage, and Apple beyond your Asking."[39] These observations at least indicate what could be made available in western Virginia by the end of the colonial period.

Yet commercialism can not be measured simply by subtracting consumption from production to arrive at surplus, whether or not the amount of data is adequate, for that expresses only a quantitative measure of productivity and fails to address the question of motivation. Commercialism was the expression of a desire to produce surplus above and beyond subsistence levels and to respond quickly to opportunities for sale. The critical question is the extent to which the populations of frontier areas were content to rely on importing outside items from time to time with-

36. See Frederick Co. Will Book 1:409; Augusta Co. Will Book 1:136–39.
37. Frederick Co. Will Books 1:309, 3:68–70.
38. Rose, Diary, June 3, 1751, p. 102, Colonial Williamsburg, Inc.
39. Fithian, *Journal*, pp. 145, 151.

out developing their own economies and local market opportunities. A fact of commercial behavior in the transfer of one surplus commodity, land, has already been demonstrated. Why should behavior in the treatment of surplus commodities have been any different?

The Nature and Disposal of Surplus Products

Two sets of commercial opportunities were always available to local farmers: the immediate needs of new settlers in the region who had not yet harvested their first crop and the small but frequent demands of transients passing through the valley. Such disposal was highly localized, in the vicinity of newly established farms or along the main highways, and largely unrecorded. Moreover, as the Beverley Manor accounts indicate, many pioneer settlers paid for their land at least partially in kind, principally in horses or butter. Others paid their accounts in cash, which they either had brought with them to the region or they had obtained through the sale of agricultural products or land within the region. But throughout the 1740s and early 1750s, Moravian missionaries traveling through the valley often found it difficult to obtain extra food supplies, for themselves and their horses, from local settlers. When they did manage to buy supplies, it was usually in the form of a bushel of corn or oats at one farm and another bushel at another farm farther on.[40]

The processing of commodities produced from agriculture and hunting was being carried out at the same time as pioneer farming was being established. The nature and distribution of the mills established in the upper valley by 1760 is instructive in this regard. Jost Hite had built a gristmill on Opequon Creek in the lower valley by 1738, and there were at least 3 gristmills in the upper valley by 1740. William Beverley had a mill built on the future site of Staunton by 1740. By 1750 there were at least 34 gristmills in the upper valley, with notable concentrations in and around Staunton and along the upper reaches of the main Shenandoah River (fig. 20A). Ten years later there were some 60 mills, and by 1775 at least 100, including 13 within a five-mile radius of Augusta County Courthouse (figs. 20B and C). All but 6 of these colonial mills were gristmills, grinding wheat for flour. During the 1740s and early 1750s, almost all of this flour was made for local consumption.

With the increasing range and intensity of French and Indian hostilities

40. Hinke and Kemper, "Moravian Diaries of Travels through Virginia," *Va. Mag. Hist. Biog.* 2 (1904):134–53; *Travels in the American Colonies,* ed. Newton D. Mereness (New York: Macmillan Co., 1916), pp. 334–42.

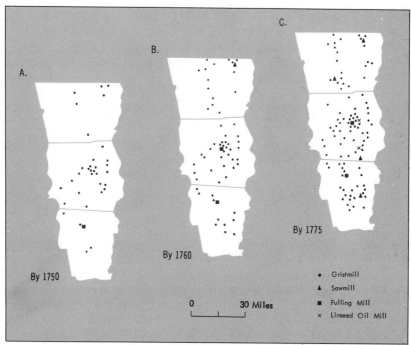

Fig. 20. Upper Shenandoah Valley: distribution of mills, 1740–75 (data from Orange County Order Books 1–4; Augusta County Order Books 1–6)

after 1754, settlers in the valley found a new market for their products which was brought, as it were, to their doorstep. Mounting military activities in western Virginia made it necessary to obtain regular food supplies for the colony's troops and Indian allies serving west of the Blue Ridge. Both Washington and Braddock used Winchester as a militia station during the war, and the troops accompanying them generated demands for food and drink from local townspeople and farmers. During the first nine months of 1757, Augusta County farmers supplied food and other goods worth over £320 for militia and Indians operating out of the southern Valley of Virginia.[41] This bill included 36 beef cattle, 41 beeves, (i.e. beef carcasses), about 8,300 pounds of beef, and 2,518 pounds of pork, as well as 480 bushels of wheat and about 10,450 pounds of flour (the product of some 250 to 260 bushels of wheat).

Although such demands hardly encouraged large-scale production, they

41. John Buchanan, An Account of Provisions, Aug. 29, 1757, Preston Papers, Va. Hist. Soc.; and Preston Papers, 1QQ142–145, 161, Draper Mss., Wis. State Hist. Soc.

did provide a ready market for agricultural produce for the next few years. At the same time, the movement of flour and bread from the Shenandoah Valley to forts between the James and New rivers proved a boon not only to local millers but also to wagoners. They were paid 2s. for every 100 pounds of flour they carried an average distance of forty miles. Flour and beef continued to be the main items supplied to the militia between 1758 and 1760. Fort Fauquier, on the south bank of the James near the present site of Buchanan, had a flour room which contained up to 5,400 pounds of flour a month during the year 1759.[42] These demands for basic foodstuffs for militia and Indians undoubtedly encouraged local farmers to grow more wheat and slaughter more beef cattle and swine during the period of the French and Indian War than they had done previously.

By 1760 the upper valley also maintained two fulling mills and at least one sawmill. The paucity of sawmills seems surprising considering the need for lumber for construction purposes. Only four were specifically mentioned in the county records by the end of the colonial period, and none before 1755. Three of them were located at the foot of the Blue Ridge close to a major source of wood supply, while the fourth was on the north fork of the North River (see fig. 20). None were reported in the vicinity of Staunton. One possible explanation is that some gristmills may have been converted to sawmills during the spring and early summer, since changing the milling operation from grinding grain to cutting wood was a relatively simple if rather expensive operation.

The two fulling mills for finishing cloth were an index of an equally necessary, but seemingly more thriving, industry. Although a variety of crafts were practiced in the upper valley by the early 1760s, by far the most commercially important was the production of textiles. Linen manufacture from flax was the most prevalent skilled occupation, with woolen manufacture a distant second. As early as 1739 Governor Gooch reported that "the common people in all parts of the colony and indeed many of the better sort are lately got into the use of looms, weaving coarse cloth for themselves and for the negroes. And our new inhabitants on the other side of the mountains make very good linen which they sell up and down the country."[43] Amounts of linen cloth recorded in inventories and sales during the 1740s indicate that some settlers possessed up to seventy-five yards, which at the prevailing price of 1s. 3d. per yard would have been worth almost £4 15s. By 1750 there were at least half a dozen weavers living in Beverley Manor, and the linen trade appeared promising enough

42. Preston Papers 2QQ15 and 20, Draper Mss., Wis. State Hist. Soc.
43. Percy S. Flippin, "William Gooch: Successful Royal Governor of Virginia," *Wm. and Mary Qtly.*, 2d ser. 5 (1925):240.

to encourage Solen Hays to build a fulling mill as well as a gristmill on Moffett's Creek in northern Rockbridge County between 1747 and 1749.[44] By 1751 one had been built in Staunton and another located on the Roanoke River in present-day Roanoke County.[45] So much enthusiasm for linen manufacture was engendered at this time that a petition was sent to the House of Burgesses "for allowing a greater Premium to the Linen Manufacturers than they have now."[46] It was rejected, and that seems to have dampened the enthusiasm for large-scale production at this time. Most of the craftsmen associated with the early linen industry were of Scotch-Irish origin and had learned their trade in Ulster. It was the presence of this national group which gave the upper Shenandoah Valley a reputation for linen production. Linen remained largely a small-scale, domestic industry supplying coarse cloth and clothing for local consumption. Very little linen or woolen cloth was involved in the external trading ventures conducted by Augusta county settlers before 1760.

The Cattle Trade

In a region which was located west of the Blue Ridge, on a river with limited navigability, and at some distance from large markets, one would expect the earliest major commercial contracts with the outside world to be developed through the cattle trade. Beef was always in demand in eastern urban areas for local consumption or for export to the West Indies, and cattle provided their own transportation. Though a cattle trade could not be built up overnight, there were indications of some developments before 1742. In June of that year, Augusta County petitioned the House of Burgesses to impose a duty "on all Horses and cattle drove thro' the said Inhabitants, from the Northern or Southern Provinces."[47] It was from more southerly areas that the settlers of the Shenandoah Valley were first exposed to the cattle trade, and perhaps in a negative manner, as the petition hints, through drivers from Southside Virginia or the North Carolina Piedmont who were moving northward to Pennsylvania and collecting a few local cattle on the way. In September 1742, a court case brought by a Maryland merchant against one valley settler could not proceed because the defendant

44. Augusta Co. Order Book 2:297; Augusta Co. Deed Book 4:392–99.
45. Augusta Co. Order Book 2:585–86.
46. Ibid., 3:242, and *Journals of the House of Burgesses,* ed. McIlwaine and Kennedy, 9:52.
47. *Journals of the House of Burgesses,* ed. McIlwaine and Kennedy, 7:56. Farmers in southeastern Pennsylvania were complaining about Virginia cattle drives by 1747 (Lemon, *Best Poor Man's Country,* p. 161).

"was gone to Carolina for Cattle."[48] Livestock drives from the south continued to pass through the Valley of Virginia to Philadelphia during the 1740s, and drivers no doubt added to their herds on their trips northward through the valley.

The more northerly settlers had the advantage of being closer to the Philadelphia market and no doubt organized their own drives, although the record is not explicit on the matter. Many valley farmers may not have owned enough steers to participate in such drives; Augusta County inventories indicate potentially larger supplies than in Frederick County. Through the early 1760s the ratio of steers to total cattle maintained by the average farmer was about 1:4, and in both counties the average number of cattle owned by propertied farmers was fourteen, so that only three of these animals were likely to be steers. At least one of these steers would be slaughtered each year to provide beef for the family. Of the inventories containing references to cattle before 1760, 17% in Augusta County (36) and 12% in Frederick County (33) owned more than twenty cattle. Only these few settlers would have been able to supply ten to twenty steers to the northward drives.

Settlers in the upper valley began to organize their own drives during the early 1750s. James Patton was active in this enterprise and tried to collect 200 cattle by accepting payment of debts to him in the form of "Black or Fatt cows" at 12s. 6d. per 100 pounds.[49] Whatever steps were taken at this time to conduct local cattle drives to northern markets were interrupted by the French and Indian hostilities after 1754, and cattle which might otherwise have been taken north were slaughtered locally to supply fresh or salted beef for the militia and the Cherokees.

Even before the end of the war local settlers had begun to conduct their own independent cattle drives again. In 1758 two Augusta settlers, James Leister and John Givens, whose partnership as retail traders had failed, decided to go into the cattle business and drive cattle to Pennsylvania. They found the Pennsylvania markets not up to expectations and decided to slaughter the cattle there, barrel them, and send them via Philadelphia to the West Indies. They seem to have sold the barrels of beef at a profit, for they returned to the valley in 1759 with a large assortment of goods from Philadelphia.[50] Leister and Givens received financial help from two local merchants, and this became a common financial arrangement.[51]

William Crow, a Staunton merchant, was the most important cattle

48. Orange Co. Order Book 3:241.

49. James Patton to William Preston, undated (but ca. 1753), Preston Papers, Va. Hist. Soc.

50. James Leister v. John Givens, 1761, Augusta Judgments, 1762 (file 404).

51. See William Boone v. Campbell, Moore, and Walker, ibid., 1772 (file 422).

dealer in the Shenandoah Valley during the late 1750s and early 1760s. He and a few associates organized regular cattle drives to the north. If there was not a sufficient market for them in Winchester, they drove their herd, by then usually 150 to 200 head, to Philadelphia and sold the cattle there.[52] Considerable profit derived from this trade. In 1762 Crow bought 50 cattle in the upper valley at 14s. per 100 pounds and expected to sell them for 40s. per 100 pounds, or almost 200% profit. Crow and his drivers often came in for criticism because it was believed that they were pilfering other settlers' cattle on their northward drives. The cattle trade as an organized enterprise declined markedly after the mid-1760s. Crow seems to have moved to Botetourt County about 1764, and cattle rearing was already being replaced by other commercial activities.

The Early Road Network

The movement of cattle to northern markets did not as a rule cause new drive roads to be blazed through the valley. The cattle drives made use of the developing road network west of the Blue Ridge, particularly the main Indian trail which was made into the Great Wagon Road from Philadelphia during the decade after 1745 (fig. 21). This road formed the backbone of the highway system that developed in the southern interior, and along it linear patterns of rural settlement and nodes of urban settlement were established. During the 1730s and 1740s much of this highway within the Shenandoah Valley remained nothing more than a trail along which wagon transportation was extremely difficult, if not impossible. As late as 1753 Moravian missionaries were informed by settlers in the lower valley that they would not be able to proceed beyond Augusta Courthouse. This they found to be true. "Immediately beyond Augusti Court House the bad road began, it was up hill and down and we had constantly to push the wagon or hold it back by ropes."[53] Despite the fact that this road through the Valley of Virginia as far as the New River had been authorized as a public road since 1745, few major improvements were made in the original trail south of Staunton before 1755.[54] It was not

52. Ibid., Sept. 1760, and Feb. 1762 (file 407), Mar. 1764 (file 413), and Aug. 1767 (file 415). Hart has claimed that Crow also drove cattle to Fort Pitt and to eastern Virginia (*Valley of Virginia*, p. 12) but there is no indication of this in the judgment reference which he gave.

53. Hinke and Kemper, "Moravian Diaries," *Va. Mag. Hist. Biog.* 12 (1904): 143–47; Mereness, *Travels in the American Colonies*, p. 338.

54. For information on roads, see Edward G. Roberts, "The Roads of Virginia, 1607–1840" (Ph.D. diss., University of Virginia, 1950).

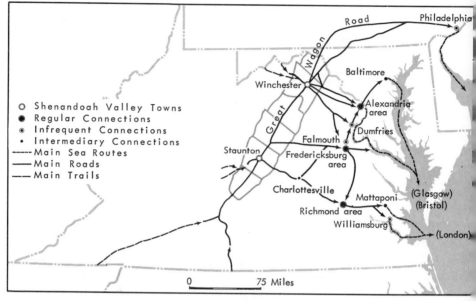

Fig. 21. Trading connections of the Shenandoah Valley by 1760 (data from Augusta Judgments and Orders, 1745–60; Bliss, *Tuckahoe in the Valley*; Coulter, *Virginia Merchant*; Roberts, *Roads of Virginia, 1607–1840*; Thomson, *Merchant in Virginia, 1700–1775*)

until the early 1760s that the road became extensively used by wagon traffic.

One reason for the general lag in improving the road was the paucity of settlement, particularly south of Lexington, and thus the lack of available labor, until after 1760. Moreover, in the period of pioneer settlement, it was difficult to impose and collect enough taxes to pay for construction. The location and construction of roads were under jurisdiction of the county court, the members of which ordered new roads to be built when and where they thought necessary. The county was laid out in precincts, to each of which was allotted a part of the road system. The tithables in each precinct were responsible for the construction and maintenance of the roads, and road conditions often varied greatly from one precinct to another.

Despite the long-term significance of the Great Wagon Road, the earliest efforts to develop external contacts concentrated on building roads west to east rather than north to south. The inhabitants of the lower Shenandoah Valley led this activity during the 1730s and 1740s. As early as 1736 there was a petition from the lower valley settlers complaining that they had no road to trade with eastern Virginia and wished one to be built over the Blue Ridge from the forks of the Shenandoah through Chester Gap (see fig. 7).[55] This road was begun in 1737 and was soon followed by others. Settlers in Beverley Manor made their first requests two years later, and soon a road was being cleared through Rockfish Gap which eventually linked Staunton with Richmond.[56] Despite the proliferation of additional road requests, the Orange County court gave most encouragement to the road through Ashby's Gap, which was to run through the future site of Winchester, and petitions to continue this road westward to the upper reaches of the Potomac were presented as early as 1742. During the 1740s and early 1750s road building in the lower Shenandoah Valley was conducted at a much faster pace than in the upper valley. By 1755 Winchester was the most important route center linking western with eastern Virginia. Three roads from eastern Virginia via Ashby's, Snicker's and Gregory's gaps, focused on Winchester, while farther north a branch road went through Vestal's Gap. These roads, capable of taking wagons, linked the lower valley to the markets of Alexandria, Dumfries, Falmouth, and Fredericksburg.

Local road building in the upper valley went on at a constant pace during the 1740s and early 1750s, although this often meant little more than clearing a trail and leveling the rougher areas. The county courthouse in Staunton was a focal point for roads. Secondary focuses were mills, meetinghouses, churches, and ferries. Major rivers were crossed by ferries, but because many local roads were no more than bridle trails along which one traveled on horseback, fords were the most common way of crossing streams. Road connections between the upper valley and eastern Virginia by 1755 were neither so centralized nor so well developed as in the lower valley. Settlers in the upper valley were working under greater physical constraints—gaps in the Blue Ridge were higher and more difficult to negotiate, and the region was located farther from the main trading centers of eastern Virginia. These handicaps were particularly acute for the inhabitants of the future Rockbridge County, and for wagon transportation they had to travel up to Rockfish Gap. The road from Staunton to this gap was completed early in 1747, and Augusta County officials asked the House of Burgesses that it be joined as quickly as possible with the road leading to Fredericksburg.[57] But the upper valley was working under a further constraint, for Piedmont counties were less inclined to acknowledge

55. Orange Co. Court Judgments, 1735, as cited in John F. Dorman, *Orange County, Virginia, Deed Books 1 and 2, 1735–1738, Judgments, 1735* (Washington D.C., 1961), p. 72.

56. Orange Co. Order Book 2:3.

57. Augusta Co. Order Book 1:175.

the need for road links with the upper valley, and several of these Augusta County requests failed to elicit response.[58]

The decade after 1755 saw the completion of several important east-west links as well as an expansion of roads south and west of the Shenandoah Valley. By 1765 a road had been built through Manassas Gap, giving Winchester and the lower valley four important connections with eastern Virginia. A road through Swift Run Gap was joined to the Charlottesville-Fredericksburg road, giving the upper valley two important links with eastern Virginia. Moreover, trails were completed through Thornton's Woods's, and James River gaps, providing additional eastern contacts. The military activities conducted during the French and Indian War hastened new road building in the west. In particular, the military roads built west of Winchester further strengthered that town's reputation as the major route center of western Virginia. The road between Winchester and Fort Cumberland on the Potomac, which was well established by 1756, was extended northwestward to Fort Pitt and became Virginia's main road link with the upper Ohio Valley.

External Trading Contacts

The inhabitants of the Shenandoah Valley, while primarily subsistent during the first decade of settlement, were far from self-sufficient. Indeed, the most prominent characteristic of their early trading patterns was the evident desire to establish contacts with outside markets. Settlers wished to obtain a variety of goods from the outside world, both necessities and luxuries. To do so, of course, they had to sell or trade off their surplus products. During the pioneer occupance phase, as demonstrated earlier, surplus products were not available on a regular basis until after 1750. Before that time over 90% of all farm products were used for subsistence. By the mid-1760s 25% of the average valley farmer's output was available for trade, and some farmers in the northern part of the valley between Winchester and the Potomac probably had an even larger surplus. Physical and locational conditions certainly favored the lower valley over the rest of the region; however, time and circumstances have not, because few records have survived to permit a detailed reconstruction of its trading structure and mercantile activities.

The most critical import into the valley during the colonial period was salt, for domestic use and the preservation of meat and butter. Most of the salt brought in during the pioneer period came from Philadelphia, with

58. See ibid., 2:381, 4:257.

small orders being supplied from Fredericksburg and Alexandria. It was an expensive item to buy; from the Virginia towns it was purchased at 4s. per bushel during the 1740s and 1750s, but over the longer haul from Philadelphia it could cost as much as 7s.[59] In addition to salt, cloth, rum, and sugar were mentioned often in early trading accounts. Since only coarse linen and woolen cloths were made in the valley, a wide variety of higher-quality cloths was imported. Irish linen, shalloon (a twilled woolen fabric mainly used for linings), silk, osnaburg, and check were most in demand. A variety of clothing was also imported, especially hats, shoes, coats, and breeches. Presumably these were of higher quality than homemade clothes. Rum and sugar were by far the most frequently imported food and drink items. Both were transported in bulk; it was common for a local merchant to import 200 to 250 pounds of sugar and 100 to 150 gallons of run at a time.[60] After these items a large number of smaller goods were always in demand. In order of frequency, the more important of these were powder and shot, knives, buttons, nails, paper, pins, and bar iron. The last, the heaviest of all the most commonly sought items, was imported in amounts ranging from one to five hundredweight at 35s. per hundredweight.[61]

These items could be imported from eastern or northern markets in one of three ways. Probably the most common, and least recorded, method was bringing goods in by packhorses. Much of the initial trade with eastern Virginia was based on this means of transportation. Individuals operating the pack trade would often be the intermediaries between a group of valley residents and the eastern merchant. In 1740 one of these local traders, who imported goods from several eastern merchants, was charged with breaking the Sabbath by traveling "with loaded horses" to the upper valley.[62]

While the pack trade meant that some effort had to be made by valley settlers to obtain needed commodities, the itinerant peddler brought the smaller items of trade to the valley itself. Peddlers were active there by the

59. Since the Frederick judgments appear not to be extant, most of the data on trading activities through the early 1760s are derived from Augusta Judgments (files 385–414), supplemented by occasional references in other county records and private manuscripts (especially the William Allason Papers, Va. State Lib., and the Thomas and Francis Walker Papers, Lib. Cong.).

60. See, for example, William Pearce's account with Anthony Strothers (1745–1746), Augusta Judgments, 1747–48 (file 386), and Hugh Hay's account with Isaac Hislop (1763), ibid., 1763–64 (file 407).

61. James Bartley's account with George Mifflin (1753–38), ibid., 1745–46 (file 385). Bartley appears to have bought over 3 tons of iron and 360 pounds of Bristol and London steel from Mifflin, a Philadelphia merchant. The total bill came to more than £111. It is possible that this judgment reflected past debts incurred in Pennsylvania.

62. Orange Co. Order Book 2:280.

late 1730s and remained prominent in the Virginia backcountry throughout most of the eighteenth century.[63] Most of the peddlers who frequented the valley during the colonial period operated from supply bases in southeastern Pennsylvania.[64] Particularly during the pioneer period in western Virginia, peddlers played an important role by filling in gaps in the trading network in areas where there were no country stores. On the other hand, as outsiders and competitors, they incurred the animosity of botn the Virginia government and local merchants. During Governor Gooch's administration (1728-49), laws were passed to have peddlers licensed, a recurring practice thereafter, and to make them pay excessively high license fees, which they generally managed to avoid.[65] In 1764 a group of Winchester merchants complained about the encroachment of peddlers on the local trading activities and requested that they be banned from Virginia.[66]

The third, and increasingly the most important, trade was the wagon trade. Some form of cart transportation must have been available from an early date; heavy or bulky items such as iron, lead, and salt could hardly have been carried by any other means. Because of the initial use of the north-south route through the valley and its early improvement as far as Staunton, the earliest wagon and cart traffic used this road to obtain heavy goods from Philadelphia. Wagon transportation between Winchester and its eastern Virginia trading centers was possible by the late 1740s, but it only became feasible from Staunton to the east after 1755.

The organization of the backcountry trade in the Shenandoah Valley was dominated by the frontier merchant and the country storekeeper. During the early development of the region's commerce these two functions were embodied in the same man. Moreover, the country store as it appeared before the early 1760s was little more than a remodeled room or two in the settler's house. Only in Winchester and Staunton were stores gradually built as separate buildings or at least as the dominant part of an individual dwelling. The country store performed three main functions for local settlers. It was generally the only source of goods from the outside world; it operated as a market for local farm surplus, which was used to pay for

---

63. Ibid., p. 76.

64. For example, in 1759 Archibald Cunningham, a peddler from Lancaster County, Pennsylvania, was charged with owing Philip Benezet, a Philadelphia merchant, almost £86. See the bond of Archibald Cunningham (1759), Augusta Judgments, 1763 (file 405).

65. Gooch to Board of Trade, P.R.O., C.O.5/1326, Lib. Cong. Transcripts. See also Calvin B. Coulter, Jr., "The Virginia Merchant" (Ph.D. diss., Princeton University, 1944), p. 37; Robert P. Thomson, "The Merchant in Virginia, 1700–1775" (Ph.D. diss., University of Wisconsin, 1955), pp. 134–35.

66. *Journals of the House of Burgesses,* ed. McIlwaine and Kennedy, 10:250.

accounts within a trading system always characterized by a shortage of actual money; and it functioned as the most reliable source of credit, generally on a relatively long-term basis.[67] Most pioneer storekeepers were farmer-merchants who lacked trading contacts with the outside world. Before 1750 such men as Patrick Gillespie, James Ross, and Robert White near Winchester, Moses Thompson and Andrew Johnston in Beverley Manor, and John McDowell in Borden's Tract operated in this manner.[68] However, to obtain goods from outside markets, wealthier or more enterprising individuals made their own external contacts, or several settlers banded together and made contacts with eastern merchants. This latter method remained quite common throughout the colonial period, and perhaps more than any other form of trading connection best expresses the decentralized patterns of trade that existed. Thus, for example, at least seven or eight settlers in Borden's Tract had accounts with Andrew Berkeley, a merchant in Henrico County during the early 1740s. During the early 1760s over a score of farmers in the upper valley maintained accounts with Patrick Coutts and John Cross, a Richmond partnership, mostly for amounts under £5.[69]

The development of specialized resident merchants who kept stores began in the late 1740s. Felix Gilbert had a store in Staunton by 1748, and he was soon followed by Israel Christian. Both of these men began to acquire regular connections with eastern Virginia merchants during the early 1750s.[70] The vicinity of the county courthouse was the most logical place to establish a store. The periodic meetings of the county court brought people, especially the wealthier and more powerful county settlers into town, where they could conduct business affairs after taking care of official matters. Moreover, early road building was focused on the courthouses, providing both Winchester and Staunton with better transport connections than elsewhere. Staunton was the only place in the upper valley during the colonial period at which major trading activities were conducted, and this function did not come easily to the settlement. As early as 1749 a petition was sent to the General Assembly requesting that the town of Staunton be established and that annual fairs be set up, but Staunton had to wait until

67. For an extensive exploration of pioneer merchanting, see the works of Lewis E. Atherton: *The Pioneer Merchant in Mid-America,* University of Missouri Studies, vol. 14 (Columbia, Mo., 1939); *The Southern Country Store, 1800-1860* (Baton Rouge: Louisiana State University Press, 1949); and "The Services of the Frontier Merchant," *Miss. Valley Hist. Rev.* 24 (1937):153-70.

68. Augusta Judgments, 1745-46 (file 385); Augusta Co. Deed Book 2:397; Frederick Co. Will Books 1:152-54, 2:46-51, 160-62.

69. Augusta Judgments (files 386, 404).

70. Ibid. (files 387, 393).

1762 for such official recognition, nine years after Winchester. By 1764 at least five well-established merchants or partnerships were operating out of stores in Staunton, and probably more than that number were resident in Winchester. They represented the most centralized aspect of frontier trade. Not only did they gradually build up trading contacts with eastern and northern merchants; it was they in turn who supplied goods to the other two merchandising elements in the local trading network, the more isolated country storekeepers dispersed throughout the valley and the growing number of tavern and ordinary keepers located along the major highways. Yet much local trade was not closely associated with these urban centers. As was pointed out earlier, some farmers maintained their own contacts with outside merchants, so that they did not have to depend on goods redistributed from Winchester and Staunton.[71]

Valley merchandising involved small amounts of goods and payment in money, kind, or services. Few accounts were for more than £10, and they usually involved the buying of sundry domestic goods, sugar, cloth, nails, liquor, and ammunition. Only a small proportion of the total bill was actually paid in cash. Nevertheless, half of all the local accounts examined for the period from 1740 to 1765 involved a cash payment of some amount. Some customers were in the habit of paying cash and some in kind. In one third of these accounts cash represented more than 50% of the payments that had been made. Another third largely involved payment in kind, from skins and hides to wheat and horses. Accounts paid mainly in services comprised the remaining third.

In external trade, accounts could rarely be paid in services (except for wagoning) and were almost entirely made in cash and local produce. A wide variety of produce was exported from the valley in partial payment of trading debts to eastern and northern merchants. Butter was by far the most common item. Although it was generally exported in small amounts less than fifty pounds, some individuals exported several hundredweights at a time.[72] Tobacco was another valuable export, especially from the lower valley. As early as 1752 Frederick County joined four northern Piedmont counties in petitioning for an additional tobacco inspection point at Falmouth, although warehouses in the Alexandria area were actually the nearest markets for this commodity.[73] In 1759 George Washington produced 16,056 pounds of "best mountain sweetscented tobacco" on his estate in Berkeley County and, together with Lord Fairfax, sent his tobacco via

71. See the comments on decentralized trade in Merrens, *Colonial North Carolina,* pp. 169–70.

72. Augusta Judgments, 1756 (file 398), 1763–64 (file 407).

73. *Journals of the House of Burgesses,* eds. McIlwaine and Kennedy, 10:11.

either Alexandria or Falmouth to Bristol, England.[74] Other items sent east or north included horses, beef, whiskey, cider, tallow, cheese, and small amounts of wheat, as well as deer and elk skins, shoe thread, twine, and shoe leather.

Most of the accounts that valley farmers and merchants had with outside merchants were for amounts ranging between £5 and £30. In Augusta County the largest account recorded before the mid-1760s was Israel Christian's 1758 account with W. Dickenson and Company of Williamsburg for over £816, mainly for cloth and sugar.[75] Samuel and Walter Cowdon ran up a bill of more than £387 with Jeremiah Warder of Philadelphia in 1761 and 1762.[76] Thomas Fulton, a Staunton tavern owner, had accounts with three Fredericksburg merchants for the years 1760 and 1761 that totaled £225, largely for rum and wine, and also for salt and sugar.[77]

The majority of the upper valley's early trading connections were with the Fredericksburg and Richmond areas, although connections were made with a large number of other centers. Of the nine accounts examined for the 1730s and 1740s, five were with Fredericksburg area merchants and only one with a Richmond area merchant. The three earliest accounts were with the Philadelphia area.[78] During the 1750s and early 1760s trading ventures became more extensive and represented both a further search for markets and some consolidation of the region's commercial links with Fredericksburg and Richmond. Fredericksburg continued to be the main trading center of upper valley merchants, and no fewer than ten merchants or merchant partnerships from that town had clients in the upper valley.[79] Richmond's interests in the valley trade at this time

74. *Writings of George Washington,* ed. Ford, 2:160, 330, 338.

75. Augusta Judgments, 1759–60 (file 402).

76. Ibid., 1765 (file 410). The account was for "sundries."

77. Ibid., 1763–64 (file 407). The Fredericksburg merchants were Anthony Strothers, Robert and James Duncanson and Co., and the Fraser and Wright Co.

78. Ibid., 1745–55 (files 385–95). Hughen Mathews had an account for rum and punch with James MacCuan of Sussex-on-Delaware in 1732–33; James Bartley's account for iron and steel with George Mifflin of Philadelphia has already been discussed; and Richard Cradock had a large account during the years 1740–42 with James Bayard of Cecil County, Md., for sundries, nails and cloth. The dates of these accounts make it probable that most of them were opened before the individuals moved to Augusta County.

Merchants working out of Fredericksburg with interests in the trade of the upper valley were Anthony Strothers, Alex Wright (who speculated in Staunton town lots), Pendleton and Clayton, and Richard Bernard of Stafford County. The Richmond area was represented by Andrew Berkeley of Henrico County.

79. These merchants were Anthony Strothers, Isaac Hislop, Fraser and Wright, Fraser and Strachan, George McCall, Nicholas Smyth, Woodrow and Ramsay, Robert and James Duncanson, Charles Yates, and Peter How.

appear to have been represented mainly by the firm of Coutts and Cross, although it was as late as 1759 before they made any serious attempt to attract customers.[80] They had over twenty clients by 1761, but a store which they established in Staunton failed within a year.[81] Competition from local merchants probably led to this failure.

A similar venture was being conducted about the same time in the lower valley. William Allason, a Scottish factor who had established a store at Falmouth around 1757, sent his brother to set up a store near Winchester in 1761. Although the venture failed after eleven months because of less than anticipated sales and unreliable payments, Allason, like Coutts and Cross in the upper valley, retained many of his 155 clients, who traded directly with his store in Falmouth.[82] Among the most prominent were Lord Fairfax and Isaac Zane, Jr. The presence of Fairfax and his small entourage at Greenway court added a demand for luxury items which had no parallel in the upper valley. However, Allason operated more as a freight agent for Fairfax than as a merchant, for he generally arranged for the direct, periodic shipment of British goods through Falmouth to the Fairfax residences in Frederick County. Tobacco, leather goods, hats and stockings, cheese, and deerskins were the most common items sent to Falmouth by his valley customers. Most of his customers had accounts of between £15 and £30.

The spottiness of the data for the lower valley should not disguise the fact that Alexandria was probably the most frequently used market center for lower valley trade during the pioneer period. Alexandria, Falmouth, and Fredericksburg in that order were the focal points of this northern commercial activity, while Richmond area merchants seem to have focused almost entirely farther south. Although valley settlers had also a number of contacts with the Piedmont, the activities of Piedmont merchants in Shenandoah Valley trade were largely preempted by or controlled through the trading operations of the fall-line towns. For example, as a result of his surveying, military, and political activities in the valley between 1755 and 1761, Dr. Thomas Walker of Albermarle County attracted an important clientele from the region for his mercantile and financial services during the remainder of the colonial period, but most of the actual trans-

80. Augusta Judgments (file 404). In addition, four other outside merchants had dealings with the upper valley but their location was not given. Three of them, Thomas Underwood, Johnson and Branch, and Andrew Johnson, seem to have been from Richmond.

81. Augusta Co. Order Book 7:71.

82. A considerable amount of information on trading conditions in the lower valley is contained in the William Allason Papers (1752–75), Va. State Lib. Allason actually did about £1,000's worth of business during the 11-month operation of the store.

actions were made through Walker's account in Fredericksburg.[83] Williamsburg was the only Tidewater settlement which valley settlers used with any frequency.[84]

For scarce items such as iron, the highest-quality cloth, china, rum, and wine, few Virginia markets would suffice, and contacts with Philadelphia and Great Britain were required. It was in these markets that the largest debts were incurred by valley merchants. In 1757 Samuel Moore in Augusta County owed Mathias Bush of Philadelphia almost £133 on his account.[85] Of Samuel and Walter Cowdon's £387 account with Jeremiah Warden in 1761 and 1762, only £124 10s. had been paid by 1765, and Samuel Wilson and Thomas Hughart still owed Samuel Hudson of Philadelphia almost £73 in 1762 on a total bill of £107, the value of the high-quality cloth they had purchased from him three years earlier.[86] Contacts with British firms in Glasgow, Bristol, and London were made through eastern ports, especially Philadelphia and Alexandria, and to a minor degree through Baltimore and Falmouth.[87] Winchester was clearly much better placed to trade with these centers than Staunton. But the difficulty of collecting debt payments in the backcountry led some merchants to demand a considerable amount of advanced payment on larger purchases. George McCall, a Spotsylvania County merchant operating out of Fredericksburg, charged advances as high as 85% on large orders. This was 10% higher than the Glasgow firm of Andrew Cochrane and Company charged merchants from the valley who traded with them.[88]

83. Thomas and Francis Walker Papers, Boxes 162–64, Manuscript Div., Lib. Cong. Walker had accounts with at least five valley merchants, Alexander Boyd, Israel Christian, Robert Gamble, Felix Gilbert, and Sampson Mathews. In 1761 Felix Gilbert bought 21 slaves in Fredericksburg partly by borrowing £200 (sterling) from Walker's account (Gilbert to Thomas Walker, July 16, 1761, ibid., Box 162).

84. Israel Christian's account of over £816 with the Williamsburg firm of Dickenson and Co. not only included a large variety of cloths and over 800 pounds of sugar from Williamsburg, but also almost £100's worth of "sundries" from Newcastle, Del. (Augusta Judgments, file 403). William Cowne, a Mattaponi merchant with ties in London, had some trade with the upper valley (ibid., file 393), as did the Warwick firm of Chapman and Chamney.

85. Ibid. (file 407).

86. Ibid. (files 407, 410).

87. In 1751 the Glasgow firm of Andrew Cochrane and Co. supplied two Augusta settlers with cloth and small domestic items through their agent in Fredericksburg, and in 1753 the Glasgow partnership of Andrew Cochrane and James Murdoch supplied five Augusta County inhabitants with small amounts of goods through William Lusk, who may have operated out of Baltimore (ibid., files 392, 397). Williams Givens owed Alexander Spiers and John Bowman of Glasgow £46 10s. on his accounts with them before 1762 (ibid., file 408).

88. Ibid. (files 392, 410).

The early search for markets, characterized by small-scale trade by individual settlers with a large number of widely distributed centers in Virginia, Maryland, and Pennsylvania, appears to have been out of all proportion to the generally localized, limited commercial capabilities of early agriculture.[89] Yet by the late 1740s there was already a concentration of external contacts in Alexandria for the lower valley and Fredericksburg for the upper valley. Falmouth developed into an important rival for valley trade during the late 1750s and early 1760s, while Richmond's influence, limited as it was, was directed mainly at the upper valley. Contacts were also sustained with Philadelphia, although earlier writers have probably exaggerated its influence at the expense of the Virginia fall-line towns. At the same time, well-established contacts had been created by the early 1760s with British markets, and the Shenandoah Valley, if as yet only on the extreme western margins of the colonial mercantile system, was intimately affected by the activities of the Atlantic trading world.

89. For some theoretical comments on the development of tributary trading areas, see R. G. Golledge, "Conceptualizing the Market Decision Process," *Journal of Regional Science* 7, supplement (1967):239–58.

6 Specialization: Agricultural Development

In 1752 a letter appeared in the *Virginia Gazette* admonishing the colony for its neglect of the large numbers of religious dissenters settling in the Shenandoah Valley and requesting that they be granted religious freedom. Part of the letter stated:

The particular Case I refer to, is that of the Presbyterians in the Frontier Counties of this Colony. . . . Augusta, the largest County perhaps in Virginia, is almost wholly settled by them. . . . tho' they are Dissenters, they have as much Religion as renders them good Subjects, and entitles them to an extensive Toleration. They are also a laborious People, and very much improve the Colony. As the Products of their Land and their Manufactures are different from those of the Virginians, they strengthern the Colony in its weakest Parts, and furnish us with those Necessaries and Accomodations which our eternal Piddling about the Sovereign Weed Tobacco, hinders us from providing in sufficient Plenty.[1]

The writer, although prophetic in his own time, could not have foreseen how accurate his economic estimates would be a decade or so later.

The processes of agricultural change that occurred in the valley between the early 1760s and the beginnings of the nineteenth century reflected the enormous strides that were made in economic development and regional interdependence. All the elements of the changing agricultural geography of the valley during the eighteenth century reflect changes in the degree of commercialism present rather than a complete reorientation from subsistence to commercialism. The pioneer phase of development might be termed as one of predominantly unspecialized farming accompanied by an emerging commercialism and extensive external contacts. The early postpioneer phases of development were founded upon increasing commercialism and specialization in the agricultural sector of the economy, accompanied by substantial but slower population growth and by the expansion and intensification of manufacturing and service activities. Although these economic divisions are functionally interrelated, it is useful for understanding the developmental implications of economic change to distinguish between agricultural and nonagricultural sectors.

The timing of the postpioneer transition was determined by the links between the external forces encouraging change and the internal predisposi-

1. Park's *Virginia Gazette* (Williamsburg), Mar. 5, 1752.

tion for change as reflected in the settlers' actions themselves. The mid-1760s saw the beginnings of sustained interest in the lower Shenandoah Valley by eastern Virginia planters as well as the first large-scale commitment to commercial agriculture by farmers throughout the valley. These trends were associated with the economic fluctuations of the 1760s, especially the decline in tobacco prices and the search for viable alternatives in eastern Virginia. However, the mid-1760s did not mark any major break in development. What did occur was an increasing rate of involvement in commercial activities to the point that commitments were rapidly made to distinct agricultural specialties. This specialization had important geographical repercussions on the changing emphasis between crop farming and livestock husbandry, on land utilization, on the functions of labor supply and population composition, and on the structure and orientation of the region's external contacts.

Thus, economic development after the early 1760s was characterized by four major processes: (1) more distinct agricultural specialization, especially in crops; (2) increasing diversification in manufacturing and service functions; (3) elaboration of a network of urban places; and (4) consolidation of commercial contacts with specific eastern market centers. Spatial variations in the patterns and timing of specialization and diversification provide the framework within which it is possible to discern trends in regionalization during the second half of the eighteenth century. In relations with eastern Virginia, significant similarities begin to emerge between agricultural specialization in the valley and the northern Piedmont. In terms of westward expansion, the valley became integrated into the sequential patterning of a developing upper southern agricultural economy.

The Initial Significance of Hemp

The marked changes in the content and orientation of the region's agriculture after the 1750s were a continuation of previous agricultural patterns. The mixed farming structure remained intact. No new major crops were introduced, and agricultural techniques remained substantially unaltered. What was new, and what increased the rates of spatial and socioeconomic change, was the increasing emphasis on production for outside markets. Much of the pioneer commercialism had been fostered under conditions of irregular and temporary patterns of demand. Contacts with outside markets, although widespread, had not yet encouraged the sustained production of any specific frontier produce for commercial purposes. This situation changed during the mid-1760s with the development of commercial hemp production.

The Virginia government had been encouraging the cultivation of hemp since 1722 as a means of promoting the settlement of the colony's western Piedmont. However, not until settlement was well under way west of the Blue Ridge was more serious subsidization considered. In 1745 the Virginia Assembly renewed the existing bounty of 4s. per hundredweight of hemp harvested and added a bounty of 2s. per hundredweight for all hemp exported to England.[2] Most of the money appropriated for this purpose was spent in eastern Virginia, not only because that area had distinct production and transportation advantages but also because the production and processing of hemp in the valley was not encouraged by the bounty. Western frontier settlers used a winter-rotting process to separate fiber from stalk: the harvested plants were spread out in the fields to allow the fall and winter rains and ground frosts to leach out the gum substance binding the lint to the main stalk, a process which could take up to three months. But until 1748 bounties were only given for water-rotted hemp, produced more laboriously by tying the plants in bundles and leaving them to soak in ponds or streams for up to two months after harvest, a process which yielded a cleaner fiber in a shorter period of time.[3] The House of Burgesses did consider passing an act in 1748 to establish inspection and storage warehouses in Frederick County and in Lunenberg County in Southside Virginia,[4] but no warehouses were built, and it seems likely that these locations had been chosen to encourage new production rather than to facilitate current production.

Most hemp produced during the 1750s and early 1760s was for local consumption, and the bulk of it was cultivated in eastern Virginia as a commercial supplement to tobacco. When tobacco prices were low, planters turned to other crops, including hemp. During the depression in tobacco prices between 1758 and 1764 initial attention was focused on indigo, and a short boom occurred between 1760 and 1764. Then, within a year of a new hemp bounty, hemp replaced indigo and became an important secondary staple of Virginia's agriculture.[5] However, in the Tidewater both wheat and corn remained more important commercial crops than hemp, and in the Piedmont not only did hemp remain a secondary crop to tobacco, but in the northern Piedmont it had to compete with the expanding wheat and flour industry.[6] It was in the Valley of Virginia, where its cultivation did

2. Hening, *Statutes,* 3:81, 148, 254, 5:358. See also George Melvin Herndon, "The Story of Hemp in Colonial Virginia" (Ph.D. diss., University of Virginia, 1959).

3. James F. Hopkins, *History of the Hemp Industry in Kentucky* (Lexington: University of Kentucky Press, 1947), pp. 39–67.

4. *Journals of the House of Burgesses,* ed. McIlwaine and Kennedy, 7:298–99.

5. Herndon, "Story of Hemp," pp. 39–41.

6. Avery O. Craven, *Soil Exhaustion as a Factor in the Agricultural History of Virginia and Maryland, 1606–1860,* University of Illinois Studies in the Social Sciences, vol. 13, no. 1

not compete with other commercial staples, that hemp attained its greatest relative significance.

The Shenandoah Valley had no peculiar physical advantages for the growing of hemp any more than it had for flax, but local agricultural conditions were conducive to the production of a fine, strong, long-fibered hemp.[7] Although it did not have the soil-depleting reputation of tobacco, it required a great deal of labor for ground preparation, sowing, weeding, and especially for harvesting.[8] The plants were pulled up by the roots to insure the highest possible yields, with a mature man covering half an acre per day. Average yields per acre seem to have been an unspectacular 500 pounds.[9]

After the hemp had been winter-rotted, further processing necessitated much additional labor. The outer bark and other woody parts had to be reduced to small pieces and separated from the bark, resulting in a minimally processed "gross" hemp. An additional procedure, involving the scraping of the hemp so that only the fiber remained (scutching), resulted in a more finely processed "neat" hemp. Before the Revolution 90% of the valley's processed hemp was in this latter form. Although it had not gone through the final procedure of hackling, whereby the fibers were individually separated, neat hemp was suitable for sail and tent cloth and a variety of coarse materials for clothing. During the pioneer period it was incorporated into osnaburg for everyday clothes, and it was sometimes used as warp along with a wool weft to produce linsey-woolsey, a cloth which easterners associated with the frontier. In the production of coarser textiles, therefore, hemp could be competitive with flax.

The production of hemp on a larger scale for export to eastern Virginia or the Middle Colonies occurred before the new bounty inducements of 1764 and seems to have been initially a response to the temporary shift to indigo and hemp east of the mountains during the late 1750s. However, the response was slow and cautious. Though James Craig had a certificate recorded for 687 pounds of cleaned hemp in Augusta County in November 1759, his lead was not followed for over two years, when Thomas Lewis

---

(Urbana, Ill., 1925), pp. 61–65; Gaspare J. Saladino, "The Maryland and Virginia Wheat Trade from Its Beginning to the American Revolution" (M.A. thesis, University of Wisconsin, 1960), pp. 13–18, 26–27.

7. Nicholas Cresswell, on a visit to the lower valley in the mid-1770s, claimed to have seen hemp 14 feet tall (*The Journal of Nicholas Cresswell*, ed. R. B. Cunningham Graham [New York: P. Putnam's Sons, 1924], p. 198).

8. Hopkins, *History of the Hemp Industry in Kentucky*, pp. 41, 48–49, and Herndon, "Story of Hemp," pp. 58–60.

9. Herndon, "Story of Hemp," pp. 61–63; Herndon, "Hemp in Colonial Virginia," *Ag. Hist.* 37 (1963):86–93.

recorded a certificate for 3,393 pounds in February 1762.[10] Regular sustained cultivation for export throughout the valley began a year later in response to rising colonial demands, especially in the Philadelphia market.[11]

The production of hemp for external markets could be a very profitable enterprise. It required about six tons of harvested hemp to produce one ton of neat hemp. Assuming a yield of 500 pounds per acre, Craig's 687 pounds of neat hemp were probably the output from eight acres of sown hemp, and Lewis would have planted some forty acres to produce his 3,393 pounds.[12] Both men could have earned a tidy profit for their efforts. In 1760 the price of neat hemp was 25s. to 26s. per hundredweight; with the bounty of 4s. per hundredweight added, Craig would have received about £9 and Lewis some £45. However, wagon costs to fall-line markets or to Philadelphia could have reduced these profits by up to one tenth.

The Geographical Impact of Hemp Production

The development of hemp production for external markets had substantial effects on the organization of land, population, and economy in the valley. Expanding production placed unprecedented demands on land and labor supply. The increasing involvement by local farmers in hemp cultivation provided many of them with their first sustained contacts with the external mercantile world. Despite the plant's widespread cultivation throughout the valley, it was integrated differently into the farming systems of the upper and lower parts of the region. And the demands of the Revolutionary War period enormously expanded and accelerated its production and helped to encourage already existing tendencies toward increasing socioeconomic differentiation of the region's population.

Between 1764 and 1769 the upper Shenandoah and James valleys produced almost 500 tons of hemp for external sale, rising from less than 5 tons in 1764 to almost 150 tons annually between 1767 and 1769 (fig. 22).[13] The average farmer was producing between 1,100 and 1,200

10. Augusta Co. Order Books 6:318, 7:166.

11. David C. Klingaman, "The Development of the Coastwise Trade of Virginia in the Late Colonial Period," *Va. Mag. Hist. Biog.* 77 (1969):26–45, especially p. 35.

12. Even if Lewis had been getting yields of 600 pounds per acre he would still have required 34 acres. However, it is possible that his 3,393 pounds represented not only his own input but also the production of other settlers who either paid debts to him with hemp or were in tenant partnership with him.

13. From the same sources used here for fig. 22, Herndon derived much higher figures of 120 and 231 tons, respectively, for the years 1767 and 1768 (Herndon, "Story of Hemp," p. 135).

pounds annually, the output of 12 to 14 acres of sown hemp, double the normal cultivated acreage on the average farm. The 250 acres devoted to specialized hemp production in 1764 had expanded fourteenfold to almost 4,000 acres within five years. Before 1765 only a handful of farmers participated; by 1769 almost 300 were involved.

During the same years production in the lower Shenandoah Valley averaged between 25 and 30 tons annually, or less than one third the output of the upper valley.[15] Even if these figures reflect incomplete returns, the regional disparity is not too surprising. Hemp was the premier commercial crop of the colonial small landholder, and it had to compete with tobacco and wheat in Berkeley and Frederick counties. There were really two levels of production in these two counties—a small number of large landholders or planters who grew hemp as a secondary commercial crop (following the eastern Virginia precedent), and a larger number of small farmers for whom hemp was the primary commercial crop. Moreover, the lower valley constituted a more substantial local market than farther south, which helps to explain its lower production for export. By 1767 a small ropewalk had been established near Winchester, and by 1776 ropes and cordage were being manufactured there from locally produced gross hemp.[16]

The expansion of hemp production created additional demands for field labor. Slavery and tenancy had already been established farther north, but in the upper valley the first significant importation of Negro slaves coincided with hemp expansion, and it appears likely that tenancy was given a boost also. Moreover, the valley's hemp industry was dominated by settlers of Scotch-Irish and English origins; in the upper valley before 1776, 75% of the producers for export appear to have been Scotch-Irish. German participation was minimal; even in Shenandoah County they comprised less than half of all large-scale hemp producers. Although initial labor costs were increased, good profits were to be made as external demand increased. By 1765 prices in Virginia for winter-rotted hemp had risen to 35s. per hundredweight, and they fluctuated between 33s. and 35s. until the early 1770s.[17] The average hemp producer in the valley was thus able to earn between £13 and £15 annually before haulage costs. At the same time, the number of local wagons increased, especially in the upper valley.

14. Some farmers produced or collected huge amounts of hemp. At least two men recorded between 10 and 12½ tons each between 1764 and 1769, and one farmer had 9 tons recorded between 1769 and 1770.

15. Frederick Co. Order Books 11–14; Hart, *Valley of Virginia*, p. 9.

16. G. Melvin Herndon, "A War-Inspired Industry: The Manufacture of Hemp in Virginia during the Revolution," *Va. Mag. Hist. Biog.* 54 (1966):301–11, especially p. 306.

17. Water-rotted hemp was usually worth about 2s. more per hundredweight (Herndon, "Story of Hemp," p. 137).

Despite the loss of half of its total hemp output when Botetourt County was formed in 1770, Augusta County's production for the three years before the outbreak of the Revolutionary War probably ranged from 150 to 160 tons annually (see fig. 22).[18] By 1773 twice as many farmers in the upper Shenandoah Valley were cultivating more than twice as many acres of hemp (over 4,500 acres) than had been the case before 1770. And the average output per farmer also continued to rise, to between 1,400 and 1,500 pounds. The growers for 1773 produced 5½ tons more hemp than the same number of growers had done in 1769.

Hemp and the Revolution

Until 1774 hemp production in the valley had to rely on growing but uncertain markets. With the increasing fiscal and political conflicts with Britain and the inauguration of the nonimportation agreements in May 1774, the American colonies were forced to supply their own demands for hemp. These demands were further increased by the military needs of the Revolutionary War, for the supply of which hemp had no real competitor.[19]

These events had two immediate effects on hemp production in the valley. First, they shifted emphasis from the production of neat hemp to gross hemp, which was more suitable for the manufacture of ropes, sacks, cordage, and sailcloth than for textiles. This change reduced the amount of labor required in processing, but the upper valley in particular did not have the facilities to produce the heavier items now in demand. Consequently, the region was forced to become an even greater primary producer than it had been before the war, with further processing and manufacturing being conducted largely outside the area. This shift would have occurred in any case as the colonists moved to centralize hemp manufacturing after 1775 at government factories, as in Richmond, or at ports such as Norfolk, Alexandria, and Philadelphia.[20] Second, with the state emerging as a major market for hemp, transportation to market was government subsidized, thus reducing transportation costs for western producing areas. Farmers merely had to haul their hemp to the nearest local collecting station, from

18. Although the hemp returns for 1775 were incomplete, they were probably as great if not greater than those for the previous two years.

19. For an evaluation of the Revolutionary War's impact on the agriculture of the valley, see Robert D. Mitchell, "Agricultural Change and the American Revolution: A Virginia Case Study," *Ag. Hist.* 47 (1973):119–32.

20. See Virginia State Auditor's Item No. 218, Va. State Lib.; Herndon, "Story of Hemp," pp. 107–8, 116; Robert Johnson, "Government Regulation of Business Enterprise in Virginia, 1740–1820" (Ph.D. diss., University of Minnesota, 1958), p. 52ff.

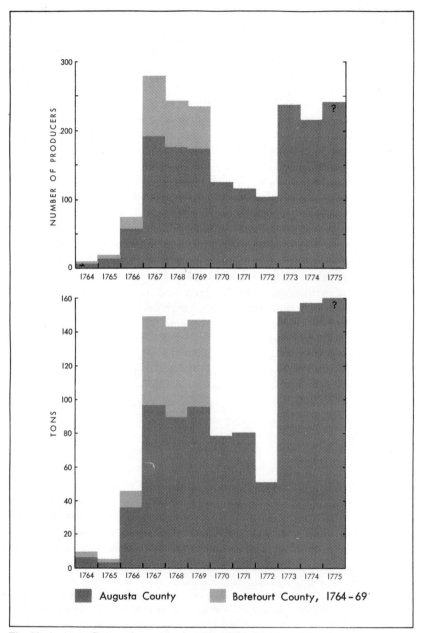

Fig. 22. Augusta County hemp production, 1764–75 (data from Augusta County Order Books 8–16)

which point the government employed wagoners to haul the commodity to market. Hemp brought less money in Winchester or Staunton than in Richmond, but by selling in the valley a farmer could avoid the risks and transportation costs to Richmond. In 1776 the government agent in Augusta County paid 30s. per hundredweight if the hemp was delivered in Staunton and 40s. if the farmer delivered it to Richmond.

Virginia became the leading producing area for hemp in North America, producing at least 5,000 tons annually. Although no precise figures are available, western Virginia produced between 25% and 30% of the state's output of commercial hemp during the Revolutionary War. Hemp was also a major crop of the Piedmont, especially in its northern and west-central counties, between 1760 and 1780; the Peidmont contributed between 60% and 70% of Virginia's hemp output, while the Tidewater's contribution was relatively insignificant (fig. 23). Within western Virginia, Augusta, Botetourt, and Frederick counties, in that order, were the leading hemp-producing counties. The now much-reduced Augusta County alone was producing between 250 and 300 tons annually during the war. The upper Shenandoah Valley was contributing just over 10% of Virginia's total output, the lower valley about 8%, and Botetourt County about 6%.

As one of the leading hemp-growing areas in Virginia during the Revolutionary War, the Shenandoah Valley continued to undergo substantial geographical changes in the wake of its commercial development. With output almost doubling after 1775, the acreage devoted to hemp and the number of farmers engaged in commercial hemp growing increased proportionately. Between 1776 and 1783 probably about 15,000 acres annually were sown to hemp (9,000 in the upper valley and 6,000 in the lower), while some 700 to 750 farmers (approximately one in every ten farmers) specialized in hemp production.

However, the significance of hemp must be kept in perspective. Even at peak production Virginia hemp never attained the commercial importance of tobacco or wheat, especially as an export crop. Although hemp production probably altered the economic life of the Shenandoah Valley more than any other area of the colony, it by no means dominated local agriculture. Nearly every farmer in the valley grew wheat, initially for subsistence but also for sale when conditions were favorable. By 1783 about 15,000 acres were also devoted to wheat. But the significance of hemp was much more localized and of more limited duration. Hemp production, like that of tobacco, was characterized by a "boom and bust" cycle as a result of the peculiar characteristics of its sources of demand.

The fluctuating nature of the industry is best seen in the price trends of the Revolutionary period. Between 1774 and 1776 prices in the valley

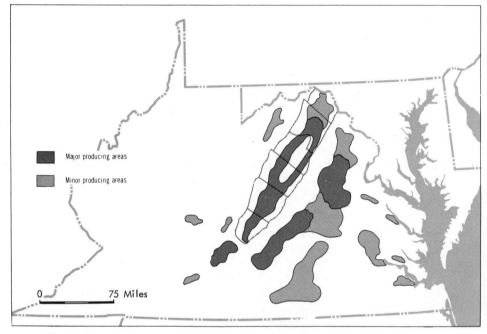

Fig. 23. Commercial hemp-growing areas, 1776 (generalized); (data from Herndon, *Hemp in Colonial Virginia*; Hart, *Valley of Virginia*; Virginia State Auditor's Items, Nos. 218, 231, Va. State Lib.)

ranged from 27s. 6d. to 35s. per hundredweight. However, with the intensification of military activities prices rose steeply to 100s. (£5) by late 1777. By October 1778 Alex Sinclair, a government agent, was paying 180s. (£9) per hundredweight for hemp delivered at his house in Rockbridge County.[21] By the beginning of 1779 the Navy Board in Norfolk was paying up to 220s. (£11) per hundredweight for gross hemp from western Virginia. The period of peak hemp prices, of 300s. (£15) per hundredweight, lasted from January 1780 until the early fall of 1782, after which prices declined precipitously to 50s. by the end of 1782.[22] By the summer of 1783 hemp prices in the valley were back to their immediate prewar level of 30s. to 35s.

21. Virginia State Auditor's Items Nos. 218 and 231, Va. State Lib. See also William A. Anderson Ledger, 1775–85, University of Virginia Library, Charlottesville; Andrew Reid Account Book, 1776–97, Cyrus H. McCormick Collection, Wis. State Hist. Soc.; Herndon, "Story of Hemp," pp. 137–42.

22. Virginia State Auditor's Item No. 218; Herndon, "Story of Hemp," pp. 140–42. See also W. A. Low, "The Farmer in Post-Revolutionary Virginia, 1783–1789," *Ag. Hist.* 25 (1951):122–27.

In October 1783 Virginia passed a tax law which rated various goods that could be used to pay taxes. The hemp certificates of the Piedmont counties were rated 15% higher than those of the lower Shenandoah Valley, which in turn were rated almost 8% higher than those of the upper Shenandoah Valley and 15% higher than those of Botetourt County.[23] These ratios suggest that the quality of hemp produced in western Virginia was inferior to that of the Piedmont and that within the Valley of Virginia quality tended to decline southward from Berkeley County. However, growers in the valley were eager to consolidate their commercial advantages by petitioning for a hemp inspection system to maintain quality control.[24] The General Assembly finally acted in 1784, when it established hemp warehouses in Alexandria, Fredericksburg, and Richmond, but not in the valley. This system was only designed to inspect hemp going out of the state by water or being made into cordage in eastern Virginia.[25] Valley hemp going by wagon to Philadelphia or Baltimore was not subject to inspection, although its quality was governed by buyer demands in these cities.[26]

The absence of a comprehensive inspection system after the war was one reason for the failure to sustain Virginia's hemp production. The Valley of Virginia was the only region in the state to grow commercial hemp after 1783, and there were varying responses to the task. Farmers in Frederick County were discouraged by the drastic price reductions of 1783, while those in Augusta County were optimistic about future production, if the Virginia government gave them some "encouragement."[27] Yet most valley hemp went into local textile production again. Few farmers produced more than 500 pounds annually after 1784, and exports, mainly to Maryland and Pennsylvania, rarely amounted to more than twenty tons a year.[28] Cheaper Russian hemp and cordage

23. Hening, *Statutes,* 11:300.

24. Augusta County farmers had been petitioning for such a system since 1769 (*Journals of the House of Burgesses,* ed. McIlwaine and Kennedy, 11:253).

25. Hening, *Statutes,* 10:508, 11:98–99, 412–15.

26. Some evidence for this trade can be· gleaned from Valentine White's Receipt Book, 1781, Va. State Lib. During the fall of 1781 the state of Virginia spent over £4,186 to transport hemp from the Shenandoah Valley and Botetourt County to Philadelphia.

27. Legislative Petitions, Frederick County, Nov. 18, 1783, and Augusta County, June 8, 1784, Va. State Lib.

28. See James McDowell Papers and Andrew Reid Accounts Books, McCormick Coll., Wis. State Hist. Soc. Some valley merchants continued to trade in hemp into the 1790s. Between 1788 and 1791 the Staunton firm of Mustoe and Chambers paid off part of a Richmond debt with 3½ tons of hemp worth £105 (Augusta Co. District Court Order Book [1789–93], pp. 495–502). In 1792 Alexandria merchants were willing to pay 38s. per hundredweight for valley hemp (*Virginia Centinel* [Winchester], Sept. 17, 1792, copy at Lib. Cong.),

began to be imported into the United States during the late 1780s, by which time the locus of American hemp production had moved to central Kentucky.

The Commercial Dominance of Wheat

Viewed from a long-term perspective, wheat was the most significant commercial item in the agriculture of the Shenandoah Valley. Its emergence as an export crop was more gradual and more lasting than that of hemp, and more difficult to document. Its production, processing, and marketing differed from those of hemp and tobacco, especially in its integration into subsistence patterns, its lower labor requirements, and its external markets. Yet it would be misleading to view the agricultural development of the valley in terms of a dual economy in which some areas were dominated by specialization in hemp or tobacco and others by wheat. Agricultural change was more complex than that because commercial trends occurred within a mixed farming framework in which wheat was always a key item.

The expansion of wheat cultivation beyond general subsistence requirements first occurred during the French and Indian War to satisfy militia demand for flour and bread. The removal of this demand during the early 1760s did not eliminate the search for other markets, especially among farmers in the lower valley. The difficulties of tobacco production in eastern Virginia and the emergence of wheat specialization in Loudoun County immediately to the east of the Blue Ridge did not go unnoticed by farmers in Berkeley and Frederick counties. It was here that commercial wheat production was most consistently sustained, in the same areas in which Tidewater influences were strongest and tobacco and slavery were most firmly established. The accounts of the Falmouth merchant William Allason clearly indicate that flour was sent down regularly to his store after 1765 by Berkeley and Frederick county customers.[29] Both small farmers and some of the largest landholders in the area participated in this trade. Two of Berkeley County's most prominent settlers, Adam Stephen and Horatio Gates, were regular

and two years later valley hemp was worth 41s. in Richmond (George Nicolson to Zachariah Johnston, June 10, 1794, Zachariah Johnston Papers, Va. State Lib.).

29. Day Books (1751–1800) and Ledgers (1757–1801), William Allason Papers, Va. State Lib. See also Miles S. Malone, "Falmouth and the Shenandoah: Trade before the Revolution," *Amer. Hist. Rev.* 40 (1935–36):696–99; Edith E. B. Thomson, "A Scottish Merchant in Falmouth in the Eighteenth Century," *Va. Mag. Hist. Biog.* 39 (1931):108–17, 230–38.

exporters of flour to Alexandria before the Revolution.[30] Nicholas Cresswell, who visited Berkeley and Frederick counties on several occasions between 1774 and 1776, took note of their increasing wheat production and was so impressed by their agrarian landscapes and the apparent ease with which a living could be made that he declared: "I am exceedingly pleased with these two Counties, and am determined to settle in one of them, if ever these times are settled. Here is every encouragement. Land is purchased at 30 shilling, this currency per acre, that is 26 shillings sterling. It will produce any sort of grain, the average of wheat is about 12 bushels to the acre, but it is not half ploughed and manure of any sort is never used."[31] He also noted that wheat was selling for 3s. a bushel in the lower valley in 1774 but was bringing up to 5s. in Alexandria.

The shift toward wheat specialization was much slower in the upper valley and was partly delayed by the focus on hemp. However, here too surplus wheat was being incorporated into local trading accounts. Between 1766 and 1775 one Staunton merchant sent over 3,000 pounds of flour to Richmond to help pay off outstanding debts.[32] It may be an exaggeration to say that there was an incipient wheat belt extending through the Piedmont areas of Maryland, Virginia, and the Carolinas on the eve of the Revolution, but such a specialization already existed in the lower valley and was to spread throughout the entire region during the Revolutionary period.[33]

Wheat and the Revolution

The demands of wartime in the 1770s, which again expanded markets for bread and flour, elaborated already existing trends in wheat production. The increasing demands for these commodities within the colonies and for export to the West Indies during and after the war provided secure and growing markets for wheat after the exaggerated war demands had subsided. The war created increased demand in Virginia for

30. See Adam Stephen Papers, particularly item 138, Manuscript Div., Lib. Cong; Horatio Gates Papers, N.Y. Public Lib. Gates was receiving 10s. 6d. per barrel of fine flour in 1775.

31. Cresswell, *Journal*, p. 50. He went so far as to calculate the costs and profits from a 500-acre farm and concluded that he could make a profit of £385 sterling within a short time (pp. 195–97).

32. Augusta Co. District Court Order Book (1789–93), pp. 237–54.

33. See Gray, *History of Agriculture*, 2:606–7; Merrens, *Colonial North Carolina*, pp. 118, 239; Saladino, "The Maryland and Virginia Wheat Trade," pp. 13–18, 26–27.

wheat at the expense of tobacco and helped to develop wheat as a second major commercial crop throughout the Shenandoah Valley. Between 1779 and 1783 the valley was probably producing over two million pounds of flour annually for sale, with 75% of this output coming from the three lower valley counties.[34] The official claims records indicate that Frederick County farmers were best prepared to expand their grain production, supplying large amounts of both wheat and corn to the militia. Indeed, the evidence for the Revolutionary period clearly indicates the strength of the lower valley to have been in grains, while the upper valley concentrated on hemp and livestock.[35]

Commercial wheat production was sustained after the war by the increasing civilian markets for flour and bread and by the rise of Alexandria and Richmond as major flour-milling centers. Prices for both wheat and flour in the valley continued to remain high after the war. During the mid 1780s wheat prices ranged between 3s. and 4s. per bushel, 6d. to 1s. higher than they had been before 1775, but they continued to rise after 1785 and had almost doubled by 1800. Similarly, the better grades of flour continued to fetch 14s. to 16s. per hundredweight after 1783, and these prices too had almost doubled by the end of the century.[36] An increasing number of advertisements of

34. See Public Service Claims, 1779–83, Va. State Lib.; Mitchell, "Agricultural Change and the American Revolution: A Virginia Case Study," *Ag. Hist.* 47 (1973):119–32. The official claims only account for about one-third of the commodities sold to the government during the war. There were many other opportunities for disposal, including commissary activities. Commissaries were active throughout the state during the war, and many of them were supplied with large amounts of cash to make immediate purchases. The commissary for Shenandoah County, for example, was provided with over £20,000 during 1781 and 1782 (see John Pierce [Commissary General] Account Book, 1781–82, and "The State of Virginia against the United States for Supplies to the Army during the late War," Winchester, Mar. 1, 1780–Dec. 1, 1780, both in Va. State Lib.). I am grateful to Harold B. Gill, Jr., for information concerning commissary activities.

Hart, *Valley of Virginia*, p. 10n, suggests that Berkeley and Frederick counties were each producing over a million pounds of flour a year during the war, but his sources do not support this statement. In these two counties production for the militia was dominated by a few large landowners. For example, in 1782–83 Thomas Bryan Martin of Greenway Court supplied 27% of Frederick County's flour deliveries to the militia and 5% of its corn deliveries.

35. Mitchell, "Agricultural Change and the American Revolution," pp. 122–23, 128–30. See also Virginia State Auditor's Item No. 160 (Culbertson Papers), Va. State Lib.

36. These prices were calculated from the data in Augusta and Frederick County Order Books and Will Books for 1775 and 1800. They parallel the price rises in both wheat and flour in eastern Virginia over the same period. See Low, "The Farmer in Post-Revolutionary Virginia 1783–1789," *Ag. Hist.* 25 (1951):122–27, and Low, "Merchant and Planter Relations in Post-Revolutionary Virginia 1783–1789," *Va. Mag. Hist. Biog.* 61 (1953):308–18. A settler who sold 2½ bushels of wheat at 4s. per bushel would receive

farm sales in the valley after 1780 made references to potential opportunites for commercial wheat production. Grattan's Merchant and Saw Mills on North River in Rockingham County were put up for sale in 1792: "These mills are situate in the heart of a fine wheat country, and in excellent order for manufacturing and sawing. Richmond and Fredericksburg affords convenient cash-markets for flour, and the growing towns of Staunton and Harris[on]burg, contiguous to these mills, ensure a demand for plank and scantling."[37] The 100-odd gristmills that existed before 1775 in the upper valley had increased to about 200 by the end of the century, and there were over twice that number in the lower valley. Ninety percent of the mills added since 1775 were built after 1783.

By the last decade of the eighteenth century the Shenandoah Valley had become one of the most important wheat- and flour-producing regions in the entire South.[38] Travelers such as Count Castiglioni, Harry Toulmin, and La Rochefoucauld-Liancourt frequently commented on the region's wheat cultivation and flour production. In 1793 Robert Gamble, a Staunton merchant who had moved to Richmond after the war, wrote to Thomas Jefferson:

As a Virginian, I am truly anxious that our markets should not be always dependent on Philadelphia or any other port. Our planters are turning farmers. Our mills make flour that is not surpassed by any in America. In 4 years the 3 little counties of Augusta, Rockbridge and Rockingham, which is contiguous to your seat, from having but one manufacturing mill only has upwards of 100 merchant mills in great perfection, and our adventuring farmers are coming with their Batteaus loaded down James River thro' the Blue Ridge within 3 and 4 miles of Lexington. Yesterday and today I have rec[eive]d upwards of 500 Barrells sent to me by this mode, and the men assure me 2000 will come the same route in this month [May] exclusive of the quantities that now come to Milton and Warren in your neighbourhood over Rockfish Gap.[39]

State paternalism, as in the case of hemp production, began to play an important part in the organization of the flour industry during the last two decades of the century. In 1780 flour, as well as hemp, tobacco, and

10s. If he sold a hundredweight of fine or second-grade flour, the product of 2½ bushels, he would receive about 14s.

37. *Virginia Centinel* (Winchester), Jan. 28, 1792.

38. Lewis C. Gray has written, "During this period [1783–1800] the most important wheat producing regions of the South were around Frederick, Maryland, the upper [northern] Shenandoah Valley, and the northern piedmont section of Virginia" (*History of Agriculture,* 2:608).

39. "Letters to Jefferson from Archibald Cary and Robert Gamble," *Wm. and Mary Qtly.,* 2d ser. 6 (1926):130.

flax, was decreed as a suitable tax payment in lieu of money, and no doubt some farmers grew wheat specifically for that purpose.[40] In 1787 thirty inspection centers were set up for flour, but none of these centers was located in the Shenandoah Valley, despite the fact that the merchant community of Alexandria declared that "the Manufacturing of Wheat has been for some years past carried to such an extent by the Inhabitants of the Western Counties as to render Flour and Bread Staple Commodities of the State."[41] The nearest centers to the valley were Alexandria, Fredericksburg, Richmond, and Lynchburg. The same law established four grades of flour and specified that a barrel of flour had to contain a standard weight of 196 pounds of flour.[42] The increasing export of flour from the upper Shenandoah Valley through Rockfish Gap led to several petitions for more conveniently placed inspection stations.[43]

Wheat Cultivation and Land Use

It is difficult to gauge the acreage changes that occurred during the Revolutionary period as a result of shifts in crop emphasis, but wheat was certainly the largest gainer. With the relative decline in hemp and tobacco production after the war, many farmers changed to wheat. The acreage shifted from tobacco to wheat could not have been very substantial, if indeed there was any, but much of the acreage previously devoted to hemp was planted in wheat. The production of wheat required less management and less labor than hemp, but not necessarily less acreage. Of the approximately 12,000 acres in wheat at the outbreak of the Revolution, probably no more than one-sixth was devoted to wheat for sale and no more than 200 farmers produced regularly for export. If indeed the valley was producing two million pounds of flour for sale annually during the early 1780s, this output would have required about 4,000 acres sown to wheat (assuming an average conversion ratio of forty-two pounds of flour per bushel and an average yield of twelve bushels per acre).[44] Thus, the acreage of wheat devoted to commercial purposes

40. Hening, *Statutes*, 10:245. In 1781 John McCulloch of Rockbridge County was repaid for making 220 flour casks "to contain a part of the Specific Tax Collected in this County" (Rockbridge Co. Order Book 1:257).

41. "Inspection of Wheat," *Wm. and Mary Qtly.*, 2d ser 2 (1922): 288–91.

42. Hening, *Statutes*, 12:515–20. An act summing up all earlier legislation on flour and bread was passed in 1792 (ibid., 13:517–24).

43. See, for example, Legislative Petitions, Augusta County, Oct. 28, 1789.

44. In 1796 La Rochefoucauld-Liancourt found that on well-manured fields in the lower valley wheat yields of up to 25 bushels per acre were achieved (*Travels*, 2:99–100).

presumably doubled during the war years, and the proportion of wheat output for sale rose to about one-quarter.

The region's output of wheat and flour continued to increase rapidly during the last fifteen years of the century, but much emphasis had to be placed on feeding the large increases in population that occurred locally after the war. Wheat was not a basic part of the slave's diet, its place being taken by corn, but the doubling of the valley's white population after 1775 produced some constraint on the wheat production allotted for sale. By 1800 about 20,000 acres of wheat were required to maintain the region's own population, with about 12,000 acres of this total located in the lower valley. Yet the output of commercial wheat continued to rise steadily during the later 1780s and quite rapidly during the 1790s. By 1790 the lower valley was producing about four million pounds of flour annually for sale and the upper valley about two million. This entire amount would have been the output of about 12,000 acres of wheat. By 1800 the lower valley was probably producing about ten million pounds of flour annually for export and the upper valley about four million pounds, requiring a total of some 28,000 acres. In terms of land use, total acreage under wheat in the lower valley by 1800 would have amounted to about 32,000 acres (four times the peak hemp acreage), and to some 15,000 to 16,000 acres in the upper valley (just under twice the peak hemp acreage).

In 1810, according to the tabulations of the then purveyor of public supplies, Tench Coxe, the Shenandoah Valley was by far the leading wheat-producing region in Virginia, with an output of over 224,600 barrels of flour (over 40 million pounds) which represented 30% of the state's recorded total of almost 148 million pounds.[45] In fact, Berkeley and Frederick counties, with an output of some 84,000 pounds each, produced almost 21% of the state total together and ranked only behind Madison and Loudoun counties in the northern Piedmont in individual production.

The increasing commercial orientation of the region's agriculture, especially toward wheat, was also reflected in increased proportions of cleared land by the end of the century. Evidence from newspaper advertisements and estate inventories suggests that the average amount of cleared land per farm had doubled to between 18% and 20% of the total farm area, and had reached 25% in Berkeley and Frederick counties.[46] Some farms were advertised at up to 30% cleared,

45. Coxe, *A Statement of the Arts and Manufactures of the United States of America for the Year 1810* (Philadelphia, 1814), pp. 112–14.

46. Data for these estimates were derived from the following newspapers which were examined for the years 1790 to 1801: *Virginia Gazette* (Richmond; on microfilm, Va. State Lib.), *Staunton Eagle* and *Staunton Gazette* (Huntington Lib. and Lib. Cong.), and *Virginia Centinel* (Winchester; Lib. Cong.).

and inventories indicate that arable acreages of forty to fifty acres were common. These ratios compare favorably with conditions not only in western Pennsylvania (12% to 15%), eastern Massachusetts (14% to 16%), and the Connecticut Valley (20%), but also southeastern Pennsylvania (20% of 25%).[47]

The commercial dominance of wheat after the Revolution was no more evident than in the decision of some of the lower valley's largest landowners to convert some or all of their commercial acreage to wheat. On the one hand, these men were conscious of the social implications of their shift from planter status to that of farmer. Yet this very shift in their commercial orientation indicates a flexible response to changing market conditions and, indeed, may demonstrate that those eastern planters who had developed quarters in the valley or who had moved to its lower region during or after the Revolution were more responsive to new economic trends than the majority of the valley's small holders. Thus, Thomas Bryan Martin, at Greenway Court in 1791, wrote his brother in Kent, England: "Are you all starving that you give such prices for our flour? Farming is now my Object, Tobacco is not worth raising."[48] Although Nathaniel Burwell of Carter's Grove did not abandon tobacco production in Frederick County, he diversified his valley quarters by cultivating wheat for the finest grained flour and rye for whiskey production and had two merchant mills and a sawmill built.[49] This example illustrates the changing significance of tobacco and wheat in the lower valley. Before the Revolution wheat was a secondary commercial crop to tobacco except among a few grain specialists. After the war, with a few exceptions such as the Robert Carter estates, the situation was reversed, and tobacco was never able to reclaim its primary position.

Tobacco in the Valley's Economy

As a crop which was exported to Britain, tobacco production trends were subject to considerable fluctuations because of distant and somewhat

47. Solon J. and Elizabeth H. Buck, *The Planting of Civilization in Western Pennsylvania* (Pittsburgh: University of Pittsburgh Press, 1939), p. 267; Percy W. Bidwell and J. I. Falconer, *History of Agriculture in the Northern United States, 1620–1860,* Carnegie Institution of Washington, publication no. 358 (Washington, D.C., 1925), pp. 119–21; Edward N. Torbert, "The Evolution of Land Utilization in Lebanon, New Hampshire," *Geog. Rev.* 25 (1935):211–12; Lemon, *Best Poor Man's Country,* p. 168.

48. Thomas Bryan Martin to Rev. Denny Martin, Mar. 10, 1791, Wykeham-Martin Papers (on microfilm, Colonial Williamsburg).

49. Burwell-Millwood Records, pp. 87–103 (on microfilm, Univ. of Va. Lib.).

unpredictable markets. These fluctuations were quite different from those for hemp, and indeed, the production history of tobacco was almost the complete opposite of hemp production.

Tobacco cultivation continued to expand during the last decade of the colonial period, particularly in the lower valley, although the total acreage involved was small. Lord Fairfax, George Washington, and a few other large landowners with Tidewater connections continued to send their crop to Virginia ports for export or to William Allason in Falmouth. The migration of small planters had begun only during the late 1760s, but their contributions to the agriculture and trade of Berkeley and Frederick counties is evident in Allason's account books for the early 1770s. Tobacco was the most frequently mentioned crop sent down by his lower valley customers, and he was collecting over 50,000 pounds annually by this means.[50] Washington continued to have his valley lands cultivated for tobacco as an absentee landowner. Some absentee Tidewater planters developed their lower Shenandoah Valley quarters to such an extent that they relied upon the output of these estates to provide their margins of profit. In 1775, for example, most of the profit made by Nathaniel Burwell came from the 32,000 pounds of tobacco produced on his two Frederick County estates, the Marsh and River quarters. These two estates accounted for £270 or 30% of his total plantation expenses, which involved overseers' wages and about 5,000 pounds of pork and 400 barrels of corn sent westward over the Blue Ridge to feed his slaves. The estates together produced tobacco worth £754, some 37% of his total crop production by value.[51]

By 1775 the total acreage under tobacco in the valley was probably no more than 350 to 400 acres, with 90% of this acreage located in Berkeley and Frederick counties. Tobacco had scarcely penetrated the agriculture of the upper valley. A few of the large slaveowners cultivated an acre or two along with their hemp, and small amounts were used to repay debts to local merchants.[52] But for all practical purposes tobacco was not part of the farming activities in the upper valley.

Further activity was drastically curtailed by the outbreak of the Revolution, for no crop was more negatively affected by the war than tobacco. The plant virtually disappears from the records between 1776

50. Day Books (1751–1800), and Ledgers (1757–1801), William Allason Papers, Va. State Lib., and Malone, "Falmouth and the Shenandoah: Trade before the Revolution," *Amer. Hist. Rev.* 40 (1935–36):696–99.

51. Burwell-Millwood Records, on microfilm, Univ. of Va. Lib., especially pp. 21–52.

52. Francis Kirtley, the upper valley's largest slaveowner, left tobacco worth £6 12s. (about 750 pounds) in 1775 (Augusta Co. Will Book 5:335–37.).

and 1782.[53] The larger planters shifted their emphasis to more profitable alternatives, such as hemp, wheat, corn, and livestock, while some smaller planters dropped tobacco production entirely to concentrate on the immediate gains to be made in supplying flour and meat to the Revolutionary army.

Tobacco production was resumed on a more widespread basis after the war, but on two different levels and for two different purposes. The rapid fall in the price of hemp after 1782 and the Virginia legislature's attempt to bail out the tobacco planter caused many small farmers throughout the valley to shift to some cultivation of tobacco, mainly to pay off their taxes. This trend is apparent in every county except Augusta. Berkeley County, for example, petitioned in 1786 for a tobacco warehouse within the county "as many of the Inhabitants at this time Cultivate large quantities of Tobacco to enable them to defray their Taxes."[54] The sheriff of Shenandoah County had collected "a large quantity of tobacco" in 1787 to pay taxes but had been unable to transport it by June 1 to Richmond.[55] In Rockingham County, where almost no tobacco had been grown before the Revolution, ninety-nine farmers petitioned for a tobacco warehouse in Harrisonburg. They expected to produce about 100 hogsheads of tobacco during the first year and, with some official "encouragement" (again), could easily produce much larger quantities.[56] In Rockbridge County during the late 1780s, 30,000 to 35,000 pounds of tobacco were collected annually to pay taxes, and by the early 1790s the county was petitioning for a warehouse near the James River gap.[57] All this activity, though it involved more extensive tobacco cultivation than before, did little to extend total tobacco acreage. No more than 500 acres could have been cultivated for tax and local trading purposes.

Eastern planters who moved to the lower valley after the Revolution might have been expected to boost tobacco production there, but they were faced with a new set of economic circumstances. They shifted their primary emphasis to wheat while maintaining tobacco as a secondary

53. Lord Fairfax did leave 10 hogsheads of tobacco in his inventory in 1782 (Frederick Co. Will Book 4:589–95), but other references are rare, and William Allason's accounts with valley customers contain little mention of tobacco during this period.

54. Legislative Petitions, Berkeley County, Nov. 22, 1786.

55. Ibid., Shenandoah County, Nov. 4, 1789.

56. Ibid., Rockingham County, Nov. 20, 1784. By this time tobacco was worth 3s. per hundredweight in the upper valley compared to 25s. for hemp (Augusta County Order Book 18:213).

57. Rockbridge County Tithables (1787), and Legislative Petitions, Rockbridge County, Oct. 20, 1790, and Oct. 11, 1792. During the 1790s Rockbridge County tobacco was selling for only 12s. to 15s. per hundredweight.

staple.[58] The response of absentee planters was varied, but many continued to concentrate on tobacco. Robert Carter expanded his tobacco acreage and slave labor on his six estates in Frederick County. Nathaniel Burwell, although he did diversify, continued to produce tobacco, doubled the number of slaves he had operating in Frederick County, and set up his son with his own quarters nearby. Although some of the 9,500 slaves in the lower valley in 1800 may have been employed in farming pursuits other than tobacco, the costs of maintaining field hands would have been higher than the periodic costs of hired wage labor. The fact that every county in the valley increased its slave numbers during the last two decades of the century indicates that tobacco cultivation experienced a gradual revival and even cautious expansion throughout most of the region despite the market uncertainties of the 1790s.[59]

Minor Commercial Crops

Although the major crops involved in the increasing commercialization of agriculture were wheat, hemp, and tobacco, valley farmers continued to diversify and experiment with other commercial possibilities. Rye remained a significant grain crop, especially for whiskey production, and oats, barley, and, to some extent, buckwheat continued to be cultivated, but none of these grains achieved commercial importance as crops. The growing of white potatoes was first recorded during the Revolutionary War, and they appeared with increasing frequency as a subsistence item thereafter.[60] Sweet potatoes were introduced during the early 1790s, probably from eastern Virginia, but were reputed not to grow well west of the Blue Ridge.[61] Of the crops that became minor commercial items, flax, ginseng, and indigo, only the latter had not been grown during the pioneer period.

Flax remained an important element in the crop patterns of the valley well into the nineteenth century. Very little of it was ever

58. Bliss, "Tuckahoe in the Valley," pp. 57–70; Bliss, "The Tuckahoe in New Virginia," *Va. Mag. Hist. Biog.* 59 (1951):387–96.

59. In April 1791 John Harket, a Baltimore merchant, wrote Adam Stephen in Berkeley County that flour was fetching 32s. 6d. per hundredweight while tobacco was hardly getting any price (Adam Stephen Papers, Lib. Cong.). Prices remained low until 1797 and then rose slowly over the next 5 years (Gray, *History of Agriculture,* 2:605, 765).

60. See, for example, Frederick Co. Will Books, 4:468–71, 5:15–20, 70–74, 252–54; Augusta Co. Will Book 5:440–44, 472–76. Amounts up to 50 bushels were mentioned.

61. See Thomas Jefferson to Archibald Stuart, Oct. 30, 1794, Archibald Stuart Papers, Va. Hist. Soc. In 1797 one of Andrew Reid's customers in Rockbridge County paid back part of his account with 10 bushels of sweet potatoes at 6d. per bushel.

exported since it remained the most important fiber in the domestic textile industry and since it was so widely grown throughout the colonies. Farmers seldom grew more than an acre or two, and only small amounts were reported in inventories. In addition to its use in linen production, flax did enter the trading relations of the valley in two other forms. Flax was often cultivated for its seed, particularly after 1775. Small amounts of seed were exported from the region, and some may have eventually found its way to Ireland.[62] Second, several attempts were made to crush the seeds to produce linseed oil for outside markets. Two oil mills were erected in the upper valley during the early 1770s. The importation restrictions imposed by Virginia in 1775 and the demands of the Revolutionary War no doubt encouraged the increased production of linseed oil in the Shenandoah Valley as a drying agent in paints or for the manufacture of soft soap. Oil production continued after the war, and by 1810 the valley almost monopolized Virginia's production of linseed oil. It contained twenty-three of the state's thirty-two mills, and Shenandoah County alone produced almost 15,000 gallons annually, or about 45% of Virginia's total recorded output.[63]

The small-scale production of ginseng continued after 1765, but whereas it had originally been important only in local trade in the upper valley, it had become a minor export crop by the late 1760s. Staunton became a collecting point for the ginseng of the entire upper Shenandoah and James valleys. Probably no more than 1,500 to 2,000 pounds was collected annually, but it was sent to pay off trading debts in the Virginia fall-line towns and some was exported to Glasgow and London.[64] By 1774 markets for ginseng were drying up, and the outbreak of war ended the trade completely.

Indigo was the only new experimental cash crop attempted in the region after 1765, and it also appears to have been confined to the upper valley. A few farmers experimented with it during the Revolutionary

62. Gray, *History of Agriculture*, 2:574, 611–12. Flaxseed was selling for 4s. per bushel during the 1790s.

63. Coxe, *Statement of Arts and Manufactures*, pp. 103–5. Linseed oil was selling for 5s. to 6s. per gallon during the 1790s.

64. The Staunton partnership of Reed and Johnston collected hundreds of pounds of ginseng from growers as far away as the headwaters of the James during the late 1760s (Ledger of Read and Johnston, Nov. 1766 and Nov. 1768, Coll. of Wm. and Mary Lib.). Between 1767 and 1775 John Bowyer exported almost 4,200 pounds of ginseng to Richmond, earning him about £420 at an average price of 2s.per pound (Augusta Co. District Court Order Book [1789–93], pp. 237–54). See also Papers of the Breckenridge Family, vol. 1, Sept. 1, 1767–Nov. 9, 1768, Manuscript Div., Lib. Cong.; Augusta Judgments, 1770 (file 419); Thomas Stuart to Thomas Adams, June 12, 1771, Adam Papers, Va. Hist. Soc.; Edward Johnson to William Preston, July 2, 1778, Preston Papers, Va. Hist. Soc.

War, and several hundred pounds were sent to Richmond during the late 1780s and then exported to London.[65] Despite a doubling in the price of indigo during the 1790s, it evoked no further interest among valley farmers. A few farmers continued to grow small amounts of cotton after the 1760s, and cottonseed was frequently imported from Richmond.[66] Of all the major crops in southern agriculture, only cotton and rice never achieved commercial significance in the Shenandoah Valley.

The Livestock Trade and Livestock Products

Livestock and livestock products had formed the backbone of the early mixed farming patterns of the valley. They continued to be integral parts of the region's economy throughout the remainder of the century. Although there is no evidence to suggest that large numbers of cattle continued to be driven to northern markets after 1765, former associates of William Crow probably continued to drive cattle northward during the last decade of the colonial period. There were no major declines in livestock numbers, and an actual increase in the number of sheep. Livestock products, particularly butter, continued to be important items in both local and export trade. Between 1772 and 1776 one Rockbridge County merchant sent over 4 tons of butter to eastern Virginia merchants; and between 1766 and 1775 a Staunton merchant sent 5 1/2 tons of butter, 812 pounds of cheese, and 200 pounds of tallow to Richmond.[67]

Extraordinary demands were made upon livestock, livestock-supporting activities, and livestock products during the Revolutionary War. There were considerable demands for meat to supply the troops, guards, and prisoners of war stationed in or near Winchester and Staunton; cattle and horses were driven from the Shenandoah Valley to supply other centers in eastern Virginia; and considerable amounts of corn, hay, oats, and natural pasturage were required to feed the cattle, draft

65. See Augusta Co. Will Book 6:20–22; Augusta Co. District Court Order Book (1789–93), pp. 495–502; and A. Walkeep's account with Andrew Reid, 1796–98, in Reid Family Collection, Box 1, McCormick Coll., Wis. State Hist. Soc.

66. See Augusta Co. Will Books 5:23–26, 271–74, 6:311–14, 350–51, 9:20–27; Rockbridge Co. Will Books 1:355–57, 2:23–26, 99–103; Edward Johnson to William Preston, June 30, 1777, and Mar. 29, 1780, Preston Papers, Va. Hist. Soc.

67. Between 1772 and 1776 William Anderson, à merchant in Rockbridge County, sent over 4 tons of butter to eastern Virginia merchants. At 6d. per pound he was able to earn £225 (William Anderson, Ledger, 1775–85, Univ. of Va. Lib., and Augusta Co. District Court Order Book [1789–93], pp. 237–54).

oxen, and draft and pack horses maintained by the Virginia regiments in the valley. The valley's livestock supplied the militia with an annual average of about 300 tons of beef, 6 tons each of pork and bacon, and 3 tons of mutton, with two-thirds of this coming from the upper valley. However, in monetary terms, the profits to be made from livestock products were much lower than from crop products. In 1779 the army's quartermaster in Staunton spent just over £1,000 for livestock products but £25,000 for flour, meal, rum, whiskey, and salt.[68]

Yields from livestock gradually increased during the second half of the eighteenth century. The claim records for the war years indicate that the average live weight of steers slaughtered for the army was about 550 pounds, rendering about 180 pounds of final usable product. This was a 25% to 30% increase over yields during the French and Indian War. It is possible that many steers slaughtered during the late 1750s were not fully mature animals and that animals slaughtered for the Revolutionary army were of higher quality than those normally killed, but the average change is still impressive considering the general absence of improved breeding or stall fattening until after 1783. A few farmers contributed superior animals. Mathew Patton of Rockingham County, who was to become one of the leading cattle breeders in post-Revolutionary Virginia, contributed six steers in 1779 with an average live weight of 804 pounds, and William Thompson of Augusta County supplied two animals totaling 1,800 pounds.[69]

Backcountry drovers were active in transporting cattle to military centers in eastern Virginia, often on their own initiative. This led one army supervisor in the upper valley in 1781 to complain to Governor Thomas Jefferson that "unless more severe laws are passed against speculators, or Ingrossers the Country will not be able to supply any more beef. Large droves are being carried off from the back country, greatly to the distress of the good men in the field."[70]

The war exerted unusual pressure upon the valley's capacity to produce livestock. The heaviest demands were made on cattle and hogs for meat and horses for transportation. In the case of swine, the

68. Public Service Claims, Augusta County, List II (Feb.-Dec. 1779), Va. State Lib. During the war veal, beef, and pork were selling for 3s. per pound, bacon for 2s. 6d. and mutton, butter, and tallow for 6d. per pound.

69. Ibid., Rockingham County Court Booklets I and II, and Augusta County, List II (Feb.-Oct. 1781). Livestock production was one category in which the small farmer could make a substantial contribution. The largest beef suppliers to the army were James Wilson of Rockbridge County in 1779 (6,720 pounds) and G. A. Bowman of Shenandoah County in 1782 (7,346 pounds).

70. *Calendar of Virginia State Papers*, ed. Palmer, 1:538.

overall demands of the war period seem to have exceeded the settlers' abilities to supply pork and bacon, especially in the upper valley. Sheep were least affected by war demands. The large amounts of mutton that occasionally were bought probably reflected temporary scarcities of other meats. The postwar economic depression and shortage of money made it difficult to refurbish depleted stocks, and farmers in the valley complained that they had not received adequate financial compensation either for their cattle and horses or for their personal services.[71]

Despite the decline in livestock numbers during the war, the Shenandoah Valley remained one of the most important livestock-producing areas in post-Revolutionary Virginia. In 1782 the region recorded 59,520 cattle and 28,375 horses. The upper valley maintained slightly more than half of these totals, and Augusta County's 13,000 cattle and 6,600 horses probably made it the largest livestock-rearing county in the state.[72] The slightly more than 2:1 ration of cattle to horses that prevailed in the tax lists during the 1780s is reflected also in the county inventories between 1780 and 1800. In the Augusta and Rockbridge inventories cattle outnumbered horses by a ratio of 5:2 compared to just under 2:1 in Frederick and Shenandoah counties. In the two upper valley counties cattle outnumbered swine 5:4 and sheep just over 5:4, while in the two lower valley counties the respective ratios were both almost 1:1. These ratios tend to sustain the view that the numbers of swine were most sharply reduced by the war while sheep were least affected. Indeed, sheep rearing became more widespread toward the end of the century, and there were serious attempts to establish a factory woolen industry in the upper valley during the 1790s. Thomas and Francis Douthat, two Huguenot brothers who had emigrated from Britain, began the manufacture of woolen knits and woolen broadcloth near Staunton and requested the General Assembly to provide them with an interest-free loan in order to finance the remaining construction and to purchased 1,000 sheep. One Staunton merchant testified that he had made a very rapid sale of some of their woolens.[73]

71. A Rockingham County petition of 1784 stated that farmers would have no money to pay taxes until "Your Petitioners have an opportunity of reaping their approaching and flourishing harvest and making sale thereof and until they have an opportunity of taking their cattle (the staples of their county) to market" (Legislative Petitions, Rockingham County, June 5, 1784). See also ibid., Augusta County, June 8, 1784.

72. See Main, "The Distribution of Property in Post-Revolutionary Virginia," *Miss. Val. Hist. Rev.* 41 (1954):251–56.

73. See Legislative Petitions, Augusta County, Nov. 1, 1793 and Nov. 14, 1794. There is also some indication that sheep drives to eastern Virginia markets were common by the early

The cattle trade emerged again after 1783, and steers were driven by local settlers and occasionally by backcountry peddlers to local markets in Winchester and Staunton for final movement to Richmond, Baltimore, or Philadelphia. Winchester became the major collection and distribution point in western Virginia. In 1793, while visiting the town, Harry Toulmin, a British traveler, observed that "you would be astonished at the multiplicity of cattle which pour through this town from the backcountry."[74] By the beginning of the nineteenth century the Valley of Virginia was becoming once again an area of transit for cattle and also hog drives northward through the valley, no longer from the Carolinas, but now from Kentucky and eastern Tennessee.[75] Valley farmers had also contributed to the emergence of these drives by providing improved breeding stock for western herds and by adopting better management practices. Stall feeding was practiced by a number of prominent farmers by the end of the century, and more frequent use was made of clover and timothy. Before the end of the war Mathew Patton in Rockingham County and the Fairfax family at Greenway Court had imported a number of English bulls which they crossed with local cows. Patton emigrated to Kentucky about 1790, and using his own stock and occasional bulls supplied from the valley, he and his sons helped to establish improved cattle breeding in the Bluegrass region. The long-horned "Patton stock" was the most prized kind of cattle in Kentucky during the first quarter of the nineteenth century.[76]

It is difficult to discern any areally distinct patterns of livestock specialization in the valley by 1800 to the degree they were later displayed in Kentucky. Farmers who specialized in either livestock or crop production did not exclude other agricultural activities from their production units. Thus, livestock was to be found on almost all valley farms, and livestock products provided local farmers with a salable "insurance" item. This was particularly true of cattle and swine, which

---

1790s. See "Home Manufactures in Virginia in 1791, Letters to Alexander Hamilton," *Wm. and Mary Qtly.*, 2d ser. 2 (1922):140–41.

74. Toulmin, *Western Country in 1793*, p. 58.

75. Sarles, "Trade of the Valley of Virginia, 1789–1860," pp. 34–35; Paul C. Henlein, *Cattle Kingdom in the Ohio Valley, 1783–1860* (Lexington: University of Kentucky Press, 1959), pp. 104, 115.

76. N. F. Cabell, "Some Fragments of an Intended Report on the Post-Revolutionary History of Agriculture in Virginia," *Wm. and Mary Qtly.*, 1st ser. 26 (1918):145–68, especially p. 168; Henlein, *Cattle Kingdom in the Ohio Valley, 1783–1860*, pp. 25–29. See also the inventory of Henry Miller, the ironmaster, in Augusta Co. Will Book 1A (Superior court, 1778–1828): 34–38. Miller left 160 beef and dairy cattle, including 3 imported English animals, and 11 oxen.

insured the widespread cultivation of corn and the maintenance of both meadow and woodland pasture as major elements in the land use patterns of the valley.

Agricultural Diffusion and Regionalization

The progress of agriculture after the early 1760s was both commercial and westward. Agricultural change in the valley was a complex set of processes dominated by a variety of crop and livestock specialties, intricate combinations of which provided the basis for the internal regionalization of farming activities. At the same time, the area did not develop in a vacuum. It was affected by a number of external influences which placed it within the broader context of the emerging regionalization of what might be termed upper southern agriculture.

It is, of course, an oversimplification to interpret agricultural change in terms of a shift from a primarily subsistent to a more commercial orientation, but even the changing subsistence-commercial ratio of production on the average farm during the eighteenth century is difficult to estimate. Before 1760 up to 90% of all farm products in the valley were used for subsistence purposes. The quickening pace of commercial activities during the 1760s suggests that the average farmer had probably reduced his subsistence proportion of total output to less than 75% by the end of the decade, with some of the larger landholders in Berkeley and Frederick counties producing up to 35% of their total output for sale. The events of the Revolutionary War certainly provided enlarged opportunities for production for market. Assuming that levels of food and drink consumption remained relatively constant and that increasing production was primarily the result of acreage conversion or extension rather than of higher yields, most valley farmers by the end of the century could devote no more than 50% of their total output for sale. Only a few farmers, principally in Berkeley and Frederick counties, had the capability of reducing their subsistence proportion much below half or, in the case of absentee planters who had the basic foodstuffs shipped in to their valley quarters, eliminating it almost entirely.

Increasing commercialization was reflected in increasing specialization of land use and, consequently, in distinctive but changing patterns of agricultural regionalization. No longer on the frontiers of settlement by the end of the colonial period, the Shenandoah Valley became, geographically, a transition area between the long-established commercial agriculture of eastern Virginia and the rapidly developing agricultural settlements in Kentucky. As such, the valley was affected directly by the major phases of the diffusion of upper southern agriculture.

Tobacco and hemp, which had been early specialty crops in the valley between the 1760s and mid-1780s, previously had been the major and the secondary commercial crop, respectively, in eastern Virginia and became important items in Kentucky agriculture from the late 1780s on. The livestock industry of the valley developed as an integral part of the region's mixed farming structure and, consequently, never developed the high degree of specialization that typified the livestock industry of Kentucky. However, the fattening of swine, as well as the improved breeding of cattle that began in the valley during the late 1770s and early 1780s, had also diffused westward by the end of the century. Commercial wheat production, which had emerged in the northern Virginia Piedmont during the late 1750s, had diffused to the lower valley by the late 1760s and to the upper valley by the outbreak of the Revolution. Although it remained the major staple of valley agriculture after the war, it also had become commercially important in Kentucky by the early 1790s. It is true that wheat specialization had developed in both southeasten Pennsylvania and western Maryland a decade earlier than in the Virginia Piedmont. If it can be established that the appearance of this specialization immediately south of the Potomac was a direct result of the Pennsylvania or Maryland precedent, it might be argued that wheat in upper southern agriculture was more a contribution of Middle Atlantic rather than eastern Virginia farming. However, even if this were to prove the case, wheat was integrated differently into the valley's agricultural patterns than into those of western Maryland or southeastern Pennsylvania. Farther north, hemp, tobacco, cattle, and swine were either absent as commercial commodities or of minor significance, and farming was conducted in the near absence of slave labor.[77]

77. For some further points on this important question of agricultural regionalization, see J. E. Spencer and R. J. Horvath, "How Does an Agricultural Region Originate?" *Annals Assoc. Amer. Geog.* 53 (1963):74–92; Robert D. Mitchell, "Agricultural Regionalization: Origins and Diffusion in the Upper South before 1860," in *International Geography*, 2 vols. (Toronto: University of Toronto Press, 1972), 2:740–42.

7 Diversification: Trade and Manufacture

THE increasing commercialization of valley life during the last thirty years of the century was evident not only in the increasing specialization and intensification of primary production but also in the diversification of manufacturing and trading activities. The success of the region's agricultural enterprise was in part the result of its diversified farming structure, which provided farmers with a relatively wide range of production options and thus considerable flexibility to respond to changes in external demand. At the same time, other processes were in operation which contributed to a more broadly based but more tightly organized economy. Internal diversification was enhanced by the expansion of the region's processing, craft, and manufacturing activities, which affected both the conduct and content of local and long-distance trade. The growth of trade in general was encouraged by the doubling of the valley's population during the last quarter of the century, creating both more producers of primary and secondary goods for sale and a larger local market for goods and services.

In order to achieve the transition to a more balanced and integrated postpioneer economy, which was fostered by these trends toward specialization and diversification, changes in two important structural prerequisites were necessary. An elaboration of the region's transportation network had to be devised to improve accessibility within the valley and between it and its most frequent trading contacts. Second, a system of towns had to emerge to provide some functional and spatial order for both the organization of services within the valley and the conduct of external trade.

Improvements in Accessibility

In the absence of any easily navigable streams, the development of valley communications during the pioneer period had focused on a rudimentary road network. The backbone of this network was the Great Wagon Road along which the region's major settlements were located and from which branched a small number of east-west secondary roads linking the valley with eastern Virginia at Winchester and Staunton. During the latter part of the century further improvements were basically an extension of this structure, although some attempts at qualitative change were made in both road and river transport, expecially after 1775. Indeed, by the outbreak of the Revolution the pioneer network had changed very little. The road system of the lower valley remained more substantial than that farther south, and there was still no mountain gap capable of taking wagons in the eighty-mile stretch between Staunton and Roanoke. However, during the next twenty-five years some critical new links were forged. By the beginning of the nineteenth century, six main roads connected the lower valley with eastern Virginia, Winchester had consolidated its highway link with Baltimore, a third main road connecting the upper valley with eastern Virginia had been opened up from Lexington, and highways had been constructed from the valley as far west as Pittsburgh and the New River valley (fig. 24).[1] Four main factors were responsible for the development of this network: (1) the increasing size and density of the valley's population: (2) westward population expansion and access to thermal springs; (3) the need to move men and materials during the Revolutionary War; and (4) the further growth and expansion of long-distance trade.

It was no coincidence that the densest road network was developed in Berkeley and Frederick counties, where almost 48% of the valley's population resided by 1800 and where the greatest proliferation of urban settlements existed (fig. 25). In response to the density of occupance in the eastern part of the lower valley, a new highway was constructed during the early 1780s from Shepherdstown on the Potomac along the south fork of the Shenandoah River as far as Elkton, finally opening up the isolated eastern section of Shenandoah County. Connections were made with the Great Wagon Road at both ends of Massanutten Mountain, while the difficult traverse across the mountain was negotiated through the wind gaps northeast of Newmarket. The Great Wagon Road itself was straightened and widened in several sections, most particularly in the Harrisonburg area during the early 1780s, when the location of the county seat of the new county of Rockingham shifted the main road westward from its original route through Keezletown. With the completion of these improvements, all the major towns of the valley had acquired excellent north-south connections, and only Woodstock in Shenandoah County was not located on or near a direct route to eastern Virginia.

1. For general comments on Virginia's road policies, see Roberts, "Roads of Virginia, 1607–1840," pp. 33ff., and for observations on the patterning of the road network of western Virginia see Mitchell, "Upper Shenandoah Valley of Virginia," pp. 407–9, 458.

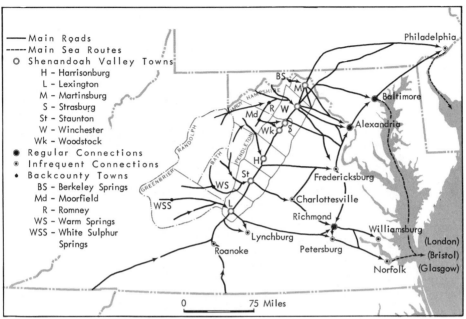

Fig. 24. Trading connections of the Shenandoah Valley by 1800 (data from Augusta Judgments and Orders, 1760–1800; Bliss, *Tuckahoe in the Valley*; Roberts, *Roads of Virginia, 1607–1840*; County Legislative Petitions, 1776–1800; merchant account books)

Although attempts had been made to provide road connections to the mountainous west during the early 1750s, they had been partially successful only in the lower valley after the formation of Hampshire County. Population remained thinly distributed throughout these western frontiers until the Revolutionary period, and the phenomenon that created an interest in pushing a road west of the upper valley was the presence of thermal springs at Warm Springs in what was to become Bath County.[2] Visitors had been bathing in the springs since at least 1750, but the clearing of a routeway from Staunton was not begun until the early 1760s.[3] In 1768 a group of Fredericksburg businessmen tried to run a lottery to speed up the slow progress of the road, and four years later the Virginia Assembly designated it a toll road to pay for

2. See Frank Reeves, *Thermal Springs of Virginia,* Virginia Geological Survey bulletin no. 36 (Richmond, 1932), pp. 6–8; Jefferson, *Notes on the State of Virginia,* ed. Peden, p. 35.

3. See Journal of Dr. Thomas Walker, July 9, 1750, Walker Papers, Manuscript Div., Lib. Cong.; Augusta Co. Order Books 4:9, 5:375, 6:236, 395, 472, 8:45.

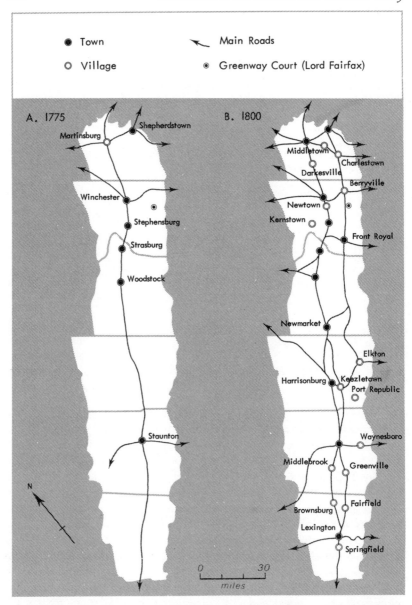

Fig. 25. Towns and villages of the Shenandoah Valley, 1775 and 1800 (data from Hening, *Statutes at Large*; Shepherd, *Statutes at Large*; county histories; Land Tax Books)

its completion about the outbreak of the Revolution.[4] Thereafter, wealthy eastern Virginians vied for the opportunity of buying up land and construction rights in the vicinity of the springs because up to 500 visitors annually spent the summer there. In the lower valley, Lord Fairfax and other wealthy residents became regular visitors to the springs at Berkeley Springs (originally Bath "Warm Springs") during the 1760s, but eastern Virginians did not appear until the early 1770s.[5] It was here that eastern Virginia planters met their few western counterparts. By the mid-1780s wealthy residents of Berkeley and Frederick counties mingled with 500 to 600 easterners at the springs every summer. Also during this decade, the rapid population growth of the western frontiers led to the formation of new counties that were linked more effectively with their traditional market centers in the valley through the improvement of western roads for wagon traffic.[6]

The events of the Revolutionary War, with the army's need to move soldiers and supplies around as expeditiously as possible, placed unusual demands upon transportation both within the Valley of Virginia and between the valley and the eastern part of the state. Because of its greater proximity to markets and its better route system, the lower Shenandoah Valley's roads posed no major problems. But in the upper Shenandoah Valley the transportation of hemp to Richmond and Philadelphia put a heavy strain on the road through Rockfish Gap and the Great Wagon Road. To a lesser extent, the transportation of hemp and flour to Fredericksburg produced a substantial traffic flow on the road through Swift Run Gap. The lack of an easy route through the Blue Ridge south of Rockfish Gap became particularly apparent during the war. One commander complained that enough stores had been lost trying to transport them by water to buy twenty wagons and teams for moving stores to and from Staunton.[7] The move to construct a road through the Blue Ridge in Rockbridge County after 1782, launched partly because of the problems encountered during the early part of the war, was consummated in 1786.[8]

After the Revolution, the Virginia government undertook two major projects to consolidate the state's western trade and reduce the northward

4. Rind's *Virginia Gazette* (Williamsburg), July 21, 1768; *Journals of the House of Burgesses,* ed. McIlwaine and Kennedy, 12:126, 167, 299; Augusta Co. Deed Book 18:291–92.

5. See Bliss, "Tuckahoe in the Valley," pp. 183–84, and the illustrated description of the spa in the late 1780s in the Journal of Samuel Vaughan, 1787, pp. 33, 71, Manuscript Div., Lib. Cong.

6. See, for example, Legislative Petitions, Augusta County, Oct. 28, 1789, Va. State Lib.

7. *Calendar of Virginia State Papers,* ed. Palmer, 2:95.

8. Rockbridge Co. Order Books 1:291, 3:71, 246, 478, 702.

flow of goods to Maryland and Pennsylvania. Both these projects, the development of turnpikes and the improvement of river navigation, would have further enhanced the accessibility of the lower valley while effecting few improvements in the upper valley. As it turned out, between 1785 and 1800 four of the six main roads connecting the lower valley with eastern Virginia, through Vestal's, Snicker's, Ashby's, and Chester's gaps, were designated as turnpikes in order to improve their upkeep.[9] Despite petitions from the counties of the upper valley for similar treatment, the best the Virginia Assembly would do was to permit a lottery for improvements on the road through Rockfish Gap. It was not until 1802 that the road through Swift Run Gap was finally made into the upper valley's first turnpike, followed six years later by the road via Rockfish Gap.[10]

A far more ambitious project was the attempt to make the Potomac and James rivers navigable for their entire length and to forge water links with the Ohio River. The Shenandoah River was bypassed in George Washington's initial scheme of 1774, and when the Potomac River Company and the James River Company were launched in 1785, initial plans were to improve the Potomac to just west of Berkeley Springs and the James to just east of Buchanan.[11] However, during the early 1790s, after some initial improvements had been undertaken, more direct steps were taken to involve the Shenandoah Valley in both schemes. Obstacles to navigation were to be removed from the south fork of the Shenandoah as far as Front Royal and the channel of the North River was to be deepened up to Lexington. Predictably, Augusta, the county which would be least affected by these inroads into the valley, made an alternative suggestion to the Virginia Assembly in 1798. Praising the attempts being made to facilitate the transport "of the produce of our country to market, by the opening and extending of the interior navigation," the petitioners went on to say: "We inhabit a country remote from the two large rivers on the improvement of which much public money has been expended: we pay with alacrity our share of such contribution, although our local situation forbids our participation in its good effects. . . . We wish you to devise some general plan for straightening and improving the roads from the backcountry to tide water.

9. See Hening, *Statutes,* 12:75–80, 524, 527.

10. See Legislative Petitions, Augusta County, Nov. 20, 1790, and Rockingham County, Nov. 19, 1794; Hening, *Statutes,* 13:175; *The Statutes at Large of Virginia, 1792–1806,* ed. Samuel Shepherd, 3 vols. (Richmond, 1835–36), 1:313, 2:377–78, 3:405–6.

11. Dunaway, *History of the James River and Kanawha Company,* pp. 10–12; Washington, *Writings of George Washington,* ed. Ford, 9:404–12; Bacon-Foster, *Early Chapters in the Development of the Potomac Route to the West,* p. 53; Hart, *Valley of Virginia,* pp. 154–58.

Particularly should we be benefitted by the enaction of a law, laying off a straight road from Staunton to Norman's Ford, thence to Alexandria and the City of Washington."[12] But the state took no action, and the Shenandoah Company, founded in the same year, soon folded for lack of private subscriptions.

Cora Bacon-Foster has maintained that if the Potomac River Company had concentrated on its original plan to improve the Potomac, it would have been successful, "but unfortunately they [the directors] listened to the importunities of the business men on its tributaries and undertook the improvement of the Shenandoah."[13] Neither company had much to show for its efforts. By 1807 only eight miles of the South Branch above Harper's Ferry had been cleared for navigation, the James River had been improved to just above Buchanan, and the deepening of the North River had scarcely begun. In short, except for settlers at the extreme ends of the valley, the region was without cheap water transport throughout the entire eighteenth century, and the functioning of its towns was entirely dependent upon the maintenance of its highway network.

Urban Structure and Hierarchy

Urban settlement during the pioneer period had developed at a very elementary level. It was only during the 1760s that moves were made to establish towns in addition to the county seats of Winchester and Staunton. One reason for this change was the general belief of the Virginia government that the highly dispersed pattern of settlements west of the Blue Ridge was not conducive to adequate protection from Indian raids. More fundamental reasons were the need to supply basic services to the valley's increasing population and to consolidate the region's external trading contacts. Yet, in terms of the widespread trading connections in existence by the outbreak of the Revolution, the concentration of service and trading functions in urban places was slow to materialize. This lack of development raises a number of critical questions about the timing and functional characteristics of local towns, about their size, growth, and spacing, and about the whole process of urbanization in frontier and postfrontier areas.

In Virginia a settlement legally became a town through statutory

12. Legislative Petitions, Augusta County, Dec. 8, 1798.
13. Bacon-Foster, *Early Chapters in the Development of the Potomac Route to the West,* pp. 103–4, and also pp. 105–7.

recognition of its rights to be governed by a group of local trustees and to conduct annual fairs. As new counties were established, county seats were designated at specific locations to carry out the administrative functions of the new unit. Such functions hardly guaranteed the formation of an urban settlement, as numerous eastern Virginia precedents demonstrated, but in the valley the locus of these functions also became associated with rudimentary commercial and, to a lesser extent, craft functions during the pioneer period. To qualify as a town, a settlement had to have a rather arbitrarily defined minimum population (about 100 to 120 people, or 20 to 25 families), living in close proximity, which was believed necessary to provide sufficient male personnel to perform the range of civic responsibilities a town acquired. Winchester (1752), Stephensburg (1758), and Staunton (1761) attained this status during the pioneer period, although a number of smaller compact settlements had begun to form as villages in the lower valley. Small service centers had begun to develop at Martinsburg and Woodstock before their establishment as the county seats of Berkeley and Shenandoah counties, respectively, in 1772, although Martinsburg was not legally recognized until 1776. By the end of the colonial period these two settlements and Stephensburg, together with Shepherdstown and Strasburg, both founded during the early 1760s, represented a second level in the urban structure of the lower valley below Winchester (see fig. 25).[14] In the upper valley no such hierarchy existed. Staunton was still the only viable central place.

This pattern, or lack of it, reflected the influence of two fundamental but sometimes opposing forces, the growth of population and the decentralization of trade. The emergence of a number of small central places in the lower valley during the 1760s coincided with several other processes. The valley experienced a rapid rate of population growth in the decade after the French and Indian War, primarily as a result of rising local birthrates rather than frontier refugees from the war zone. The development of the minimum threshold of local population density needed to support a distinct concentration of services (on the order of fifteen to twenty persons per square mile) seems to have occurred in a few areas of the lower valley during this period. At the same time, valley farmers were beginning to commit themselves to agricultural specialties on a large scale and required some basic facilities for the marketing of their produce and for coordinating their commercial contacts with eastern merchants.

The operation of these two demographic and commercial forces was

14. See Hening, *Statutes,* 6:268, 7:235, 406-7, 473-74, 600.

still very much in evidence during the last quarter of the century. After 1775, with the increasing growth of population and trade, a new phase of village and town development took place. Most of the new establishments, including county seats, were located along the Great Wagon Road and the roads connecting it with eastern Virginia. By 1800 there were eight towns in the lower valley; Martinsburg had been elevated to town status and had been joined by the new establishments of Front Royal and Newmarket. There were only three towns, the county seats, in the upper valley. About fifteen other settlements were established between 1786 and the beginning of the nineteenth century, founded and laid out by local landowners often in direct competition with an already established town or with another new settlement.[15] Some were speculative ventures that eventually succeeded, such as Charlestown on the lands of Charles Washington in Berkeley County. Others, which were less strategically placed for trade, often went unrecognized by the state government, such as Middlebrook in Augusta County and Brownsburg in Rockbridge, while still others were recognized by statute but were actually "paper towns" that were never built. Some were laid out in a regular grid pattern, similar to the county towns, with individual lots of one-quarter to one-half acre in size (compared with one-half to one and a half acres in the county towns). Others were simply one-street settlements with contiguous individual lots located along the street. Unlike the county seats, the other towns all lacked the administrative nucleus of a courthouse square, usually of two to three acres in size, with its relatively imposing public buildings.[16]

The emergence of these new settlements and the incorporation of Winchester and later Staunton produced new levels of functional significance in the developing urban hierarchy of the Shenandoah Valley. The importance of Winchester was recognized by its incorporation in

15. For the establishment of these settlements, see Hening, *Statutes,* 2:31, 121, 139, 224, 262, 270, 359.

16. See, for example, town plats of Staunton, in Augusta Co. Deed Books 2:460, 25:291, 293, which show that the town was not originally planned with a central square. The first addition to the original settlement, Alexander St. Clair's 25 acres, did have a central square (ibid., 16:192). For Lexington, see Rockbridge Co. Will Book 1:304. Although none of the surviving eighteenth-century records for Rockingham contain a plat of Harrisonburg, the town has a very distinctive courthouse square. Unlike Staunton and Lexington, it has a true square bounded by streets on all four sides with the courthouse located in the center. The morphology of the so-called Harrisonburg square has been described in Edward T. Price, "The Central Courthouse Square in the American County Seat," *Geog. Rev.* 58 (1968): 29–60. See also John W. Wayland, *Historic Harrisonburg* (Staunton, Va.: McClure Printing Company, 1949), pp. 74–75. For Winchester and Staunton, see Frederick Morton, *The Story of Winchester in Virginia* (Strasburg, Va.: Shenandoah Publishing House, 1925); Edward Aull, *Early History of Staunton and Beverley Manor* (Birmingham, Ala. 1963).

1779, a status which Staunton was not granted until 1801.[17] Incorporation was in part a reflection of the size of a settlement as well as its
functions, and permitted the town to govern itself through an elected
board of trustees headed by a mayor, to levy taxes, and to establish town
ordinances without petitioning the state legislature. Seven towns in the
lower valley operated on a second level of urban activity below Winchester, and there was keen commercial competition between them. In
the upper valley, the new county towns of Harrisonburg and Lexington
emerged on a second level, but they had little more than twenty years
of growth before the end of the century and lacked the economic and
transportational connections of Staunton. They provided many of the
same services as the older county town but on a smaller scale. None of
the three upper valley towns had any competition within its own county.
On a third level, the new settlements that were established after 1785
provided, except for Charlestown, a few local services on only a slightly
larger scale than did the individual country store or wayside tavern.

Despite the increased number of towns in the Shenandoah Valley
after 1775, the entire region remained overwhelmingly rural. In 1790
Winchester's population had reached some 1,650 inhabitants, making
it by far the largest town in western Virginia and the sixth largest in
the state. Staunton had fewer than 800 inhabitants. By 1800 Winchester had increased to 2,128 people and Staunton to about 1,100.[18] Among
the older established towns, Shepherdstown had grown rapidly to 1,108
persons, Woodstock to 634, Stephensburg to 513, while Strasburg was
almost static at 352 persons. Of the newer settlements Harrisonburg and
Lexington had about 300 people, Newmarket 290, and Front Royal
254. Charlestown was the most rapidly growing settlement in the valley.
It had acquired 568 inhabitants during its first fourteen years of existence and became the county seat of Jefferson County in 1801. At the
other end of the scale, the village of Springfield in Rockbridge County
had 86 inhabitants in 1800. By the end of the century about 15% of the
population of the lower valley lived in towns and villages, compared
with less than 10% in the upper valley. Towns were spaced ten to twelve
miles apart in the lower valley but twenty-two to thirty miles apart in
the upper valley. The disparity in the number, size, and distribution of
urban settlements between the lower and upper parts of the valley

17. Hening, *Statutes,* 10:172–73, 176; Shepherd, *Statutes,* 2:335–37.

18. Second Census of the United States, 1800. Winchester's population comprised 946
white males, 834 white females, and 348 slaves. No precise figures were given for any of
the towns in the upper valley. Both Winchester and Staunton contained about one in every
ten inhabitants of their respective counties.

clearly reflects the fact that by 1800 more than 63% of the region's population resided north of the Fairfax Line.

Yet the commercial significance of frontier urban settlements cannot be judged solely by their number, size, and status. One of the most striking characteristics of the Appalachian phase of the westward movement between 1730 and 1800 was the absence of rapidly growing urban centers of any substantial size. No settlement west of the Hudson River valley–Blue Ridge zone had attained 2,000 permanent inhabitants by 1800 except Winchester, which was larger than either Lexington, Kentucky (1,800) or Pittsburgh (1,565). In the Mohawk Valley of upstate New York there were as yet no settlements with more than 1,400 people.[19] Size, therefore, is not a true measure of the critical role played by frontier urban centers in early western expansion and development.

A key element in explaining the functional importance and different growth patterns of these settlements was the timing of the initial concentrations in relation to the emergence of later settlements and their capacity for controlling the region's import trade. Despite the fact that Winchester was elevated to town status only six years before Stephensburg some ten miles to the south, it was able to grow faster and acquire a greater number of functions initially because it was the county seat and headquarters for Virginia's western campaigns during the French and Indian War. The stationing of militia in the town temporarily provided the demand needed to establish local merchants and middlemen. As the valley's economy became more commercialized during the latter part of the century, the export of commodities continued to remain somewhat diffuse and decentralized, but the flow of imported goods came increasingly under the control of Winchester and Staunton. The market point principle was in operation. The supply of goods for export was located at a large number of production sites (farms, mills, workshops, and the like) from which the goods could be exported to prospective markets. Since the producers and the eventual consumers did not meet face to face, except occasionally at urban-based fairs, intermediaries (traders and merchants) and intermediate locations (market towns) had to be easily identifiable. This principle worked in both directions. Valley farmers could send sale goods to central collecting and redistribution points outside rather than within the valley if they wished, and they had done so frequently during the pioneer period. Most farmers could not afford to maintain independent contacts, so that the goods

19. Richard C. Wade, *The Urban Frontier: The Rise of Western Cities, 1790–1830* (Cambridge, Mass.: Harvard University Press, 1959), pp. 43, 170; *The Geography of New York State,* ed. John H. Thompson (Syracuse, N.Y.: Syracuse University Press, 1966), pp. 149–52.

which they bought from areas outside the valley rarely came back to them directly, regardless of the point of origin, and had to be acquired from local market towns. In short, during the eighteenth century the valley's import trade became increasingly more centralized, and by the outbreak of the Revolutionary War the Virginia government's marketing policies encouraged increasing concentration of the valley's export trade in Winchester and Staunton as well. The emergence of populations and small service centers west of the valley after 1775 provided the two settlements with further opportunities to enlarge their trading areas.

Winchester's commercial significance was partly the result of the composition of the local population it served. By any American postfrontier standards it was a rather unusual population. The town serviced not only the most densely settled area west of the Blue Ridge but also the wealthiest. On the one hand, it received a permanent boost in the purchasing power of its clientele with the immigration of eastern planters, especially after 1780, and summer boosts during the spa season. Thus, the influence of the wealthy Millwood society provided a specialized market for certain goods and services that were to be found nowhere else in the West—the production of quality cabinetware and snuff, summer theater, horse racing, resident artists, and the like.[20] However, some of Frederick County's wealthiest settlers and most of its absentee planters rarely required an urban locus for their trading activities. By providing their own wagon transportation, for example, they could afford to deal directly with external wholesale merchants, as Lord Fairfax, Horatio Gates, and Adam Stephen did; or they could ship in basic food supplies for agricultural workers on their valley quarters, as Nathaniel Burwell did. To some extent these practices detracted from rather than contributed to Winchester's commercial growth.

At the same time, both Winchester and Staunton supported a number of craft and manufacturing functions that further contributed to their commercial dominance. Craftsmen were present in both settlements during their early growth, but it is impossible to determine how many there were and how varied their contributions were during the latter part of the century. The large population of Berkeley and Frederick counties and their relatively high purchasing power during the last quarter of the century guaranteed Winchester a larger and more varied set of craftsmen than Staunton. Wheelwrights, cabinetmakers, and clockmakers were always in demand in the northern town, and leather and metal goods were important items of trade. Staunton, on the other hand,

20. Bliss, "The Tuckahoe in New Virginia," *Va. Mag. Hist. Biog.* 59 (1951):392–93; La Rochefoucauld-Liancourt, *Travels,* 2:90–93, 102–5.

built up a reputation as a textile center, and spinners, weavers, and clothiers were prominent among its crafts people. Yet a great deal of the valley's processing and manufacturing was highly decentralized and occurred outside of an urban environment. For example, Rockingham County had become one of the most thriving industrial counties west of the Blue Ridge by the turn of the century, but it remained one of the least urbanized areas in the valley.

Impact of Manufacturing on Trade

During the first thirty years of valley settlement, manufacturing had not only been highly decentralized, its contributions to the region's export trade had been minimal. Although there had been some trade in locally manufactured textiles within the valley itself, few domestic items were exported. To pay for imported manufactured goods, settlers had exported mainly surplus products from hunting, farming, and animal husbandry. During the ten years before the Revolutionary War, the upper valley in particular made considerable strides in the domestic production of the coarser types of cloth. It continued to produce linen and woolen goods and to specialize in osnaburg. In 1775 one Tidewater Virginian estimated that Augusta County produced enough osnaburg to supply the entire population of the state with such items as shirts, jackets, trousers, and dresses.[21]

The nonimportation agreements of 1774 and the ensuing war encouraged new attempts to expand the textile industry of the Shenandoah Valley as a source of home manufactures. In 1776 an Ulster immigrant, Smyth Tandy, established a fulling mill and bleaching green near Staunton. He requested financial aid from the Virginia government and during the war exported linen goods to Richmond and Fredericksburg. In addition, wagonloads of linens, which he originally intended for Williamsburg, were diverted to army use. When the linen trade declined drastically in 1782, the mill fell into disuse, but when the market for linens began to revive during the early 1790s, it was opened again.[22] The importance of the Shenandoah Valley as a hemp-producing area during the war encouraged the Virginia Assembly to establish a sailcloth factory in Staunton and a factory in Winchester making cloth from hemp and

21. Cited in Victor S. Clark, *History of Manufactures in the United States,* 3 vols. (Washington, D.C.: Carnegie Institution of Washington, 1929), 1:223.

22. Legislative Petitions, Augusta County, Nov. 4, 1776, and Nov. 1, 1791, and also *Virginia Gazette* (Richmond), July 27, 1782.

flax. Most, if not all, of the sailcloth produced in Staunton was manufactured into tents and bags for the use of the army. When that demand
disappeared after 1783 so also did the Staunton factory, although Winchester managed to maintain its cloth factory and a ropewalk throughout
the remainder of the century.

Between 1775 and 1800 the valley produced a wide range of textiles.
Producers were encouraged by the expanding markets for cloth
and clothing after 1790. Not only did the linen trade revive, so
also did the American market for woolens and mixed goods. Over
the next twenty years textile production throughout the valley expanded
rapidly to the extent that the region ranked second only to the six counties
of the northern Piedmont from Loudoun to Albemarle immediately over
the Blue Ridge. According to Tench Coxe's figures, by 1810 the six
valley counties were producing textile products worth $306,615, compared
with $467,000 for the six adjacent Piedmont counties.[23]

It was in Rockingham County that the major textile developments
occurred. According to Coxe, by 1810 the county had by far the most
diversified output of textiles in western Virginia, and its annual output
of over 300,000 yards of cloth made it the third leading textile-producing
county in the state (table 15). It ranked second only to Berkeley
in its output of mixed cotton goods and, with Augusta, ranked among
the top seven counties in linen production. Coxe's figures are of
questionable accuracy, however; one point making them suspect is the
absence of a return of woolen production in Augusta County, which
was probably the leading woolen county west of the Blue Ridge by the
early nineteenth century. Staunton woolens sold widely throughout
western Virginia. It is probable that with the state's two leading
producers of mixed cotton goods and the state's greatest concentration
of linen goods in Augusta, Rockingham, and Shenandoah counties,
much of this output was sold in Virginia markets outside the valley,
particularly in the form of osnaburg. Hats, too, were an important
export item, with Frederick and Rockingham counties ranking
second and third, respectively, in the state in terms of annual output.

The products of four other industries in the valley were significant in
their own right and contributed surplus output to the region's export
trade by the end of the century. These products were derived from
the iron industry, tanning and leather, distilling, and wood-using
industries. Western Virginia is much better endowed with mineral
resources than the eastern half of the state; this fact was apparent even
during the second half of the eighteenth century, when the minerals of

23. Coxe, *Statement of Arts and Manufactures*, p. 88.

Table 15. Output of manufactures in the Shenandoah Valley, 1810

Manufacture	No. of producing counties in state[1]	Berkeley County[2]	Rank	Frederick County	Rank	Shenandoah County	Rank	Rockingham County	Rank	Augusta County	Rank	Rockbridge County	Rank
Cotton goods	43	—	—	45,108 yds	28	—	—	33,893 yds	32	—	—	13,500 yds	37
Mixed cottons	34	95,191 yds	1	24,591 yds	21	—	—	84,507 yds	2	—	—	—	—
Linen goods	65	10,300 yds	61	47,463 yds	35	145,960 yds	9	157,046 yds	7	221,640 yds	5	34,801 yds	45
Woolen goods	30	19,455 yds	10	18,307 yds	11	—	—	25,764 yds	6	—	—	10,557 yds	17
Stockings	24	14,612 prs	4	—	—	—	—	360 prs	23	—	—	—	—
Hats	63	5,884	9	11,207	2	8,405	6	10,130	3	5,965	8	2,125	19
Guns	19	43	14	150	6	70	9	262	3	—	—	—	—
Gunpowder	20	1,000 lbs	13	—	—	490 lbs	17	6,650 lbs	5	—	—	9,000 lbs	3
Iron	15	—	—	—	—	1,754 tns	3	25 tns	14	3,158 tns	1	200 tns	9
Copperware	8	—	—	—	—	$2,043	5	—	—	—	—	$5,000	2
Clocks, watches	6	$1,300	3	—	—	$560	5	—	—	—	—	—	—
Soap	17	—	—	—	—	—	—	43,157 lbs	5	—	—	—	—
Candles	17	—	—	—	—	—	—	4,285 lbs	14	—	—	—	—
Footwear	68	12,948 prs	7	13,517 prs	5	—	—	21,029 prs	1	3,032 prs	26	—	—
Saddles	52	$10,325	7	—	—	$8,385	9	$8,100	10	$15,000	5	4,245	21
Beer, liquor	76	102,915 gals	7	119,500 gals	3	91,600 gals	8	138,894 gals	2	250,520 gals	1	108,936 gals	6
Snuff, tobacco	12	—	—	—	—	25,000 lbs	6	—	—	—	—	—	—
Cabinetware	38	$3,300	12	$9,650	2	$3,081	14	$3,350	11	$3,992	9	$2,400	17
Carriages	28	$3,500	12	$28,800	1	—	—	—	—	—	—	—	—
Paper	4	$5,000	3	$5,600(?)	2	—	—	—	—	$14,400	—	—	—
Windsor chairs	3	—	—	$1,250	2	—	—	—	—	—	—	—	—

SOURCE: Tench Coxe, A Statement of the Arts and Manufactures of the United States of America for the Year 1810, (Philadelphia: A. Cornman, Jr., 1814), pp. 88–114.
[1] Includes the cities of Richmond, Norfolk, and Petersburg.
[2] Includes Jefferson County.

the Appalachians were just beginning to be exploited. Although the lead ores at Chiswell Mines in the southern Valley of Virginia had been-worked since the French and Indian War, it was the iron resources of the region which were most exploited after 1760. Small pockets of iron ore (brown and red hematites) were found along the foothills of the Blue Ridge and the North Mountain in the Shenandoah Valley. As early as 1742 a German settler named Vestal established a small ironworks near the main branch of the Shenandoah River in Frederick County.[24] And by 1750 George William Fairfax, in conjunction with merchants in Alexandria and Norfolk, had established a furnace and forge east of Winchester known as the Bloomery.[25] Lewis Stephens founded another ironworks, the Malboro, six years later on Cedar Creek near the future site of Stephensburg, and it was in this works that Isaac Zane, Jr., became involved in 1767. A year later he acquired the full rights to the Marlboro furnace by buying out his three partners.[26] About the same time, the first ironworks in the upper valley had been completed on Mossy Creek in Augusta County, almost on the Augusta-Rockingham boundary. The founder was another Pennsylvania German, John Miller, father of the Henry Miller who was to become, along with Zane, one of the two largest iron manufacturers in western Virginia during the eighteenth century.[27] In 1774 Henry Miller, in partnership with his friend Mark Bird of Berks County, Pennsylvania, bought three tracts of land on Mossy Creek with the intent of expanding the ironworks; within five years Miller had acquired sole ownership of the entire works, which he retained until his death in 1796.[28]

The Mossy Creek Ironworks produced bar iron for local blacksmiths and a whole series of domestic items such as stoves, pots, kettles, and agricultural tools. So far as it can be determined, these ironworks had little direct influence on the location of other craft and industrial activities, which remained widely scattered. In any case, there were no other

24. Kathleen Bruce, *Virginia Iron Manufacture in the Slave Era* (New York: Century Company, 1931), p. 21.

25. Bliss, "Tuckahoe in the Valley," p. 56.

26. Roger W. Moss, Jr., "Isaac Zane Jr., a 'Quaker for the Times,' " *Va. Mag. Hist. Biog.* 77 (1969):294–95.

27. Smith et al., *Pennsylvania Germans of the Shenandoah Valley* (p. 202), state that Miller's ironworks was first established in the early 1750s, while Kathleen Bruce, *Virginia Iron Manufacture* (p. 21), suggests 1760 for the building of the furnace and five years later for the completion of the forge. She attributes the ironworks to John Miller. The earliest mention of a Henry Miller in the county records is for March 1764 (Augusta Co. Deed Book 11: 821).

28. Augusta Co. Deed Books 20:350–64, 21:424–26, 22:138–42, 244–46, 23:27. Miller acquired Bird's half of the ironworks for almost £18,000.

large iron-using concerns in the upper valley. Unlike Zane, who exported considerable quantities of iron to William Allason in Falmouth and Hall and Gelpin in Alexandria during the 1760s and 1770s for export to Britain, Miller primarily supplied local markets.[29] During the Revolutionary War the demands of the army in western Virginia benefited both Miller and Zane, and they went on to war production. By 1780, according to Jefferson, both ironmasters were producing about 150 tons of bar iron annually and some 600 tons of pig iron, placing them among the four leading iron producers in the state.[30] Moreover, Miller by this time is said to have been producing iron pots, pans, and other items "that were successfully peddled through the valley and over the mountains to a growing market."[31]

Ironmasters in the lower valley had other local iron-using manufactures to support even before the outbreak of the war. The most notable was Adam Stephen's armory near Martinsburg, which was producing about a dozen high-quality muskets weekly by the eve of the Revolution. During the war the gunnery was kept extremely busy supplying firearms to the Virginia militia and sending them by wagon to Williamsburg. More than thirty men were employed in this war production, about twice the peacetime level.[32]

The demands of the army during the Revolutionary War and the growing demands for iron manufactures after the war encouraged the development of other iron interests in the valley. During the 1780s two furnaces were opened in southwestern Shenandoah County and an ironworks was erected near Lexington.[33] Between 1790 and 1804 at least two successful and one abortive attempt were made to establish ironworks near Staunton and Lexington.[34]

29. Letter Book (1770–89), pp. 5, 10, 43, and Letter Book (1757–70), Allason Papers, Va. State Lib.; Hart, *Valley of Virginia*, pp. 23–24; Moss, "Isaac Zane Jr., a 'Quaker for the Times,'" 296–97.

30. Jefferson, *Notes on the State of Virginia*, ed. Peden, pp. 27–28. Miller obtained his charcoal from the woodland areas he owned along the Mossy Creek and from occasional arrangements with local settlers "to coal fifteen hundred cords of wood" (Augusta Co. District Court Order Book [1789–93], pp. 521–22.

31. Bruce, *Virginia Iron Manufacture*, p. 21.

32. Adam Stephen Papers, Manuscript Div., Lib. Cong., especially correspondence between Stephen and Anthony Noble for the years 1774 through 1779.

33. Bruce, *Virginia Iron Manufacture*, p. 65; Smith et al., *Pennsylvania Germans*, pp. 202–3. Bruce (p. 22) has also suggested that a nail factory in Staunton flourished during the late 1770s, but there does not seem to be any local evidence to support this nor the presence of a slitting mill. See also Augusta Co. Order Books 21:474, 23:337; Rockbridge Co. Order Book 3:422; *Virginia Gazette* (Richmond), Nov. 26, 1799.

34. *Virginia Centinel* (Winchester), June 27, 1798; Augusta Co. Order Book 22:242; *The Industrial South* (Richmond), Dec. 13, 1884. In April 1801 William Dougherty of Augusta

By 1810, according to Tench Coxe, most of the iron production in the valley had shifted to the central and southern counties. At least eight ironworks were in operation, and the iron output of Augusta and Shenandoah counties ranked them first and third, respectively, in the state (tables 15 and 16). On the other hand, the manufacture of nails and, to a lesser extent, guns was concentrated in Frederick and Berkeley counties, which indicates that there were probably several ironworks in Frederick County to supply the needed iron.

The manufacture of leather, together with tanning, was the leading small-craft industry in the valley by the end of the eighteenth century. During the years of pioneer settlement, the production of leather goods had generally been for local consumption, although small amounts of leather, footwear, and shoe thread had occasionally been sent to eastern Virginia. This trade continued throughout the remainder of the century but was reoriented during the Revolutionary War to supply the western militia. The raw materials for the leather and tanning industry had been derived initially from the products of hunting, particularly deerskins, supplemented by hides and skins off the farm. The expansion of western settlement during the 1770s eliminated the supplies from hunting so that by the early 1780s the raw materials were derived mainly from calf and sheep skins.[35] Tanning was a widely distributed activity in the valley, and tanners formed an integrated group, often meeting socially or to fix prices.[36] The leading branches of the leather industry were footwear and saddlery, with clothing (coats, breeches, and caps) a poor third. Some geographical concentration of tanning and leather activities had occurred by the beginning of the nineteenth century, especially in footwear. By 1810, according to Coxe, there were probably about 100 tanneries in the valley, with about 30 in Frederick County alone, making it the second leading tanning county in the state, and another 20 in Shenandoah County. The production of footwear, however, was concentrated in Rockingham County, the leading producer and exporter in the state, with significant outputs also from Frederick and Berkeley counties. Augusta was one of Virginia's leading producers of saddleware, and Shenandoah had a number of leathercraft industries and

County sold Philemon Towson, the Baltimore merchant, 450 acres on Irish Creek in Rockbridge County including a furnace for £200 (Augusta Co. Deed Book 1A [Circuit Court, 1789–1801]:349–50).

35. Account Books, Rowan Family Collection, Box 1 (1774–1905), McCormick Coll., Wis. State Hist. Soc.; Frederick Co. Will Book 6:338–44. The tanning vats were made mainly from black and chestnut oaks.

36. In October 1792, 10 Rockingham County tanners met in Harrisonburg to fix prices for hides, skins, and finished leather. See *Virginia Centinel* (Winchester), Nov.12, 1792.

Table 16. Industrial facilities in the Shenandoah Valley, 1810

Mills and machinery	No. of active counties	Berkeley County	Rank	Frederick County	Rank	Shenandoah County	Rank	Rockingham County	Rank	Augusta County	Rank	Rockbridge County	Rank
Looms	85	286	66	384	48	606	22	764	11	419	41	—	—
Spindles	9	158	2	—	—	—	—	6	7	—	—	—	—
Spinning wheels	5	—	—	—	—	—	—	—	—	3,701	2	—	—
Carding machines	22	8	3	13	2	6	5	7	4	6	5	2	8
Fulling machines	22	5	2	7	1	5	2	3	6	3	6	3	6
Furnaces	9	—	—	—	—	2 (1,254 tns)	3	—	—	3 (3,158 tns)	2	—	—
Forges	13	—	—	—	—	3 (500 tns)	1	2 (25 tns)	12	—	—	2 (200 tns)	6
Trip-hammers	7	—	—	1	3	—	—	—	—	—	—	3	1
Naileries	9	c. 4,500 lbs	8	40,320 lbs	3	—	—	—	—	—	—	—	—
Stills	10	—	—	139	2	—	—	20	8	314	1	—	—
Distilleries	74	c. 85 (98,000 gals)	7	38 (109,000 gals)	5	44 (92,000 gals)	8	116 (139,000 gals)	2	250 (251,000 gals)	1	125 (109,000 gals)	5
Breweries	5	c. 2 (5,300 gals)	5	c. 2 (10,400 gals)	4	—	—	—	—	—	—	—	—
Tanneries	65	c. 10 (12,938 hides)	6	c. 20 (28,100 hides)	2	c. 15 (15,761 hides)	4	14 (12,137 hides)	8	10 (12,850 hides)	7	c. 10 (9,750 hides)	9
Linseed oil mills	14	1 (750 gals)	9	4 (3,000 gals)	3	5 (14,812 gals)	1	4 (1,750 gals)	5	6 (6,530 gals)	2	4 (1,600 gals)	6
Paper mills	4	1 (2,000 reams)	2	1(?)	?	—	—	—	—	1 (6,000 reams)	1	—	—
Sawmills	5	—	—	—	—	—	—	44	1	40	2	—	—
Potteries	2	—	—	—	—	—	—	3	—	3	1	—	—
Gunpowder mills	21	1 (1,000 lbs)	16	—	—	1 (490 lbs)	19	7 (6,650 lbs)	4	(1,400 lbs)	—	9 (9,000 lbs)	3

Source: Tench Coxe, *A Statement of the Arts and Manufactures of the United States of America for the Year 1810* (Philadelphia: A. Cornman Jr., 1814), pp. 88–114.

undoubtedly a footwear industry which was not recorded in the 1810 figures. Tanyards were to be found in all the major towns in the valley by 1800; Winchester had five.

In the minds of eighteenth-century Virginians, the industry most associated with the Shenandoah Valley was distilling, and with good reason. The valley was the largest regional producer of liquors in Virginia, if not in the entire South, by the end of the century. In 1810 Augusta was by far the leading county, with an annual production of over 250,000 gallons of whiskeys and brandies. Rockingham and Frederick counties ranked second and third, respectively, with the other three counties ranked not far behind. In total, the approximately eighty valley distilleries were producing almost 800,000 gallons annually, one-third of Virginia's entire recorded output, but the value per gallon was only half that produced in the Tidewater counties. Brewing, on the other hand, was not a significant industry in Virginia and was found only in Berkeley and Frederick counties in the valley.

Much of the whiskey, brandy, and beer that was produced supplied the increasing number of ordinaries and taverns serving the travelers passing up and down the valley or going westward to the mineral springs. The first significant increase in the number of ordinary licenses had occurred during the French and Indian War, when about two dozen were issued annually throughout the valley. Another increase of the same magnitude took place during the Revolutionary War, and an average of six new licenses were supplied every year in the upper valley between 1785 and 1800.[37] In 1796 La Rochefoucauld-Liancourt reported no fewer than eight inns on the fifty-mile stretch of road between Staunton and Warm Springs.[38] In addition to supplying local demand, whiskey gained some importance as an export item after 1765, considerable quantities being sent to Berkeley Springs and Warm Springs and to the settlements located along the roads leading from the valley to Richmond, Fredericksburg, and Alexandria.

Wood-using industries comprised another important sector in the valley's manufacturing structure during the last third of the eighteenth century. Surprisingly few sawmills were recorded during the colonial period, but a considerable expansion of milling activities occurred during and after the Revolutionary War, and the emergence of a variety of wood-based activities provided a market for hardwoods in particular. In 1810 Coxe listed a total of eighty-four mills in Rockingham and

37. Augusta Co. Order Books 19–26; Rockingham Co. Judgments and Orders, Books 2–6; Rockbridge Co. Order Books 2–4.
38. La Rochefoucauld-Liancourt, *Travels*, 2:90.

Augusta counties, three-quarters of all the mills recorded in the state, but he gave no figures for the other valley counties. He gave no production figures either, an omission which raises several issues.

The large number of trees needed to supply the sawmills would have required a considerable amount of forest clearance each year in the areas adjacent to the mills. This cutting, in conjunction with the clearance activities that took place in the wake of commercial hemp and wheat cultivation after the early 1760s, must have produced a marked reduction in the region's forest cover by the end of the century. Thomas Bryan Martin remarked from Greenway Court in 1790 that few trees would remain soon to conceal the rocks of the Blue Ridge.[39] Despite the importance of such activities as furniture making and the production of wagons and carriages, all of which were especially prominent in Frederick County, it seems hardly likely that they could have generated sufficient demand to keep well over one hundred mills dealing with lumber in operation by the end of the century. According to Coxe's figures the Shenandoah Valley was the only significant area of paper production in Virginia at the turn of the century. Of the three paper mills in the valley, by far the largest was the one built by Henry Miller, the ironmaster, in Augusta County in the late 1780s. It was maintained after his death in 1796 largely to supply the growing demands for paper by printing companies in Staunton, Harrisonburg, and Newmarket and by local stores. Most if not all of the raw material for the mill, however, was derived from rags rather than from wood pulp.[40] Construction activities might have provided a substantial but fluctuating market for lumber. There is no evidence that logs were exported; road haulage was out of the question, and the extremely meandering path of the lower Shenandoah River rendered transport by water infeasible. It would appear, therefore, that the annual production of sawn lumber per sawmill was quite small and was limited by the demands of the local market area.

A number of specialized craft activities rounded out the very diversified manufacturing structure of the valley by the turn of the century. The hat industry continued to rely on the furs and pelts of wild animals long after the Revolutionary War, and the continued demand for headgear necessitated an ever-widening search for raw materials.[41]

39. Martin to Gen. Philip Martin, Dec. 15, 1790, Wykeham-Martin Papers (microfilm, Colonial Williamsburg).

40. Augusta Co. Will Book 1A (Superior Court, 1778–1828): 134–38. See also *Staunton Eagle,* Aug. 28, 1807; Klaus G. Wust, "German Printing in Virginia, Check List, 1789–1834," *Society for the History of the Germans in Maryland,* Report 28 (1953): 55–57.

41. The inventory of a Frederick County hatmaker, James Walker, in 1800 included

Rockingham was also a major producer of soap and, to a lesser extent, candles, and Rockingham and Rockbridge provided substantial supplies of gunpowder. Rockbridge and Shenandoah had small but valuable copperware outputs, and Augusta possessed three of the only four potteries recorded in Virginia in 1810. However, by and large, the craft activities of the upper valley were neither so large nor so varied as those farther north.

The growth and diversity of the valley's manufacturing was impressive by Virginia's standards during the last third of the century. However, the main relationship between the region's industry and trade after 1765 was not so much to add to the variety and capacity of its exports as to reduce the region's dependency on outside areas for some manufactured goods, especially gunpowder, iron, nails, and some leather and textile goods. At the same time, locally produced textiles, footwear, and whiskey were exported to northern and eastern markets, while the valley supplied gunpowder, iron, clothing, and liquor to the growing population of areas immediately to the west.

Local Trading Patterns in Western Virginia

The trading relationships maintained by the Shenandoah Valley underwent significant changes after the early 1760s, mainly in response to the increasing commercial significance of the region and to its changing locational significance within the general westward movement of population. Both the pioneer activities and the frontier location were superseded by a new set of functional and spatial relationships after the French and Indian War. The reduction in Indian activities after 1763 in the areas to the south and west of the valley had opened them up for white settlement; hemp specialization provided the valley with its first large-scale export crop.

During the last third of the century, local trading patterns within western Virginia exhibited elements of both continuity and change. Some aspects of the rudimentary trading relationships of the pioneer period lingered on until the end of the century. To the degree that they did, they maintained the initial pattern of decentralized trade. The most obvious example was the country store.

Local stores in the valley continued to supply settlers with goods and services and to market local farm and craft produce. The types of

---

skins or furs from beaver, rabbit, red fox, wildcat, mink, raccoon, muskrat, wolf, and panther (Frederick Co. Will Book 6:523–40).

goods sold and the services rendered remained much the same as they had been before the early 1760s. The items in most common demand were cloth, powder and shot, salt, sugar, shoes, knives and forks, liquor, and a large variety of domestic sundries. Salt remained the single most critical item because it still had to be entirely imported.[42] Salted meat remained a basic part of the local diet, and "salted pork, boiled with turnip tops by way of greens, or fried bacon, or fried salted fish, with warm sallad, dressed with vinegar and the melted fat which remains in the frying pan after dressing the bacon, is the only food to be got at most of the taverns in this country."[43]

The size of local merchants' accounts and the methods of payment varied more from place to place and with individual merchants than over time. Table 17 indicates the kind of payments made to three local merchants during the period 1761 to 1797. The Massachusetts account is included for purposes of comparison. Because these are sample accounts, it would be unwise to make too many generalizations from them. However, a few trends may be suggested. With the exception of Andrew Reid's accounts, payment in money was responsible for at least 60% of the payments made, and payment in services contributed only 9% to 10% of the whole. Goods usually accounted for 28% to 31% of the payments. William Anderson's accounts therefore would seem to be the most typical example of local merchandising, at least in the upper Shenandoah Valley, during the second half of the century. Typified by Josiah Dwight's accounts, payment in goods in the Connecticut Valley tended to decline and money payments to increase during the last third of the century.[44] This pattern may have held less true in the Shenandoah Valley, where money payments were at a relatively high level in any case. Although money payments were by far the most common, few accounts were fully paid up at any given time. Only 107 (29%) of the 364 accounts recorded with Read and Johnston were actually paid in full by 1770.[45]

Payment in money most often meant small amounts of cash, and local merchants frequently acted as bankers, lending small amounts of

42. Salt was particularly scarce during the Revolution and local citizens' committees were formed to allocate supplies. A bushel of salt cost 7s. during the war compared with 3s. normally. See Larry G. Bowman, "The Scarcity of Salt in Virginia during the American Revolution," *Va. Mag. Hist. Biog.* 57 (1969): 464–72.

43. Weld, *Travels,* p. 136. Although Weld did not mention them, potatoes must have been part of daily fare by the 1790s.

44. Margaret E. Martin, *Merchants and Trade of the Connecticut River Valley, 1750–1820,* Smith College Studies in History, 24, nos. 1–4 (1938–1939): 150–51.

45. Thirty-six accounts had no payment entered at all, explaining the difference between the total of 364 accounts and the 328 listed in table 17.

Table 17. Payment of local accounts, 1761–97

Merchant account	Location	Period	Payment			No. of Accounts
			Money	Goods	Service	
Josiah Dwight	Springfield, Mass.	1755–67	59.1%	31.4%	9.5%	?
Read & Johnston	Staunton, Va.	1761–70	73.2%	17.7%	9.9%	328
William Anderson	Rockbridge, Va.	1775–85	62.7%	28.0%	9.3%	374
Andrew Reid	Rockbridge, Va.	1776–97	40.0%	28.6%	31.4%	140

SOURCES: Margaret E. Martin, *Merchants and Trade of The Connecticut River Valley, 1750–1820*, Smith College Studies in History, vol. 24, nos. 1–4 (1938–39), p. 150; Ledger of Mathew Read and Hugh Johnston, College of William and Mary Library; William A. Anderson Ledger, University of Virginia Library; and Andrew Reid Account Book, Cyrus Hall McCormick Collection, Wisconsin State Historical Society.

cash (£2 or £3) or discounting bonds (generally between £2 and £5). Payment in goods, particularly during the 1770s and 1780s, largely involved hemp and butter; over 65% of the payments in goods contained in William Anderson's ledger were for these two items. Corn and wheat were the grains most commonly mentioned; animal produce also included beef, pork, bacon, cheese, beeswax, and skins. Linen cloth, shoe thread, and whiskey were occasionally mentioned. Payment in work involved a large variety of services depending upon the needs and accommodations of individual merchants. Andrew Reid's accounts reflect the fact that he owned a farm, a gristmill, and a brewery and sought a number of services in order to maintain them.

Trading accounts with local settlers were usually small, seldom amounting to more than £10 per annum. Of the accounts held by Matthew Read and Hugh Johnston between 1761 and 1770, 50% were for sums rangingbetween £1 and £10, 42% for sums of less than £1, and only 8% for sums over £10. Their largest account was for £146, which was spread over almost a seven-year period. Data on the size of local accounts were best recorded during periods of economic recession. Although largely immune from external economic crises during the pioneer period of settlement, local merchants began to feel the repercussions of Virginia's heavy financial indebtedness to Britain during the early 1770s. The British bank crisis of 1772 and the resultant claims by British merchants on their colonial debtors were felt as far inland as western Virginia.[46] Between 1773 and 1775 William Bowyer of Staunton, for example, called in debts on almost one hundred customers. Less than 5% of these debts were for more than £10.[47] Another period of economic recession occurred in the immediate postwar period, between 1783 and 1787. Evidence from available merchant accounts, however, suggests that during these difficult years, although there may have been an overall contraction of trading activities, there was also a considerable extension of local credit and payment by service because of the lack of hard cash.

Two of the most difficult questions to answer about local trade afte. 1765 are the number of merchants in operation in the valley at any given time and the extent of their trading areas within western Virginia. After the Revolution, retail merchants in Virginia had to apply each year for a trading license, for which they had to pay £5.[48] Twenty-four individuals in Augusta County and five in Rockbridge County were recorded as retail merchants between 1786 and 1790.[49] By 1800 the total number of merchant licenses issued in the upper valley was fifty-nine, sixteen each in Rockingham and Rockbridge counties, and twenty-seven in Augusta County.[50] The lower valley records are less comprehensive, with no report for Berkeley, twenty-five licenses in Frederick excluding Winchester, and seventeen in Shenandoah.

Available information indicates that although most retailers served the immediate population, some had a remarkably extensive service area. Most of Read and Johnston's customers lived in the Staunton area, but they had at least seven customers at Rockfish Gap, one on the Cowpasture River, another on Catawba Creek in Botetourt County, and one at Roanoke. William Anderson's customers came mainly from Rockbridge and Augusta counties, but he had sixteen customers in Amherst County east of the Blue Ridge and ten customers on the Holston River and one on the Clinch River in southwestern Virginia. Andrew Reid had several customers in Amherst County and in southwestern Virginia, as well as a small clientele in Greenbrier County to the west.

46. Richard B. Sheridan, "The British Credit Crisis of 1772 and the American Colonies," *Journ. of Econ. Hist.* 22 (1960):161–86.

47. Augusta Judgments, 1775–79 (files 427–29).

48. Hening, *Statutes*, 12:286–87, 13:114–15.

49. Augusta Co. Order Books 20–21; Rockbridge Co. Order Books 2–3. These records are far from complete since a comparison of the merchant accounts in the Augusta judgments for the years 1786 to 1790 reveals the names of several retail merchants who were not included in the county lists.

50. County personal property tax records for 1800. During the last decade of the century the number of licenses issued annually fluctuated between 40 and 59 in the upper valley.

Most valley merchants also were the beneficiaries of the transient trade of travelers moving through the region in all but the coldest winter months. Local merchants could develop a small but reliable trade selling liquor to the ordinary and tavern keepers who serviced these customers. The average liquor bill for an ordinary during the last two decades of the century seems to have been between £4 and £5 a year.[51] However, local merchants who were engaged only in retail trade were not able to supply ordinaries and taverns with two of their most important needs, rum and wine. These products were usually imported by valley merchants who were engaged in both wholesale and retail trade, and who therefore had more extensive commercial contacts with the outside world. This distinction poses additional questions. What were the characteristics of the mercantile hierarchy within the Shenandoah Valley, and to what extent did they change after the early 1760s? Second, to what degree can one define the existence of a specialized mercantile class as an expression of western economic development by the end of the eighteenth century?

The Development of a Mercantile Hierarchy

Merchant class may not be the most appropriate term to describe merchant groups in the valley during the latter part of the century. If specialized merchants operated as functioning social groups, they were most likely to be those involved in both retail and wholesale trade. The proclivity for individual settlers to conduct their external purchases independent of local merchants and to own a substantial number of slaves who contributed little to consumer demand may have retarded the emergence of such groups, especially in the lower valley where these practices were more widespread. That prominent and wealthy members of the propertied classes continued to conduct much of their trading activities in this manner well after 1775 is clearly expressed in the attitude of Lord Fairfax's successor at Greenway Court, Thomas Bryan Martin, who viewed merchants as freight agents and

51. These figures are derived from an examination of local merchant accounts contained in the Augusta judgments between 1780 and 1800. Such accounts were not always with licensed tavern or ordinary owners. Thus, one traveler during the early nineteenth century complained that "the good people throughout this part of the country [Augusta County] . . . have an uncouth way of conferring an obligation. They will neither take out licenses, nor suffer their houses to be called taverns, and yet they entertain guests in what, they term, private entertainment. They tell the way worn traveller he m—a—y stay all night, but they make him pay tavern prices in the morning" (T. Caldwell, *A Tour through Part of Virginia in the Summer of 1808* [New York: H. C. Southwright,1809], p. 25).

distrusted their profit-oriented ways.[52] Adam Stephen and Horatio Gates also bypassed local merchants during the last quarter of the century. Their contacts were widely distributed. Stephen maintained at least two agents in Alexandria during the 1780s, James Adam and Robert Hood, and had dealings with four or five other Alexandria merchants as well as accounts with merchants in Richmond and Williamsburg and John Harket in Baltimore.[53] Horatio Gates's mercantile contacts were even more extensive. Before the Revolution his trade appears to have been primarily with Alexandria, but after it he expanded the number and distribution of his trading outlets through accounts with William Alexander in Richmond, Nicholls, Harrison and Company in Williamsburg, James F. Nourse in Annapolis, Carey and Tilghman in Baltimore, and with two Philadelphia connections, Mordecai Lewis and Willing, Morris and Stanwick.[54] Most of these accounts were from £10 to £30 for luxury items such as wine, clothing, china, and citrus fruits.

Such independent trading was much less common in the upper valley. Two locally prominent families, the Breckenridges and the Prestons, who had members living in Augusta, Rockbridge, Botetourt, and Montgomery counties, continued to trade directly with three Richmond merchants, John Howard, James Lyle, and Edward Johnson (on whom William Preston was especially dependent.)[55] The annual purchases made by individuals ranged from £25 to £100 and generally included salt, sugar, nails, and powder and shot, as well as more luxury items such as high-quality cloth and clothing, molasses, rum, and wine. After the Revolution one of the few citizens to indulge in this kind of trading relationship was Archibald Stuart, a Staunton lawyer, who had accounts in Albemarle' County through Thomas Jefferson and in Richmond with two merchants, Robert Gamble and Zachary Rowland.[56] It was no coincidence that both Stuart and William Preston had served as members of the Virginia legislature before they established private trading accounts with Richmond merchants.

52. Martin to Rev. Denny Martin, Nov. 1, 1791, Wykeham-Martin Papers (microfilm, Colonial Williamsburg).

53. Adam Stephen Papers, Manuscript Div., Lib. Cong.

54. Horatio Gates Papers, N.Y. Public Lib.; Gates, Miscellaneous Manuscripts, Chicago Historical Society (microfilm, Colonial Williamsburg). Gates also had contacts with Bristol before the Revolution through John Winstone, a merchant at Pages Warehouse, Hanover County, north of Richmond (Gates to Winstone, Mar. 15, 1774, Misc. Mss., Chicago Hist. Soc.). See also Hart, *Valley of Virginia,* pp. 149–51.

55. See Papers of the Breckenridge Family, vol. 1, Manuscript Div., Lib. Cong., and Preston Papers, Va. Hist. Soc.

56. Archibald Stuart Papers, Va. Hist. Soc., especially his accounts for the construction and repair of houses (1789–94) and his correspondence with Jefferson (1786–94).

The basic network of trading relationships in the Shenandoah Valley after 1765 remained in the hands of the local retail merchant. He not only served local farmers, townspeople, ordinary keepers, tavern owners, and travelers but also maintained close relations with local merchants engaged in the external, wholesale trade. There was no clear-cut division of labor between retail and wholesale merchandising. Several merchants functioned in both aspects, but none were solely engaged in the import trade. So far as can be determined, more than seventy individual merchants were almost entirely engaged in local retail trade in the lower valley by 1800 and about fifty in the upper valley. Many of them remained merchant-farmers rather than fully specialized merchants. A good example was Felix Gilbert, an early settler in the upper valley who had established a store in Staunton during the late 1750s. In 1764 he bought a 690-acre farm in Rockingham County at the intersection of the Fredericksburg and Winchester roads one mile from the site of Keezletown and five from the site of Harrisonburg. He kept a store there until 1785 when he put both the farm and store up for sale and later moved to Wilkes County, Georgia.[57] Similarly, the Rockbridge County merchant Andrew Reid conducted his merchant activities during the last quarter of the eighteenth century from a 180-acre farm. Thus, one may well ask to what extent a specialized merchant community actually did exist in the valley by the end of the century.

It is difficult to answer this question for the lower valley, where the record is extremely patchy. In the upper valley such a community, if it did exist, was certainly small, and consisted mainly of those merchants who were engaged almost full-time in both retail and wholesale trade. Although even these merchants at the top of the commercial hierarchy were widely distributed within the upper valley, the most important members were to be found operating out of Staunton—Sampson and George Mathews, William Bowyer, Anthony Mustoe and William Chambers, and Roger North.

The most prominent merchants in the upper Shenandoah Valley during the last third of the eighteenth century were the Mathews brothers, Sampson and George. Their careers indicate some of the processes involved and the opportunities available in western economic development after the French and Indian War. Both brothers had been active in land acquisition and trade in the upper valley since the early 1750s. By the early 1760s they had established themselves as ordinary keepers and merchant partners, dealing mainly in local retail trade and supplying

57. Augusta Co. Deed Book 8:181; *Virginia Gazette* (Richmond) Sept. 24, 1785; Rockingham Co. Deed Book 0:469.

imported liquors to ordinary and tavern owners.[58] Both men were active in military and civic services before the Revolutionary War; these interests also proved to be good for their business.[59]

The Mathews partnership had branched out into the import trade before 1775, largely through the trading connections Sampson Mathews had established in Richmond. Thus, by the early 1770s, they had trading accounts with Perkins, Buchanan and Brown in London through Thomas Adams in Richmond and with Cunningham and Company in Glasgow through John Turner in Rocky Ridge just west of Richmond.[60] The two brothers also bought slaves in eastern Virginia and on one occasion acquired an English servant who had just disembarked at Hampton Roads.[61] Yet even merchants with such eastern connections and activities as the Mathewses remained partially merchant-farmers throughout the colonial period. Although they maintained a house, store, and ordinary on the main street in Staunton and speculated in town lots, they also had a 2,080-acre farm on Mill Creek, which was run by George Mathews, a store nearby on the Little Calfpasture River, and another farther west in Greenbrier County.[62]

Sampson and George Mathews were well-established merchants before the outbreak of the Revolutionary War, but it was the opportunities made by or given to them during the war that left them both wealthy and preeminent after 1783. In the Revolutionary militia George rose to the rank of general; he became less interested in the commercial aspects of the partnership, moved to Georgia about 1786, and became its governor in 1790.[63] Although Sampson performed a number of military and civic

58. Augusta Co. Deed Book 6:276–79; Augusta Co. Order Book 6:318; Augusta Judgments, 1763, 1768, 1770 (files 405, 414, 419).

59. Augusta Co. Order Books 12:253, 13:48; Augusta Co. Deed Book 9:98–100; Purdie and Dixon's *Virginia Gazette* (Williamsburg), June 27, 1771; Hugh Blair Grigsby, "The Founders of Washington College," *Washington and Lee University Historical Papers* 2 (1890): 12–13; Herndon, "George Mathews, Frontier Patriot," *Va. Mag. Hist. Biog.* 77 (1969):308–14.

60. Account of Messrs. Perkins, Buchanan and Brown with Thomas Adams, 1772, Adams Papers, Va. Hist. Soc.; Cunninghame, William and Co., Accounts of a Virginia Firm Dealing in General Merchandise, 1770–1809, Brock Coll., Huntington Lib. Their account with the London firm for 1772 involved some goods worth £1,301 8s. at 50% credit advance, while their account with the Glasgow firm for 1773, mainly for gunpowder, leather breeches, and steel goods, amounted to only £25.

61. Rind's *Virginia Gazette* (Williamsburg), July 13, 1769; Purdie's *Virginia Gazette* (Williamsburg), Mar. 10, 1775.

62. Augusta Co. Deed Book 9:98–100; Augusta Co. Order Books 12:253, 15:327; Purdie's *Virginia Gazette* (Williamsburg), Aug. 8, 1777; Greenbrier Store, Day Book, Sampson and George Mathews (1771–73), Va. State Lib.

63. Herndon, "George Mathews, Frontier Patriot," *Va. Mag. Hist. Biog.* 77 (1969): 322–23; Grigsby, "The Founders of Washington College," *Washington and Lee Univ. Hist. Papers* 2

duties during the war, no doubt aided by his brother's influential position, most of his activities were commercial in nature. As a prominent merchant, landowner, and magistrate who also had extensive connections in Richmond, he was a logical choice of the Virginia government to organize the merchandising and transportation of hemp from the upper Shenandoah Valley during the war. Thus, he was made hemp purchasing agent in Augusta County for the Virginia government. He maintained hemp warehouses in Staunton and Richmond and was intimately connected with the public ropewalk in Richmond. Together with Alex Sinclair, another local merchant and government purchasing agent, Mathews superintended the establishment of the sailcloth factory in Staunton. At the same time, he continued his local trading activities and had a new store built on the road to Warm Springs, twenty-eight miles west of Staunton.[64] With so many commercial interests in Richmond after the war, including ownership of a tanyard, Mathews chose to remain there until about 1790. He had a house built in Staunton, but soon retired to his farm which by then was in Bath County, and served as that county's first high sheriff.[65]

Although Bowyer, Mustoe and Chambers, and Roger North were essentially urban-based wholesale and retail merchants in Staunton, Alex Sinclair, like the Mathews brothers, had farming as well as trading interests. Most of these men also served in public office. In the upper valley by the end of the colonial period and thereafter, the small nucleus of wholesale-retail merchants were at the top of the local commercial hierarchy. To a large degree they were on a socioeconomic par with the landed families of the region, the Prestons, the Pattons, the Breckenridges, and the Lewises, except perhaps in their greater financial indebtedness to outside interests. A similar status was denied the merchants of the lower valley.

Retail merchants in the upper valley during the last third of the century remained widely distributed throughout the region. Of the fifty registered merchants in 1800, the largest concentration was in Staunton, where approximately ten of Augusta County's twenty-seven merchants resided. Smaller clusters, of three or four merchants each, were in Harrisonburg and Lexington. As a rough estimate, therefore, about 30% of each county's

(1890): 87–88; *Calendar of Virginia State Papers,* ed. Palmer, 3:49–50; Augusta Co. Deed Books 25:324, 27:490.

64. Augusta Co. Order Books 17:184, 19:17; Virginia State Auditor's Item No. 218, Va. State Lib.; Legislative Petitions, Augusta County, June 2, 1777; *Virginia Gazette* (Richmond), Jan. 3, 1784.

65. *Virginia Gazette* (Richmond), April 3, 1784, June 26, 1784, Nov. 2, 1791; Augusta Co. Deed Books 26:104, 409–10, 27:371; Grigsby, "The Founders of Washington College," *Washington and Lee Univ. Hist. Papers* 2 (1890): 87–88.

merchants was located in the county town, with the largest number living in Staunton. With the exceptions of Keezletown and Waynesboro, none of the new settlements established in the upper valley after the Revolution had merchants among their founders or earliest settlers. The large number of rural merchants, or merchant-farmers, were dispersed throughout the valley, especially along the main roads leading out of the region and often close to one of the county towns. In location, therefore, much of the local trade conducted in the valley after 1765 remained decentralized, although all of these merchants depended upon merchants in Staunton for access to imported goods.

Changing External Relationships: The West

With the westward and southward expansion of settlement after the French and Indian War, both Staunton and Winchester became more than just frontier towns exporting local produce and importing necessities and luxuries from the outside world. Both settlements developed into backcountry collecting and service centers with much larger hinterlands than they had served before 1760.

Staunton's hinterland came to include not only the upper valley but also the area immediately to the west, which was to be divided into Greenbrier, Bath, and Pendleton counties by the end of the century (see fig. 24). To a lesser extent, both Harrisonburg and Lexington were serving as secondary service centers by 1800. The development of the mineral springs, especially Warm Springs, enlarged Staunton's western hinterland. Before 1783 Staunton merchants had supplied western frontier settlers particularly with imported manufactured goods, powder and shot, salt, rum, whiskey, and cloth, receiving deerskins, butter, and ginseng in part payment.[66] After 1783 Staunton merchants began to take a more active part in encouraging western trade. In 1784 the German traveler Johann David Schoepf described Staunton as "a place by no means inconsiderable, carrying on much trade with the farther mountain-country."[67] During the following decade, the growing profitability of this trade encouraged Staunton merchants not only to increase their volume of trade with the frontier counties through the Warm Springs firm of White, Kirk and Company but also to establish store "outposts"

66. Day Book of Mathew Read, Merchant, Staunton, Virginia, 1771–76, Coll. of Wm. and Mary Lib., and Greenbrier Store, Day Book, Sampson and George Mathews, 1771–73, Va. State Lib. The Mathews brothers had about 85 customers at their Greenbrier store.

67. Schoepf, *Travels in the Confederation,* 2:69. Isaac Weld made a similar comment in 1796 (*Travels,* p. 135).

in the west. In 1788 William Bowyer, the Staunton merchant, bought two lots in Warm Springs with a dwelling house and store on them. During the 1790s he and the Staunton firm of Mustoe and Chambers set up other stores in both Bath and Greenbrier counties. Indeed, Anthony Mustoe had moved to Warm Springs by 1794 and was instrumental in finding a western market for some of Staunton's textile products.[68]

The political and commercial significance of Staunton to the western settlements can best be appreciated in the 1790 petition by 125 settlers in western Augusta County against the establishment of Bath County, which would draw "most of us Back over the mountains from our Common market at Staunton where we trade on very Equitable terms, and are served with Every Necessary we want and also the Distances are much neigher to some and to all of us [there is a] much Better Road to Staunton than [to] the Common Center of the Bounds of the Petition . . . which along with [the] Present Still growing Scarcity of Money, for the Present market of Grain is of no Benefit to the frontiers."[69]

La Rochefoucauld-Liancourt observed at first hand the processes and relationships involved in Staunton's western trade. The town's fifteen to eighteen stores were busy during the twice-weekly markets, receiving small quantities of wheat, corn, rye, hemp, linseed, wax, and honey from the western county, which also supplied the town's tanyard with skins and hides. Yet, "the trade of Staunton has decreased of late years on account of the establishment of several small towns in the county of Greenbrier, as the store-keepers in those places buy up some of the commodities which were formerly brought to Staunton, and supply the same parts of the country with articles of merchandise which were originally supplied by Staunton."[70] What the French visitor failed to appreciate was that Staunton, with its long-standing connections with eastern and northern markets, still continued to control much of the region's import and export trade.

Winchester, the largest settlement west of the Blue Ridge and better placed for trade with the Potomac Valley, Maryland, and Pennsylvania, had a hinterland and foreland that was more extensive than Staunton's. By the end of the century it had developed into an impressive service center with more than 350 houses, over thirty stores, a dozen taverns, about two dozen lawyers, and many craftsmen.[71] Toulmin in 1793 declared that Philadelphia, Baltimore, and Alexandria were the town's principal

68. Augusta Co. Deed Books 25:432, 26:264, 29:232–33; Augusta Co. Deed Book 1A (Circuit Court, 1789–1801):63–65; and Legislative Petitions, Augusta County, Nov. 14, 1794.

69. Legislative Petitions, Augusta County, Nov. 20, 1790.

70. La Rochefoucauld-Liancourt, *Travels,* 2:91.

71. Ibid., 102–5; Weld, *Travels,* p. 137.

markets for obtaining external goods. Winchester merchants "dispose of them to people of the town, of the neighborhood, and of the back-country. Multitudes of horses, sometimes bringing hemp, come down every spring and return loaded with the products of Europe and the West Indias, but principally with salt and iron."[72] To the west, Hampshire and Hardy counties were solidly within Winchester's hinterland, which extended into the frontier county of Randolph. Although all of the county towns of the lower valley attracted some trade from the backcountry, Winchester's only serious competitor for the import trade was Martinsburg, which, however, lacked an extensive western hinterland. Winchester's *Virginia Centinel* had by far the widest circulation of any western newspaper, and upper valley settlers frequently placed advertisements in it, a move not recip-rocated by the lower valley population in the *Staunton Eagle*. And, by the turn of the century Winchester had a weekly stage connection with Baltimore.

Changing External Relationships: The East

Most scholars have argued that the settled areas of western Virginia during the eighteenth century, with the possible exception of the lower Shenandoah Valley, were at a serious economic disadvantage to the rest of Virginia because of the transportation costs involved in importing and exporting goods; these haulage costs prevented trade between western Virginia and the outside world from reaching its "full potential."[73] Yet, although these costs, combined with distance from markets, were a major factor in the upper valley's trading relationships, they did not have a consistently detrimental effect. In the first place, even during the earliest years frontier settlers were always eager to trade with the outside world regardless of transportation hazards. Eastern merchants, while slower to encourage this trade also saw the commercial possibilities of the develop-ing settlements west of the Blue Ridge. It was, after all, to their advantage also to keep down transportation costs as much as possible. This point was clearly recognized during the Revolutionary War when the state tem-porarily took over control of much of Virginia's economy and attempted to regularize transportation costs between the various parts of the state. For example, the importation of salt played a critical role in valley transporta-

72. Toulmin, *Western Country in 1793*, p. 57.

73. Coulter, "The Virginia Merchant," pp. 35–37; Thomson, "The Merchant in Virginia, 1700–1775," p. 228; Sarles, "The Trade of the Valley of Virginia, 1789–1860," pp. 10, 19–20; Bridenbaugh, *Myths and Realities,* pp. 143–44; Wertenbaker, *Old South*, p. 200.

tion costs during the Revolution. It was the single most important item carried as "backload" when local wagoners hauled hemp or flour to eastern or northern markets. Total haulage costs were directly related to the availability of salt and, to a lesser extent, iron, for return loads. As one merchant described it in 1778, "the Price of Hemp at Richmond depends on the place Drawn from. But the Back load to Staunton [salt] Saves the State Seventeen pounds Ten shillings at the present price of Waggonage."[74]

Second, the lack of wagons to transport goods was sometimes as critical a factor to settlers in the upper valley as transportation costs themselves. Wagon transport, as pointed out earlier, did not become important in valley trade until the 1760s, when the transport requirements of the hemp industry provided the first major demand for wagon teams.[75] From then on, there were seldom enough wagons available to conduct trade between the upper valley and its outside markets. Wagons in general were expensive to construct, especially when the demand for wagonmakers and wheelwrights exceeded the supply. In addition, money had to be available to purchase nails, axle grease, harnesses, and horses for the wagon teams. The scarcity of wagons became particularly apparent during the expanded activities of the Revolutionary War and its immediate aftermath. There were frequent army complaints about the lack of wagons available in the upper valley, while local settlers voiced fears that the wagons and teams they had sent for use in the war would never be returned nor would they be suitably recompensed.[76] This fear did indeed prove valid, and the problems of the postwar depression were magnified. The situation was exacerbated by the shift to wheat and flour because transporting these products required more wagons than hemp or tobacco.

A third factor in transportation costs was the nature and location of markets for specialized agricultural products. An area specializing in a certain product or products in great demand was often able to compete economically with adjacent areas either because demand was so high that supply was not always able to keep up with it or because neighboring areas were not producing the same specialized crop. Both of these factors were operative after the mid-1760s in the upper Shenandoah Valley, first with hemp and later with wheat and flour. The importance of the upper valley's hemp contribution during the war combined with the fact that the state took over responsibility for transportation once the hemp had been de-

74. Thomas Hughes to Capt. Charles Thomas, Richmond, Nov. 21, 1778, Va. State Auditor's Item No. 231.

75. A wagon team generally consisted of four horses hauling a four-wheeled wagon under whose covers would be about 450 bushels of wheat, or 10 to 12 barrels of flour, or almost a ton of hemp.

76. *Calendar of Virginia State Papers*, ed. Palmer, 2:197, 450, 662, 3:173.

livered to local warehouses were the main reasons why transportation costs were a minor consideration during much of the 1770s and early 1780s. Though local traders encountered increased haulage costs again during the last fifteen years of the century, they were muted by the facts that the upper valley maintained some hemp specialization, unlike other settled areas of western Virginia, and that its new specialization, wheat and flour production, was in great demand throughout the state. The region's competitors in wheat production, the lower Shenandoah Valley and the northern Piedmont, largely supplied the milling industries of Alexandria and Fredericksburg, leaving the upper Shenandoah Valley to supply Richmond.

Moreover, the availability of land in western Virginia helped to keep land prices lower than those in eastern Virginia. The land market in the Shenandoah Valley was an extremely active one, and good farmland was relatively easy to obtain. In terms of production costs, the relative cheapness of land compensated somewhat for transport costs and may have evened up the cost-distance differential between eastern and western Virginia, especially since the general orientation of markets for valley products did not change substantially after the 1760s regardless of the particular commodity exported.

Before the mid-1760s Alexandria was the major focus for the lower valley's external trade, while Fredericksburg fulfilled a similar function for the upper valley's trade. Over the next decade, while the region maintained relatively extensive outside connections, the major commercial focus for the upper valley began to shift from Fredericksburg to Richmond; this change was not completed until the beginning of the Revolutionary War. The increasing reliance on Richmond merchants was evident by 1770. Some of the most prominent Augusta County merchants relied heavily upon the services of the Richmond merchant Patrick Coutts, who also had connections in London. By the end of the colonial period at least two other Richmond merchants, James Watt and Ninian Menzies and Company, were competing with Coutts for valley trade as well as with eight other Richmond area merchants.[77] Anthony Strothers, who had long been the leading Fredericksburg merchant with an interest in the upper valley, continued this involvement through the partnership of Davenport and Strothers. Yet after 1765 only two or three Fredericksburg area merchants actively participated in this trade.[78]

77. These other Richmond area merchants were Edward Johnson, John Howard, and James Lyle in Manchester, Chesterfield County; John Esdale, James Buchanan, Daniel Hylton and Co., in Henrico County; Alex Baine in Goochland County; and Hunter and Glassel, who also seem to have been from the Richmond area.

78. Most of the evidence for the Fredericksburg trade comes from Augusta Judgments,

Despite the continued dominance of Alexandria in the external affairs of the lower valley (involving some twenty Alexandria merchants or mercantile firms by the Revolution), there are indications that several Fredericksburg merchants developed commercial interest in the lower valley.[79] The relative decline of Fredericksburg, and Falmouth, in Shenandoah Valley trade was not the result of the silting up of the Rappahannock River but a function of the failure of these settlements to eliminate local competitive trading centers (including each other), the more accessible maritime location of Alexandria, and the increasing initiative taken by Richmond merchants in tapping the commercial possibilities of the valley, a connection which was consolidated by official decisions made during the Revolutionary War.[80]

Throughout the valley trade with Philadelphia seems to have declined at the very end of the colonial period. For example, only two Staunton merchants, Mathew Read and Roger North, did extensive business in Philadelphia, mainly with George Davis.[81] A few upper valley merchants continued to have accounts with British merchants, mainly through Thomas Adams or Patrick Coutts in Richmond.

The Revolutionary War produced several changes in the conduct, direction, and rate of trading activities in the valley. In the first place, the state took over the flow of trade in strategic products, especially hemp, but also food and clothing supplies for the army. The free interplay of supply and demand forces was temporarily stopped in favor of direct channeling of goods and supplies by the Virginia government to areas where they were thought to be most needed. This control, more than any other single feature, was responsible for the final link in the trading

---

1767–73 (files 413–23). Other Fredericksburg merchants who maintained connections in the upper valley were Woodrow and Ramsey, Nicholas Smyth, and Hislop and Blair.

79. Bliss, "Tuckahoe in the Valley," pp. 185–87. Fielding Lewis, Charles Dick, and Hislop and Blair were the Fredericksburg merchants most active in this trade.

80. See Arthur P. Middleton, *Tobacco Coast: A Maritime History of Chesapeake Bay in the Colonial Era* (Newport News, Va.: Mariners' Museum, 1953), pp. 48–50, 86–89; L. C. Gottschalk, "Effects of Soil Erosion on Navigation in Upper Chesapeake Bay," *Geog. Rev.* 35 (1945):219–38; R. E. Grim, "The Origins and Early Development of the Virginia Fall-Line Towns" (M.A. thesis, University of Maryland, 1971).

81. See the list of receipts in the Ledger of Mathew Read and Hugh Johnston (1761–70), Coll. of Wm. and Mary Lib., as well as Augusta Co. District Court Order Books (1789–93), p. 283 and (1789–97), p. 113, and Augusta Co. Deed Book 20:216–19. There seems to have been little or no contact with Baltimore merchants during this period, although William Lux may have imported some hemp from the upper valley (William Lux Letter Book 1763–1768, N.Y. Public Lib., microfilm Research Dept., Colonial Williamsburg, especially his correspondence with William Campbell, who may have lived in Augusta County).

chain between Richmond and the upper Shenandoah Valley. Throughout the war, the haulage of hemp to the state ropewalks and cloth factories in and around Alexandria and Richmond and the importing of goods by return load constituted the dominant trading activity of the valley. At the same time, commercial contact between Staunton and Richmond became much more frequent, speeding up commercial rapport. Richmond dominated the Virginia hemp trade, and it was Richmond merchants that the upper valley largely relied upon for its imports during the war years. Hemp was sent in smaller amounts to Fredericksburg, Williamsburg, and Norfolk, mainly to supply local ropewalks, textile factories, or navy requirements.[82] From the available records, it would seem that Philadelphia ranked second to Richmond as a market for hemp from the upper valley. Hemp was sent regularly from western Virginia to Philadelphia to pay for military supplies, and salt, sugar, and numerous smaller items were sent back in partial exchange.[83]

As pointed out earlier, the demands of the army temporarily reoriented other aspects of the valley's trade. Locally produced linens were sent to Alexandria, Fredericksburg, Richmond, and Williamsburg. Dairy products were transported both to Richmond and Fredericksburg. Although there are few surviving records of local merchant accounts for the war period, the ledger of William Anderson, the Rockbridge County merchant, reveals the impact of the government's role in altering the regular patterns of local trade. The bulk of Anderson's exports were hemp and butter, supplemented by linen, flour, and shoe thread. Most of this went to merchants or state agents in Richmond, but small amounts of produce were sent to Lynchburg and areas around Richmond. A considerable amount of wagonage was involved, not only to Richmond but also to Williamsburg and Baltimore.[84]

The postwar depression as well as the lack of a sufficient number of

82. Virginia State Auditor's Item No. 218; Herndon, "Story of Hemp," pp. 101–8, 117–19, 140–41.

83. Herndon, "Story of Hemp," pp. 107–8, 119; Valentine White Receipt Book, Sept. 8–Nov. 28, 1781, Va. State Lib. See also the hemp correspondence relating to the Philadelphia trade in the last few pages of Mathew Read's Day Book. In 1781 one hemp agent reported that "the hemp in the back Country he is reserving to be used in payment for Articles bought in Philadelphia, for the use of the Army. He has all along been aware of the impossibility of getting wagons to transport it, until the Corn is all planted and the fields drest over. Notwithstanding this, he will at once send one of his clerks to the upper Counties and to Augusta to set the business in motion with the utmost expedition, as to bringing forward the arms is of the greatest importance at this time" (*Calendar of Virginia State Papers*, ed. Palmer, 2:90).

84. Anderson's largest accounts were with James Marsden, probably of Richmond (over £1,200), John Syme, perhaps also of Richmond (£410), and Patrick Coutts (over £200).

wagons to haul local produce made it difficult to reestablish regular trading patterns until about 1785. The last fifteen years of the century reveal the increasing consolidation of the valley's external market contacts in the major commercial centers of the Eastern Seaboard between Philadelphia and Richmond. There were no radical shifts in marketing orientation as a result of the replacement of hemp by wheat and flour in the valley's export trade. The continued dominance of Alexandria and Richmond was maintained after the war because they were major markets for flour. Though the conduct of this trade placed greater demands on wagon space, it did not directly contribute to the increasing urban contacts between the valley towns and fall-line centers because most flour was exported from the processing points, the merchant mills, which were seldom located in the towns.

Some fourteen Richmond companies were involved in trade with the Shenandoah Valley after the war, of whom Heathcote and Fenwick and Nelson, Heron and Company were perhaps the most prominent.[85] Another Richmond merchant, Robert Gamble, maintained very close trading relations throughout the valley during the 1790s. This was primarily because, like Sampson Mathews before him, he had been a Staunton merchant engaged in the Staunton-Richmond trade during the Revolutionary War and remained attracted to Richmond after 1783. He finally moved to that city about 1789, established a store, and became involved in several partnerships. He also maintained a store in Staunton, under the partnership of Gamble and Grattan, which he employed partly as an outfitting store for people going to Kentucky, and from which he expected to be furnished, in due season, butter, flour, hemp, and any other profitable backcountry produce.[86]

The firm of Anthony Mustoe and William Chambers and that of Roger North were probably the two most prominent merchant companies in the upper valley after the war. The location of their outside commercial activities indicates the degree to which local traders focused on those market centers where they were ensured the best credit facilities and the widest

85. The full roster of Richmond merchants compiled from public and private records is as follows: William Alexander; Nathaniel Anderson; Robert Gamble; William Glassell and Co.; Heathcote and Fenwick; Heathcote and Dall; James Heron; Richard Heron; Hollingsworth, Johnson and Co.; John Carter Littlepage; John Mackey; Alex Nelson; Nelson, Heron and Co.; and William Nimmo. The Heathcote partnerships were Virginia offshoots of the London merchants John Heathcote and Co. (Augusta Co. District Court Order Book [1789–93], pp. 495–502). Three other partnerships whose precise locations are in doubt, Wilkinson and Oliver, Hodgson, Nicholson and Co., and Fletcher and Sunderland, might also have been from Richmond.

86. *Virginia Gazette* (Richmond), Oct. 27, 1790, Dec. 7, 1796; Augusta Co. Order Book 24:33, 61.

range of imported goods. Both North and Mustoe and Chambers conducted most of their business with the larger trading companies in Richmond, especially the Heathcote partnerships and James Heron, and in Baltimore, especially Abraham Usher for North and William Cochran and Company for Mustoe and Chambers.[87] Baltimore merchants seem to have shown more interest in the commercial possibilities of western Virginia toward the end of the century than did Philadelphia merchants, whose interests in the region were often more speculative than commercial. At least six Baltimore trading companies had regular contacts as far south as Staunton, while at the most only three Philadelphia firms extended their business that far south.[88]

After the Revolution the counties of the valley displayed some differences in their external trading patterns. Berkeley and Frederick counties relied most heavily on Alexandria and, through Winchester, had the most frequent contacts with Baltimore and Philadelphia. Shenandoah County merchants seem to have maintained regular contact with both Alexandria and Fredericksburg. The single most important market for all three upper valley counties was Richmond, but Rockingham County relied least heavily on that city. As the most southern of the three, Rockbridge County's trade was almost entirely with Richmond and other trading centers along the middle James River, especially Lynchburg. It retained few northern commercial contacts. Augusta County, although retaining its close commercial ties with Richmond, had a more extensive, diversified trading area. In addition to connections with Baltimore and Philadelphia, a few trading contacts were maintained with Fredericksburg and an increasing number with Alexandria.[89] However, it was the merchants of Rocking-

87. This information is mainly derived from Augusta Co. Order Books 23:423–40, 24:205; Augusta Co. District Court Order Book (1789–93), pp. 495–502; and Augusta Co. Deed Book 1A (Superior Court, 1789–1801): 80.

88. The Baltimore firms were Ashburner and Langton; William Cochran and Co.; Davis and Fulton; Alex Fulton; John and Isaac McKim; and Usher and Davidson. Philadelphia was represented by George Davis (who had actually moved to New Jersey during the 1780s); Kuhn and Risberg; and Usher and Ashton. Compare Hart, *Valley of Virginia,* p. 20. In a note on p. 150, concerning the Philadelphia trade during the 1780s and early 1790s, Hart wrote: "The writer has gone through the account books of at least a score of contemporary Philadelphia merchants but has failed to find a single reference to the Valley or a known Valley resident." In the light of this comment, it is interesting to note La Rochefoucauld-Liancourt's impressions of this trade in 1796: "The goods sold by the storekeepers are brought directly from Baltimore, yet more frequently from Philadelphia, as the small capitals of merchants of Richmond do not allow them to give as long credit as the Staunton traders can obtain in those two large cities, where they also find a cheaper market." (*Travels,* 2:91).

89. Legislative Petitions, Augusta County, Dec. 8, 1798; Augusta Co. Deed Book 25:236–41; Papers of Charles Simms, vol. 1, Manuscript Div., Lib. Cong.

ham County who maintained the closest upper valley contacts with both Fredericksburg and Alexandria, and occasionally with Falmouth. Most of the county's exports went by way of Swift Run Gap to Alexandria, Fredericksburg, and Richmond. During the last decade of the century the founding of the Bank of Alexandria in particular was a major boon to merchants in Berkeley, Frederick, Shenandoah, and Rockingham counties. Rockingham merchants petitioned for a twenty-year extension of the bank's charter so that the favorable prices and credit extension of Alexandria could continue.[90]

The extension of credit to, and the debts accumulated by, valley merchants continued to be a major factor in the region's trade after the early 1760s. Augusta County courts were as busy dealing with the collection of delinquent accounts from local merchants and farmers during the last decade of the colonial period as they had been during the previous twenty years. Few debt suits were for more than £50. The largest recorded debts were those of the Staunton merchant Alexander Boyd. At his death in 1766, Boyd had a total bill of £1,458, of which £824 still remained outstanding in 1770. Most of this debt was probably paid from his estate inventory, which was evaluated at almost £1,090.[91] William Crow, the cattle drover, accumulated debts of over £425 with two Richmond firms during the years 1765 and 1769. To pay back these debts, Crow was among the first of the region's debtors to employ the only real asset they had— land. In 1767 he sold two Negroes to the Glasgow firm of James Richey and Company, after which he had to resort to mortgaging his landed property. In 1768 he mortgaged off two tracts of land on Craig's Creek to one of his Richmond creditors for £322.[92] The largest private debtor in the upper valley who paid off his debts in land before 1775 was Mathew Harrison, a member of the most prominent family in Rockingham County. Between 1769 and 1774 he mortgaged or sold over 5,000 acres of land in Rockingham and Hampshire counties to pay off his trading debts of over £2,500 to creditors in Philadelphia, Baltimore, and Fairfax and Spotsylvania counties. His 210-acre country estate in Rockingham County, which had been mortgaged on at least three separate occasions, was finally sold to the Baltimore firm of Ashburner and Place, and Harrison himself moved to the Tidewater.[93]

90. Legislative Petitions, Rockingham County, Dec. 5, 1799.

91. Alexander Boyd's account with Alex Baine of Goochland County, Augusta Judgments, 1770 (file 419); Augusta Co. Will Book 3:467–74. It is difficult to gauge the rate of interest payments on trading accounts, but in general they seem to have ranged from 5% to 10% per annum. See also Myra L. Rich, "Speculations on the Significance of Debt, Virginia, 1781–1789," *Va. Mag. Hist. Biog.* 76 (1968):301–17.

92. Augusta Judgments, 1770, 1782 (files 419, 432); Augusta Co. Deed Books 14:112–13, 15:244–49.

93. Harrison was in debt to the Philadelphia firms of Richard and Peter Footman and

The problems of creditors and debtors were made more complicated by the political and economic events of the Revolution. After 1783 the solution to local trading indebtedness was to be found more in land transfers. In this manner, large amounts of land in the valley came into the hands of absentee landowners, mainly merchant creditors, during the last two decades of the century, which further encouraged land speculation on a large scale. Although there is no direct evidence, it is quite possible that this mortgage borrowing on landed property helped to create the great wave of land aggrandizement in the upper valley during the 1790s. Land transferred by valley debtors may have eventually passed through a variety of creditors to some of the largest merchant and real estate interests on the Eastern Seaboard. Between 1785 and 1800 Augusta County debtors transferred over 500 acres of land, three lots in Staunton, and one gristmill to creditors in Baltimore; several thousand acres of land and at least two lots in Staunton to creditors in Richmond; and several hundred acres of land to creditors in Fredericksburg.[94] In all, more than 20,000 acres of land and eight town lots in the upper Shenandoah Valley were transferred to nonresident owners, and probably twice these amounts were mortgaged at one time or another, during the last twenty years of the eighteenth century. There is some kind of poetic justice in all of these machinations. It was the potentialities of the lands of the valley that had attracted the pioneer settlers, and it was these same lands, now much altered by human action, that were to preserve the solvency of their thoroughly commercialized pioneer offspring.

Benjamin Marshall; the Baltimore merchant John Ashburner; Thomas Carson, Fairfax County merchant; and Henry Mitchell, Spotsylvania County merchant (Augusta Co. Deed Books 15:487–90; 16:530–34, 17:71–72, 101–14, 330–34, 19:35–39, 21:225–58; Purdie and Dixon's *Virginia Gazette* [Williamsburg], July 14, 1774).

94. The last transaction involved Jacob Kenney, a real estate speculator in Staunton. Through his associations with the Philadelphia firms of Usher and Ashton and John Boyce, he mortgaged about 14,500 acres of land on the borders of Bath and Augusta counties to the Philadelphia financier Robert Morris in 1795 (Augusta Co. Deed Book 30:278–79; Augusta Co. Deed Book 1A [Circuit Court, 1789–1801]: 206–8).

When he died, about 1790, the Staunton merchant Mathew Read transferred all of his lands (acreage unstated) and his lots in Staunton (at least two) to George Davis, former merchant in Philadelphia, to whom he owed £724 (Augusta Co. District Court Order Book [1789–97], p. 113; Augusta Co. Deed Book 1A [Circuit Court, 1789–1801]:37—38).

Small amounts of land were also transferred in this same fashion in Rockingham and Rockbridge counties (Rockingham Co. Deed Book 0:134; Rockbridge Co. Deed Books A:684–85, B:473–74). See also the comments on the general problem of indebtedness in post-Revolutionary Virginia in Rich, "Speculations on the Significance of Debt, Virginia, 1781–1789," *Va. Mag. Hist. Biog.* 76 (1968): 301–17.

8 The Transformation of the Early Shenandoah Valley

THE transformation of the Shenandoah Valley into the most effectively occupied part of western Virginia by the end of the eighteenth century was the result of the commercial predisposition and activities of its settlers in exploiting the most resource-rich area of the Applachians for permanent agricultural settlement. The valley was occupied as part of the second major phase of continental occupance, the interior settlement penetrations of the early eighteenth century. From the beginning most settlers were committed to commercialized perceptions of their new environment. Within the openness and accessibility of American space, the commercialization of the land, an institutional expression of a European cultural order, created the material foundations of the new society.[1] Social designations in terms of inherited status and position were largely replaced by evaluations in terms of levels of accumulated material wealth. Areal classifications based on long attachment to place had to be discarded for terminology more sensitive to the dynamics of colonization: *frontier, pioneer,* and *backcountry.*

After arriving for a visit at Greenway Court in 1768, Lord Fairfax's brother, Robert Fairfax, described the local social environment as primitive, uncouth, and almost beyond belief.[2] This reaction to the Virginia frontier merely fortified the image held by eighteenth-century Tidewater Virginians of the western parts of their territory beyond the Blue Ridge. This section remained in their view a relatively remote, interior area with its own characteristic physical geography and way of life, dominated by mixed agriculture, yeoman farmers of non-English tradition, and a roughness of life that was less prevalent east of the mountains. However, though the valley remained a backcountry geographically, it did not long continue as an underdeveloped, undifferentiated frontier.

Three general phases of development can be identified in the Shenandoah Valley during the eighteenth century. A pioneer phase, characterized

1. For some wider implications of this point, see Louis Hartz, *The Founding of New Societies: Studies in the History of the United States, Latin America, South Africa, Canada, and Australia* (New York: Harcourt, Brace, and World, 1964), and Richard D. Brown, "Modernization and the Modern Personality in Early America, 1600–1865: A Sketch of a Synthesis," *Journal of Interdisciplinary History* 2 (1972):201–28.

2. Robert Fairfax to Rev. Denny Martin, Sept. 29, 1768, Wykeham-Martin Papers (microfilm, Colonial Williamsburg).

by steady population growth, rapid land acquisition, and a relatively homogeneous yeoman economy and society, lasted from the late 1720s until the early 1760s. This phase merged into a period from the mid-1760s until the mid-1770s in which there was more rapid demographic change and westward expansion and increasing commercialization of agricultural life. This brief phase saw the termination of the valley's frontier status by the outbreak of the Revolution, as well as the beginning of different patterns of population growth and economic development in the lower and the upper parts of the region. During the last quarter of the century, population growth rates became more stabilized, although absolute growth was the highest of the century, and the patterns and levels of economic development within the valley tended toward increasing similarity. At a state level, these internal changes helped to create a trend toward increasing economic integration between eastern and western Virginia after the Revolution, and they forged the links within the upper southern economy and society that emerged between the Chesapeake and the Mississippi during the late eighteenth and early nineteenth centuries.

As a critical part of the second phase of early American expansion, the valley was a dependent area influenced strongly by two very different older colonial regions, Tidewater Virginia and southeastern Pennsylvania. The integration of these influences within the area was unique; the processes of transformations were not. Consequently, in exploring the manifestations of the commercial organization of space and society, it was necessary not only to evaluate extenuating environmental, cultural, and political circumstances but also to interpret the results in regional terms. Regionalization was an important consequence of commercialization, This regional variation was most evident in patterns of migration and land settlement, agricultural evolution, trade and mercantile life, and social identity and stratification.

To the early European settler land was an easily available and highly marketable commodity. The tone of landownership in the Shenandoah Valley was set by the land policies of the Gooch administration during the 1730s and the extension of the privately controlled Northern Neck proprietary west of the Blue Ridge. Land was used as bait to encourage the rapid settlement of Virginia's Appalachian frontiers. Although the goals of the Virginia government and Lord Fairfax were similar, the contrasting land distribution procedures they employed created different results in the long run. Both procedures were based on the initial distribution of large grants to individuals and partnerships of primarily Tidewater origins. But while the Virginia government ensured the rapid dissemination of large grants in smaller parcels to settlers or created the means whereby settlers could acquire land more directly, many of Fairfax's grantees retained their grants in the lower valley intact or disposed of them over several decades. Consequently, although most of the land taken up in the valley during the colonial period was settled by migrants of non-plantation traditions from the Middle Colonies and western Europe, large acreages in the lower valley remained in the control of absentee eastern planters.

The liberal distribution policies for land west of the Blue Ridge meant that most pioneer settlers could and did acquire substantial tracts, generally ranging from 100 to 400 acres, which were far in excess of basic agricultural requirements. Thus, property-owning yeoman farmers had portions of surplus land available for disposal. For this reason land speculation was a persistent characteristic of early American frontier settlement. Yet defining speculation is a difficult task. Wherever land was transferred primarily for its potential commercial value, the larger the amount of land an owner possessed, the cheaper it was sold per acre. Land speculation was characteristic of all levels of property ownership, and it was at the lower end of the ownership scale, among the so-called small farmers, that the greatest relative speculation occurred and the highest prices per acre were asked. In short, the price of land sold by individuals tended to be in inverse proportion to the amount of land each had available for disposal.

A price of £3 per 100 acres has long been said to be the standard level at which large colonial landowners disposed of lands in the valley. But this price prevailed only before the mid-1740s. Thereafter land prices rose steadily until the Revolution, during which they became highly inflated. The steady growth and rapid turnover of population facilitated land sales; the greater the rate of turnover, the higher the probability of increased prices for improved lands. Yet the widespread availability of good agricultural land at relatively low prices during the colonial period allowed for a broadly based landownership structure. By the early 1770s approximately two-thirds of the upper valley's and three-fifths of lower valley's taxable population owned land. But the good agricultural lands had all been taken up by the Revolution, and the increasing growth of population and land speculation thereafter restricted the availability of property and produced an increasing concentration of land ownership. By the end of the century more than half the valley's taxable population did not own land. Settlers without land who found such conditions constraining could choose to emigrate. But it was more common for valley landowners or their offspring to move, using the profits of land sales and their previous agricultural experience to better prepare them for occupying new frontiers.

In this manner, a steadily increasing commercial bias was spread westward, and the American farmer came to view his relationship to the land more as a stewardship than as a lasting covenant.

Despite the significance of land speculation, its geographical effects were mixed. Speculative activities in the valley had no direct influence, for example, on settlement patterns, the size and distribution of landholdings, the delineation of land use patterns, or the location of transportation routes. Small speculators did not have enough land to be influential, and large speculators who received lands from the government were concerned with selling them as quickly as possible. Their eagerness to sell did help to speed up the rate of settling, although similar results might have been achieved if the government had disposed of all land directly. Large speculators could affect the cultural composition of the valley's population as a result of their efforts to bring in settlers for their lands; the numerical superiority of the Scotch-Irish in the upper valley was partly a consequence of the recruiting attempts of Robert Beverley and Benjamin Borden. By choosing to hold on to their lands in the lower valley, absentee planters delayed their impact on settlement and land use, and used their lands to vault into the region's wealthiest social class after the Revolution.

Although the valley's agricultural development owed little to land speculators, a similar concern for profits and markets characterized the pioneer farmer. A sophisticated commercial economy did not appear overnight. The region's sparse population, small proportion of cleared land, and limited transportation facilities placed major constraints on immediate market expansion. Local markets did exist for surplus products, but they were temporary and small. Patterns of future agricultural development depended upon the identification of external areas of demand and the ability to sustain surplus production for these markets. In the absence of adequate transportation, cattle predictably were the first major export. Yet a locally organized cattle trade for northern markets did not appear until the late 1750s, after the original wagon road network had been created. Livestock and livestock products provided reliable exports for the remainder of the century despite depletions in breeding stocks during the Revolutionary War.

All the agricultural specializations that emerged in the valley were thoroughly integrated into its mixed farming structure, so that no regionally distinct dual economies based on planter-yeoman distinctions were created. The pioneer economy was based on corn, wheat, rye, flax, hemp, tobacco, and livestock. It was from this resource base that all of the region's specialties were derived, a base broad enough to assure valley farmers of a wide range of commercial options.

The distinct commitment to crop specialization during the 1760s did not represent a sharp break with previous agricultural activities but rather an increase in the rate of commercialization. In a graph of this rate over the next forty years, the curve for the upper valley would lag five to six years behind that of the lower valley until the 1790s. The agricultural contrasts that existed between the two parts of the valley at least until the early 1780s did not coincide with the original proprietary boundaries; only the two most northerly counties, Berkeley and Frederick, led the way in agricultural development.

Tobacco, hemp, and wheat dominated the valley's commercial agriculture during the latter part of the century. Tobacco best reflected the influence of the eastern Virginia planter economy on the valley. Only a few hundred acres were ever devoted to the plant at any one time, and not until after 1780 was it ever cultivated by the valley's overwhelmingly yeoman farmers. But its presence in the lower valley was primarily responsible for the introduction of slavery west of the Blue Ridge. Commercial hemp, on the other hand, was produced mainly by the small yeoman farmer throughout the valley. In the upper valley large-scale hemp cultivation during the 1760s produced the first significant demands there for slave labor. Hemp cultivation was encouraged by government bounties, and production peaked during the Revolutionary War when the state regulated much of the processing, marketing, and manufacture of the plant. The resulting price boom proved a veritable bonanza for many valley settlers, but this price level was not sustained after 1783.

Because wheat was both a subsistent and a commercial food crop, its evolution as a specialty is more difficult to trace. Wheat production was characterized by a steadily increasing output for sale after the mid-1760s. Production for export had begun in Berkeley and Frederick counties before the Revolution. The increasing demands for flour and bread within the Atlantic economy during and after the war assured for wheat its position as the principal commercial crop throughout the valley after 1783. So dominant did commercial wheat production become that, by the turn of the century, the Shenandoah Valley had emerged as the leading wheat-producing region in the South.

The increasing commitment to commercial agriculture after 1760 had two major long-term consequences. First, during the pioneer period less than one tenth of the average farm's total acreage was cleared for cultivation. By the end of the century the average proportion of cleared land per farm had risen to between one fifth and one quarter. This ratio compared favorably with conditions in many longer settled areas of the Atlantic seaboard. Second, very few pioneer farmers could put more than one tenth of their total farm output up for sale. By 1800 up to one half of the typical farmer's output was so available.

One of the most significant trends in Virginia agriculture after the 1760s was the increasing number of agricultural similarities between its eastern and western parts. Both product complementarity and the areal expansion of traditional agricultural staples demonstrate this development. Until the 1760s tobacco dominated the agricultural economy of eastern Virginia while livestock products were more typical west of the mountains. During the two decades after 1760, while tobacco remained a major but declining staple of the Tidewater and southern Piedmont, both hemp and wheat emerged as new crop specialties in the northern Piedmont and in the Shenandoah Valley. After the Revolution wheat dominated both these areas, supplemented by cattle and hog products, and tobacco remained of secondary importance. All the specialties that had appeared in the valley before 1780 were to emerge in Kentucky during the next two decades. These products and diffusion patterns laid the foundations for the regionalization of upper southern agriculture during the early nineteenth century.

In terms of a plantation-yeoman framework, this evolutionary sequence may seem unusual. After the Revolution any semblance of a plantation organization in the valley was eliminated by the dominance of wheat. The timing of this specialization in the valley was primarily the result of eastern Virginia influences. Moreover, in the valley wheat was integrated into a more diversified commercial structure than that which existed farther north, where commitments to tobacco and hemp cultivation, cattle and hog production, and the institution of slavery were absent or of minor importance. In this regard, the agricultural evolution of adjacent western Maryland and of Southside Virginia is critical in defining regionalization west of the Chesapeake. For example, was the strong emphasis on wheat in western Maryland after the late 1740s prevented from spreading earlier to the lower valley because of stronger pressures from the tobacco-oriented Virginia Tidewater?[3]

It was in the sphere of trade and mercantile life that the myths of frontier

3. The early settlement and agricultural development of both western Maryland and Southside Virginia remain largely unexplored. But see, for western Maryland, Gregory A. Stiverson, "Landless Husbandmen: Tenants on the Maryland Proprietary Manors in the Eighteenth Century, an Economic Study" (Ph.D. diss., Johns Hopkins University, 1973); Frank W. Porter, "From Back Country to County: The Role of Economics and Politics in the Settlement of Western Maryland" (M.A. thesis, University of Maryland, 1973); Porter, "From Back Country to County: The Delayed Settlement of Western Maryland," *Maryland Historical Magazine* 70 (1975): 329–49.

isolation and subsistence economy proved most inaccurate. The structure of any frontier area's economy defined the general framework of both its local and external trading relationships. What is most revealing about the early development of trade in the valley, particularly its less accessible upper half, is that both the extent and growth rate of external trade were out of all proportion to the limited level of agricultural specialization. As early as the mid-1730s trading contacts had been established with Pennsylvania and Maryland, to be followed soon thereafter with contacts in eastern Virginia. Part of this initial orientation can be explained by the very rapid influx of people during the first two decades of settlement and the conditions under which they came. Most pioneer settlers brought few material goods with them except for foodstuffs, so that they generated an extraordinary demand for basic necessities in order to establish themselves.

The range of early external contacts was extensive. Settlers were searching for the most profitable and reliable markets. As external commerce became more frequent during the 1760s, the region's trade concentrated more on the larger eastern markets where the variety of goods was greatest and the extension of credit most available. In the lower valley reliance was placed most heavily on the connections with Alexandria, with some competition from Falmouth and Fredericksburg. By the early 1740s Fredericksburg had already become the major market center for upper valley produce. Richmond, more favorably located for upper valley trade, did not begin to reorient the region's trading patterns until the early 1770s, when it became a leading importer of backcountry hemp. Philadelphia provided a market for the region's cattle and hemp and was a source of scarce and luxury items during the colonial period. Its importance declined after the Revolution partly because of the rise of Baltimore but mainly because Virginia's fall-line towns, especially Richmond and Alexandria, grew and began to siphon off the Shenandoah Valley trade. The emergence of these two towns as major flour-milling centers after the war ensured that this orientation would continue. Hence the shifts in agricultural specialization, insofar as they were characterized by different marketing and transactional systems, did little to influence the changing location of external markets but had a direct impact on market consolidation.

Theoretically, the growth of trading networks within the valley should have produced a local service system of small urban centers. Such a system did develop, but its appearance was late, especially in the upper valley where only one viable center existed before 1775. The major reason for this late development was the persistence of a decentralized trading structure based on individual trading contacts, peddlers, the pack trade, and most importantly, country stores operated by farmer-retailers. Throughout the century much of the valley's export trade remained highly diffuse, despite the consolidation of the western hinterlands of Winchester and Staunton after 1775. The most important changes that influenced settlement organization were the growth and distribution of population and the increasing concentration of the region's import trade. These factors explain why Winchester and Staunton became the focal points of much of the valley's mercantile life after their initial foundations as county seats. The more rapid growth of Winchester and its preeminence by 1800 resulted from the nature of the population for which it provided local service, a much larger and wealthier group than Staunton's, and from its greater accessibility to external markets. The lower valley, which contained almost two-thirds of the valley's total population after 1760, was able to support a three-level central-place hierarchy by the end of the century. While the upper valley was able to attain a level of commercial interaction equal to that of the lower valley by the 1790s, it was more sparsely settled, a fact which its less developed urban structure reflected.

Throughout the eighteenth century, the valley's development occurred within a preindustrial context. Nowhere is this more evident than in the characteristics of the valley's secondary activities and in the social features of its population. Most of the region's processing, craft, and manufacturing activities represented small-scale, decentralized, and only partially specialized enterprise. Throughout the century the valley remained a primary producing area with limited processing and manufacturing capacity except in textiles, flour, iron, and whiskey production, and a few craft specialties, particularly leather and wood. Most secondary activities involved the processing of local raw materials and the creation of finished products principally for local consumption. The main contributions of industry to the region's economic development after the pioneer period were to reduce gradually the reliance on outside sources for many manufactured products, to contribute an increasing number of finished products for export, and to supply locally produced wagons for the conduct of bulk commodity trade.

Studies of the evolution of societies on eighteenth-century frontiers have stressed the emergence of relatively homogeneous populations of small-property-owning yeoman farmers lacking many distinct elements of social differentiation. This conclusion is based on the assumption that access to wealth in early America was achieved primarily through commercial opportunities in land and trade.[4] Exploring social change at a

4. Kenneth Lockridge, "Land, Population, and the Evolution of New England Society, 1630–1790; and an Afterthought," in *Colonial America: Essays in Politics and Social Develop-*

regional level provides more insight into the structure than into the operations of society, but even at this level we should expect the increasing commercialization of the economy to be accompanied by increasing socioeconomic differences in the structure of the population. Such differences emerged slowly in the Shenandoah Valley.

There was an air of homogeneity about the approximately 18,000 settlers who occupied the valley by 1760. They were primarily farmers owning up to 400 acres of land and at least one horse and a few cattle, with sparsely furnished homes, and modest amounts of portable wealth who, when they died, left personal property worth less than £100 Va. The transformation of this pioneer society into a less fluid, more stratified form by the end of the century was the result of three processes: the growth of population, the increasing commercialization of its principal activities, and the socioeconomic influences emanating, and eventually transplanted, from eastern Virginia.

By 1775 the valley's 35,000 inhabitants were still relatively sparsely distributed; only in Berkeley and Frederick counties did overall population densities exceed ten persons per square mile. During the next twenty years the valley's population more than doubled, to almost 84,000, and overall densities had reached thirteen persons per square mile and twice that figure in the far north. The increase in population alone would have been sufficient to reduce easy access to landed property after the Revolution. By 1800 not only was half the population outside the ranks of landownership, but among those who did own land over four-fifths owned less than 250 acres. Landownership became the single most selective factor in social stratification.

The exploitation of labor was a second major factor in differentiation. The ownership of slaves reflected a certain level of social stratification, and the presence of slaves solidified the lowest stratum in the region's social structure. During the pioneer period most agricultural labor was supplied by the settlers themselves; slavery was nearly absent before the emergence of commercial tobacco and hemp cultivation. By 1782 the slave population had increased tenfold and had almost doubled again by 1800, when the almost 14,000 slaves represented slightly less than one-sixth of the total population. Throughout the century two-thirds of all the valley's slaves were concentrated in Berkeley and Frederick counties. Slaveowning reached a peak during the early 1780s, when more than one-quarter of the taxable households in the lower valley and one-fifth in the upper valley held slaves. The eastern Virginia precedent made slavery a socially

ment, ed. Stanley N. Katz (Boston: Little, Brown, and Co., 1971), pp. 466–91, is provocative in this regard.

acceptable institution. On the other hand, hired labor was always available, especially after 1760. The depression of the 1780s and rapidly declining opportunities for landholding increased the numbers of rural laborers, who may have comprised as much as one-third of the valley's adult male labor force by 1800.

It was only to be expected that the valley's social evolution would eventually be influenced by the dominant social and economic forces in the colony of Virginia. The decisions of the planter-dominated legislature and the trading links forged with fall-line market centers had a sustained impact on western frontier life. The presence of such institutions as the Anglican church, tenancy, slavery, and the tobacco plantation in Berkeley and Frederick counties, together with the conduct of civic and political affairs, attest to the Tidewater influence. But the transformation of the region from a socioeconomic extension of Pennsylvania into a western extension of eastern Virginia might not have occurred if eastern planters had not migrated to the lower valley.[5] No more than a few hundred planter families settled in Berkeley and Frederick counties after 1760, but their spatial concentration and control of large acreages of land imbued them with social influences out of all proportion to their numbers.

Eastern planters moved easily into the upper social stratum in the lower valley and, by superimposing themselves on a middle-class society of small property owners, created a more stratified society. They lived in a different social world from that of the majority of local settlers, who shared few of their conspicuous consumption habits. Where direct land control and immigration by eastern planters was lacking, Tidewater traits were much slower to spread. In the upper valley, those individuals at the top of the, social hierarchy were most often members of long-established families in the area.

How then are the contributions of different cultural heritages to be evaluated? Cultural pluralism was certainly a prominent feature of the colonial period. Yet it is difficult to identify specific ethnic contributions to the transformation of the valley. The creation of a landscape of dispersed rural settlement patterns and individual family farms transcended differences in national origins.

Three factors were of prime importance in the choice of settlement sites. First, settlers were concerned with selecting land with good agricultural potential. They avoided areas of poor soils and limited water supply.

5. For a different regional interpretation, see Wilbur Zelinsky, *The Cultural Geography of the United States* (Englewood Cliffs, N.J.: Prentice-Hall, 1972), pp. 117–28. In delimiting the present cultural regions of the United States, Zelinsky's Middle Atlantic–Upper Southern boundary bisects the Shenandoah Valley. The lower valley is assigned to the Middle Atlantic region primarily on the basis of selected settlement relicts.

Distinct group differences in land selection and in geographical mobility were lacking. Second, settlers were concerned about the price of land, and this factor was increasingly significant as they became aware of the location of markets for their produce. Third, many settlers were concerned about the cultural characteristics of their neighbors, and early patterns of migration certainly encouraged the formation of some distinct ethnic areas within the valley.

Yet many factors mitigated against the persistence of ethnic identities over time. The increasing spatial mixing of populations as good land became scarcer, the high rates of population turnover, and the widespread opportunities to accumulate wealth which permitted upward social mobility all tended to reduce ethnic distinctions after the 1760s. Moreover, most groups did not possess a tight cultural unity, exhibiting a wide range of regional and sectarian identities.

Linguistic and religious differences tended to isolate German-speaking groups from the remainder of the valley's population and to prolong their period of cultural assimilation. They participated less than English-speaking groups in the early civic, political, and mercantile life of the valley. But the more rapidly they achieved commercial success, the more rapidly they became assimilated. It is true that Germans, especially those with sectarian affiliations, were less prone to be slaveowners, but they did not participate much in the labor-intensive production of hemp and tobacco in any case.

The reduction in ethnic profiles after the Revolution was a national as well as a local phenomenon. In a period of rising national consciousness and rapid westward expansion, a different set of cultural circumstances began to emerge west of the Appalachians. The varied expressions of pluralism and regionalism that were so characteristic of the colonial period of the eighteenth century were hybridized and reduced by forces leading to national unification and identity. Thus, when Crèvecoeur posed the question, "What then is the American, this new man?", settlers moving westward as culture bearers in the creation of new environments and societies rarely would have responded in ethnic terms, might have done so in religious terms, but were clearly responding in commercial terms as they exploited the territory of the new nation.

Index

Index

Accessibility: frontier areas, 8–9; improvements in, 189–95; migration and, 18–19, 30, 83; settlement and, 39, 98; *see also* Towns; Trade; Transportation

Agriculture: agrarian systems, 8–9, 233, 235; change in, 3–5, 133, 161–62; commercial, 121, 133, 144–49, 161–87, 231; diffusion of, 138–39, 187–88; growing season, 21–22; implements, 114–16, 118–19, 143; labor for, 124–28, 165–66, 176; land use types in, 24–26, 40–43, 135–37, 163–64, 170, 176–80, 186–87, 233–35; national groups and, 130–31, 143, 166, 240; pioneer, 24–26, 133, 135–40, 162, 233; regionalization of, 138, 187–88, 235; specialization in, 161–81, 187–88, 233–34; techniques in, 129, 142–43, 163; upper southern, 187–88, 235; *see also* Climate; Crops; Land surface; Livestock; Plantation; Planters; Soils; Trade

Albemarle County, 91, 158, 215

Alcoholic beverages, 25, 138, 143, 153, 178, 181, 184, 208, 214, 237; *see also* Ordinaries; Stills; Taverns

American Revolution, 96, 167–70, 173–74, 179, 190, 193, 215, 227, 232, 235, 238, 240; *see also* Revolutionary War

Amherst County, 213

Anglicans, 47n, 56, 104, 107, 139, 239

Animal life, native, 22–24, 134–35; *see also* Deer; Fur trade; Hunting; Skins; Wolves

Assimilation, *see* Cultural traditions

Augusta County, 12, 27, 38, 161, 218; absentee landowners in, 47; agriculture, 137–40, 145, 147–48, 164–65, 169, 180, 185; boundary changes, 10–12; county seat, 14, 144; denominations in, 104–5; distribution of wealth in, 117–19; frontiers of, 39; holdings in, 31–33, 62–63, 66–70, 72, 81, 85–87, 89–90; hunting in,

134–35; industry in, 175, 201–10; inventories, 111–15, 118, 129, 140; justices in, 84; labor supply in, 126; land prices in, 74–78; merchants in, 157, 211–13, 216–17, 223; migration from, 48–49, 56; militia, 83, 94; national groups in, 43–45, 106; ordinaries in, 46; population, 99, 102; roads in, 152; slaves, 99–100, 108, 129; surveyors, 52; town lots in, 91, 197; trading area of, 216–17, 219–20, 227; *see also* Towns

Backcountry, 36, 60, 70, 84, 110, 154, 159, 184, 186, 194, 219, 221, 226, 230; *see also* Frontier

Baptists, 105

Barley, 136–38, 142, 181

Bath County, 87n, 97, 191, 218–20

Bees, 140

Berkeley County: agriculture, 156, 166, 172–73, 177–80, 187, 239; boundaries, 10–12, 113; denominations in, 104–5; distribution of wealth in, 116–17, 121, 124, 193, 239; holdings in, 120; migration to, 56; national groups in, 43, 45; plantations in, 127; population, 98–104, 238; roads in, 190; settlement in, 29, 37, 107–8; slaves, 108, 130; tenancy in, 128; Tidewater influences in, 239

Beverley family: courthouse grant by, 44; land grants made by, 33–34, 36, 41, 68; land grants to, 31–33, 62–63, 83; land speculation by, 61–62, 80; mill ownership by, 144; prices charged for land by, 74, 76, 85; settlement policies of, 33–34, 80–81, 233; tenure policies of, 64–65; Tidewater residence, 33; *see also* Beverley Manor

Beverley Manor, 31–34, 36, 52, 62–63, 67, 74, 77–84, 140, 144, 146, 151, 155

Blacks, 94, 103, 108; *see also* Slavery; Slaves

67, 135; Cub Run, 27; Cumberland Gap, 17; Great Valley of the Appalachians, 8, 18; Hawksbill Creek, 27–28; Hedgeman River, 10; Holston River, 37, 52, 82, 135, 213; James River, 19–20, 24–25, 36–37, 46, 63, 65, 70, 74, 77, 90, 95, 194–95; James River Gap, 152, 180; Linville Creek, 36, 77–78; Manassas Gap, 20, 152; Massanutten Mountain, 20–24, 37, 39, 41, 190; Middle River, 20, 77–78; Mossy Creek, 20, 204; Natural Bridge, 8, 20, 79; New River, 37, 46, 54, 56, 81, 190; North Mountain, 20, 23, 25, 204; North River, 20, 77, 146, 194–95; Panther Gap, 20; Piedmont (Virginia), 8, 34, 52; Potomac River, 8, 11, 20, 24, 28, 36, 55, 62, 151, 194; Opequon Creek, 20, 28–29, 44, 62, 144; Rappahannock River, 10–11, 37; Roanoke Gap, 17; Roanoke River, 36, 147; Rockfish Gap, 20, 25, 151, 175, 194; Shenandoah Mountain, 20; Shenandoah River, 20–29, 31, 34, 39, 45, 62, 78, 90, 92, 136, 144, 190, 194; Smith's Creek, 77–78; Snicker's Gap, 20, 151, 194; South River, 20; Swift Run Gap, 20, 25, 27, 152, 193–94; Thornton's Gap, 20, 27–28, 152; Valley of Virginia, 16, 19, 33, 47, 52, 87, 96, 135, 148–49, 163, 171, 186; Vestal's Gap, 20, 151, 194; Wood's Gap, 20, 152; *see also* Shenandoah Valley

Language, 54, 106–7; *see also* National groups
Lead, 204
Leather, 202, 206, 237
Linen, 146–47, 201–2
Linseed, 182
Livestock: breeding of, 184, 186, 188; feed for, 136, 138, 141–42, 183–84, 186–87; numbers and distribution, 139, 141–42, 145, 148–49, 184–85, 188; products from, 140–48, 156, 179, 183–87, 212; ratios, 139–40, 148; sizes of, 184; trade, 147–49, 183–87; *see also* Agriculture; Hay and forage; and individual animals
Living standards, 35–36, 107, 109–11, 120, 123–24, 126–27; *see also* Wealth, distribution of
Loudoun County 92, 108, 172
Louisiana, 26
Loyal Land Company, 83

Lunenburg County, 70–72, 163; *see also* Virginia, Southside
Lutherans, 105

Manufacturing: development of, 8–9, 161–62, 189, 237; distribution of, 146–47, 166, 174–75, 182, 185, 200–210, 218; establishments, 146–47, 166, 175, 182, 185, 201–2, 204–5, 207–10; impact on trade, 164–65, 172–76, 201–10, 222–23, 226; raw materials for, 164, 174–75, 182, 185, 204, 207–9, 218; types of, 146–47, 164–67, 174–75, 182, 185, 200–210, 222–23, 237; *see also* Crafts; Economy; Flour; Mills; Occupations
Maryland, 58, 65, 89, 113, 125, 128, 147, 160, 171, 173, 188, 194, 220, 235; *see also* Towns
Maslin, 138
Massachusetts, 178, 211
Meat, *see* Cattle; Consumption, domestic; Livestock, products from
Mennonites, 105–6; *see also* Denominations
Merchants: accounts by, 156–57, 159, 211–13, 228; activities of, 123, 147–49, 153–56, 159, 176, 179, 199, 210–21, 223–29; distribution and numbers of, 199, 214–19; and mercantile system, 152–60, 176, 205, 235–37; types of, 148–49, 153–56, 214–19; wealth characteristics of, 122–23, 217–18; *see also* Commercialism; Economy; Merchants (proper names); Towns; Trade
Merchants (proper names); Allason, William, 158, 172, 179, 205; Anderson, William, 212–13, 225; Bowyer, William, 213, 216, 218, 220; Boyd, Alexander, 159n, 228; Chambers, William, 216, 218, 220, 226; Christian, Israel, 155, 157, 159n; Cowdon, Samuel and Walter, 159; Crow, William, 148–49, 228; Gamble, Robert, 175, 215, 226; Gilbert, Felix, 155, 159n, 216; Holliday, William, 123, Matthews, George and Sampson, 33, 159, 216–18; Moore, Samuel, 159; Mustoe, Anthony (and Chambers), 171, 216, 218, 220, 226–27; North, Roger, 216, 218, 224, 226–27; Read, Mathew (and Johnston), 211–12, 224; Reid, Andrew, 212–14; Wright, Alex, 84